Ge..er and .... .f

D0538048

WITHDRAWN

Also by Harriet Bradley

MEN'S WORK, WOMEN'S WORK

FRACTURED IDENTITIES

*ETHNICITY, GENDER AND SOCIAL CHANGE
(edited with S. Fenton and R. Barot)*

* *Also from the same publishers*

Gender and Power in the Workplace

Analysing the Impact of Economic Change

HARRIET BRADLEY

First published in Great Britain 1999 by
MACMILLAN PRESS LTD
Houndmills, Basingstoke, Hampshire RG21 6XS and London
Companies and representatives throughout the world

A catalogue record for this book is available from the British Library.

ISBN 0–333–68177–0 hardcover
ISBN 0–333–68178–9 paperback

First published in the United States of America 1999 by
ST. MARTIN'S PRESS, INC.,
Scholarly and Reference Division,
175 Fifth Avenue, New York, N.Y. 10010

ISBN 0–312–21887–7

Library of Congress Cataloging-in-Publication Data
Bradley, Harriet.
Gender and power in the workplace : analysing the impact of
economic change / Harriet Bradley.
p.   cm.
Includes bibliographical references and index.
ISBN 0–312–21887–7 (cloth)
1. Sex discrimination in employment—Great Britain.   2. Sex
discrimination against women—Great Britain.   3. Women in trade
-unions—Great Britain.   I. Title.
HD6060.5.G77B73   1998
331.4'133'0941—dc21

98–34806
CIP

This book is printed on paper suitable for recycling and made from fully managed and
sustained forest sources.

10   9   8   7   6   5   4   3   2   1
08   07   06   05   04   03   02   01   00   99

Printed in Hong Kong

In memory of

Peter Lowman and **Deborah Leon**

whose energies were devoted to
improving the lives of working people

Contents

List of Tables

Acknowledgements

This book has been a long time in the making and many people have helped me in developing its ideas and in carrying out the research on which it is based. I am grateful to the Economic and Social Research Council for a year's funding (grant R000234124), to Sunderland University for a term's sabbatical which enabled me to set up the project, and to Bristol University for another in which to complete this book. Thanks are due to Richard Brown and Duncan Gallie for initial advice on the questionnaire and to Mark Erickson for helping with the interviews at one organization. People at a number of venues around the country have offered helpful comments on papers which formed the basis of some of the chapters. I would like to thank the following in particular for reading some of the chapters and for comments, reading suggestions, advice and encouragement of various kinds: Ruth Levitas, Jackie West, Steve Fenton, Gail Hebson, Theo Nichols, Steve Williams, Carol Stephenson, Paul Stewart. I owe a very special intellectual debt to Steve Fenton for debates and arguments which have helped me clarify my theoretical framework. As ever, Irving Velody has helped me through the darker days, challenged my thinking and kept me on track. Finally, the book could never have been completed without the co-operation of all the people I spoke to in the five case-study organizations: thanks to all of them.

HARRIET BRADLEY

Chapter 1

Introduction

This book is a study of social change. It has three main aims. First, it explores the pattern of relations between women and men in contemporary workplaces, tracing out continuities as well as changes. Secondly, it places these in the context of contemporary capitalist development, again considering continuities alongside change. Finally, it demonstrates how these processes combine to produce hierarchies of gender and class power within workplaces, exploring the operation of such power relations within the daily practices of working life. These relationships of class and gender are explored utilizing material from interviews with 198 employees, women and men, in five organizations in the North East of England.

Interest in such developments goes beyond the academic community. There is general social concern about the changing roles of women and men, both in employment and at home. At times this concern has veered towards becoming a moral panic, over issues such as rising male unemployment and its effects upon young men, the takeover of jobs by well-qualified young women, the challenge to the traditional notion of the male breadwinner as more women enter employment, the crisis of masculinity and the breakdown of the family. Journalists have highlighted the idea that Britain is experiencing a veritable 'genderquake' in employment. This study is concerned with how such a genderquake, if it is indeed occurring, is manifested within workplaces.

These concerns about social change relate to my broader interest in the analysis of social divisions and inequalities. The study reflects two major recent theoretical developments. First, there has been widespread recognition of the need to explore the interrelation of different types of social division and the way they combine to form

1

specific social hierarchies; secondly, it is contended that such analysis is best achieved through the study of particular sites in particular social and historical contexts (Bradley, 1996). Recently many
class theorists have argued that accounts that ignore the influence
of gender and ethnicity on class relations can offer at best a limited,
at worst a distorted, account of social inequality (for example,
Mann, 1986; Crompton and Le Feuvre, 1992: Clement and Myles,
1994). Similarly, Sylvia Walby has argued that existing analyses
of gender have proved inadequate because one or other of three
interlocking 'systems' of patriarchy, class and racial disadvantage
has been insufficiently considered (Walby, 1992); while Alison Scott
has suggested that theories of gender in the workplace which focus
either on the capitalist dynamic of deskilling *or* on the gendering
of jobs fail to account adequately for patterns of gender segregation (A. M. Scott, 1994). While some theorists still seek to develop
general accounts of the relationships between these various stratification dimensions (Walby, 1992; Marshall, 1994; Glucksmann,
1995), others believe that this is a misguided attempt: a more useful strategy is to consider the interplay of relationships of class,
gender, ethnicity, age and sexual preference within particular
locations and contexts. Accordingly, I have chosen to look at processes of gender and class specifically within workplaces and trade
unions.

These processes are explored using material obtained from a
research project based on five case studies of work organizations
in the North East of England. The case studies were carried out
between 1992 and 1993 and were funded by a research grant
from the ESRC (R000234124). The core of the research project
was 198 interviews carried out with matched groups of female and
male employees within the five organizations. These were supplemented by additional discussions, formal and informal, with managers and with union officers and representatives responsible for
organizing the workforce within the five organizations.

This project brought together a number of my personal sociological concerns. As an undergraduate student at Leicester University I became interested in the sociology of work and especially
in industrial relations and trade unions. My PhD thesis was a
study of unions in the hosiery industry; I used labour process theory as the theoretical framework for an historical investigation of
changing work relations in the industry. While working on the

PhD, I became steadily more interested in feminism and the analysis of gender. This eventually led to my first book *Men's Work, Women's Work* which was a study of the history of the sexual division of labour in employment since industrialization.

One criticism aimed at that book was that it presented women as passive victims of structural forces, ignoring their role as agents of change and resistance. This led me to decide that my next piece of empirical work would deal with women in contemporary workplaces and in particular their role as union members. In this way I hoped to set the record straight, showing how women are indeed involved as active participants in the construction of working relationships and practices. Such a project reunited my interest in gender with the older one in trade unions.

The theoretical concerns that inform the study have been developing for some years and are explored in a more general way in my second book *Fractured Identities*. This was an account of evolving theories of four major dimensions of social differentiation, (class, gender, ethnicity and age) which attempted to integrate the strengths of classical or 'modernist' analyses with the critical insights of postmodernism and post-structuralism. Using the idea of 'interacting dynamics' I tried to show how these different forms of inequality were interrelated. The book also develops a critique of existing theories of patriarchy and sketches out an approach to the study of gendered power which can give a more adequate account of the complex relations between women and men in everyday interaction. This theoretical framework, which is elaborated fully in Chapter 3, is applied in this book to the case study material as a way to unravel the intricacies of gender, class and power in contemporary workplaces.

Part of the sociological inheritance that I took from Leicester was a belief that theoretical and empirical work are inextricably related. Working towards *Fractured Identities* at the same time that I was collecting and processing the data from my research project has without doubt informed the way I have come to understand and analyse the interview material, while at the same time the arguments in *Fractured Identities* were shaped by the findings of the research. This book, however, is first and foremost a report on empirical findings. Like most field researchers, I found myself becoming absorbed into the worlds of my respondents and a major motivation for writing this book is to present the experiences

of these working lives as they were described to me and to do justice to the stories that were told to me, although it would be naive
to suggest that the stories speak for themselves. Nevertheless I
hope that this book does allow the respondents voices to be heard,
even though they are inevitably framed within, and therefore
shaped by, my own sociological preoccupations.

A project such as this one is totally dependent on the goodwill
and kindness of gatekeepers and informants. I am immensely
grateful to all the participants who made the research possible. I
owe an enormous debt to the managers who allowed me access to
their employees and helped me to carry out the research, often at
considerable cost in terms of their time, efforts and the arrangements for cover that were necessary in order for me to carry out
the interviews within working time. If they had not done so, the
project simply could not have been successfully completed. They
were busy people who generously and gracefully allowed me the
resources I needed to do the research. Faced with such gifts, one
becomes painfully aware of the parasitic nature of the academic
sociological endeavour.

Secondly, I am grateful to all the hard-pressed trade union
officers and representatives who found time to fit me into their
busy schedules and for the wealth of information, publications
and other material with which they showered me. But above all
the success of the project depended on the co-operation of the
working people I interviewed, most of whom seemed readily prepared to answer the peculiar questions of a nosy sociologist in a
thoughtful and open fashion Although it has been my experience
that generally people like to talk about their jobs, to answer questions frankly within the workplace at the request of managers can
be intimidating and the 'political' nature of some of my interests
(trade unions, equal opportunities, class) might well have been
offputting or daunting to some. Only in a minority of cases, however, did my respondents seem nervous, inhibited or hostile; and
often I was overwhelmed by the openness of the responses.
Although there can never be an acid test of the 'truth' of such
depositions, my intuition was that most of the accounts offered me
were made in 'good faith', were 'sincere performances' to use
Goffman's term (1959).

Writing up fieldwork of this kind presents the researcher with
ethical and political dilemmas. The workplace remains a 'contested

terrain' and inevitably the accounts I was offered by the different participants (managers and workers, unions and members, women and men) reflected conflicts of interests and divergent value perspectives. I have tried in analysing the fieldwork data to reflect the range of views that were offered, though to cover the varying standpoints of over 250 individuals would be an impossibility. I am aware that there is a slanting in the material, which does not arise simply from my own predilections: though to put the record straight and to follow the old sociological dictum that one should declare one's own ideological baggage in the introduction, I should state that I would describe myself as committed to gender equality and to the adequate representation of working people through democratic trade unions. What might seem problematic to some of those who participated in the study is the privilege I have given to the employees' version of the story.

There are three reasons for this. One is the simple logic of numbers: I spoke to more employees than managers or union officers so theirs was literally the majority voice. Secondly, there is an issue of power: of the three partners in industrial relations I take the workforce to be the least powerful. As will be discussed in subsequent chapters, all three groups tended to present themselves as relatively powerless, which is in itself an interesting comment on the operation of the contemporary capitalist economy. However, though managers feel themselves constrained by external forces and by the actions of those higher up in the corporate hierarchy, they do have a voice in the way decisions are made, at least at the local level in their organizations. Similarly, though operating in a situation in which unions have lost much of their former influence, trade union officers at least have a chance as formal representatives of the employees to voice their views to managers and to air them through the media. By contrast, the bulk of employees have limited input to the decision-making process.

The third point is perhaps more controversial but seems to me the nub of the issue. It is my contention that the voices of working people are less and less heard. Much contemporary research into changing work relationships is based on interviews with employers and managers, or conducted through trade unions and the contacts with their members outside the workplace that they can furnish, or through national surveys based on household sampling procedures. It is becoming rarer to come across research based on interviews with employees carried out actually within the workplace.

I would impute this tendency partly to the difficulties of gaining access to carry out interviews, in an economic climate in which time is more than ever conceived of as money; partly it may be due to firmer managerial control over workers' utterances in a political climate in which 'whistle-blowing' is very publicly disparaged as disloyalty to the organization; but most importantly it seems to me to be linked to methodological and theoretical preferences within social sciences which have recently favoured the study of texts and *discourses*, the switch from 'things' to 'words' as Barrett has put it (1992). Moreover, Skeggs, discussing work carried out within feminism and cultural studies, argues that in general 'there has been a marked tendency in recent years to move away from talking and listening to those outside of academia' (Skeggs, 1997a, p. 2). This leads to a tendency to 'normalise' the accounts offered by more powerful and privileged voices, and to use them as the basis for sociological generalization: the voices of working class people, ethnic minority members and other less powerful groups become more rather than less silenced. It is a matter of some satisfaction to me that I succeeded in my objective of talking to a fair-sized sample of employees, especially as it seemed at times that the targets would never be reached. It is important to ensure employees are not part of this gradual process of silencing; and that their opinions on current changes at work get an airing, along with the accounts offered by those with more audible voices.

There are other problems and dilemmas in carrying out research which will be familiar to anyone who has ventured out of their offices 'into the field'. Gathering data can be frustrating, intimidating and isolating. Apart from ten interviews at Trade-Fare conducted by Mark Erickson, I carried out all the field research on my own – and out there in the field, tight academic schemes tended to fall apart. Methodological designs of beautiful elegance and purity prove unworkable; one is forced to compromise and to grasp pragmatically at the chances that are offered. Coming out with anything at all becomes more important than coming out with what one went in for!

Moreover, the things one actually discovers are never quite the same as those one had hoped or expected to find. While I went into the project with the express intent of exploring gender divisions in unions and finding out about attitudes to trade unions, I found that my interviewees were more interested in the changes in working conditions which were arising broadly from processes of economic restructuring and job redesign. Class issues appeared of more concern to many people than gender issues, although, as will be discussed, 'class' was not exactly how they themselves tended to conceptualize things. There was, however, considerable interest in gender divisions within the workplace, if not within unions. Following along the lines of my respondents' concerns the project broadened out from its original narrower focus on unions – and, I think, became the more interesting for it.

As the above discussion suggests, the methodological strategy employed in this book is to present my findings primarily through drawing on the accounts offered by the employees in the five organizations. I have been concerned to give plenty of space to their descriptions of workplace relations and their views of what is going on. In trying to formulate my own interpretation of change at work, I have, of course, supplemented their accounts with my own observations, material from documents, and information offered by managers and union officers, but it is the employees' words above all that are offered to the reader.

This choice of strategy is based on assumptions that some may find unwarrantable: that these are intelligent, competent actors who are able to offer well-informed, accurate and reasonably honest accounts of the activities in which they are involved and that the accounts they offer me are not too distorted by their relationship with me as interviewer. I am reassured that these assumptions can be sustained by a number of factors: the set of accounts from each workplace were consistent with each other, but significantly different in some ways from the other sets; there was a surprising degree of unanimity on the major facets of change; what I was told tallied with what I observed; what I was told confirmed my own experiences as an employee within a variety of workplaces; the accounts of change that were offered me are in line with the findings of other recent research studies and surveys (for example, Whitston and Waddington, 1992; A. Scott, 1994; A. M. Scott, 1994; Coates, 1996; Danford, 1996) and are supported by other recent discussions of gender, class and change (Rubery and Tarling, 1988; Crompton and Le Feuvre, 1997; Walby, 1997).

This suggests that the respondents' accounts were reasonably accurate. But in any case a major objective of the study is precisely to present my *interviewees' views* of the world they inhabit, a world which they themselves help to constitute, and to explore the ways in which they themselves make sense of this world. Skeggs, arguing for the importance of continuing to study experience, states the need for a dialogic relationship between the researcher/theorist and the 'others' who are objects of research:

> Many of the concepts we have to work with are produced from those who just do not know about the experiences and interpretations of others and can only speak to those who occupy similar positions to themselves...Listening and hearing others is important for the production of accountable and responsible knowledge. This suggests that questions of methodology underpin all theoretical productions: questions of who we hear, how we listen, who we are accountable to, who we address and how we address them. (Skeggs, 1997a, p. 167)

'Listening and hearing' the voices of those I interviewed was as enriching and disturbing for me as it was for Skeggs. In the end what I offer is inevitably *my own* interpretation of *their* interpretations; but I have attempted to provide enough material in the text for readers to develop their own interpretations or to 'deconstruct' mine. This is perhaps the best we can do in an uncertain post-structural world: to listen to the play of voices and attend to their interweaving narratives.

This approach reflects what Du Gay has referred to as 'a renewed awareness of the importance of meaning in social life' (1996, p. 40). But, as I have argued elsewhere (Bradley, 1996), sociology needs to concern itself with meaning *and* materiality. Thus the next few chapters seek to locate the experiences of the interviewees within a material context, involving changing employment relations and changing dynamics of gender, class and power. Chapter 2 briefly reviews the various debates about how work is changing. Chapter 3 sets out a theoretical framework for analysing hierarchies of gender and class, which is employed in the case-study chapters. I develop a multi-dimensional model of power in terms of a range of resources deployed by actors. In Chapter 4, I introduce the five organizations and locate them in the context of economic developments in the North East region.

The rest of the book presents the major findings of the case studies. While the emphasis is on the meaning that workplace relations of gender and class hold for the employees, I have throughout tried to integrate these with discussion of the material structures which frame these meanings. Chapters 5 and 6 deal with gender relations in the five workplaces. Chapter 5 studies the dynamic of gender in the workplaces, primarily through consideration of the sexual division of labour. While the chapter shows how the structure of gendered jobs maintains inequalities between men and women, it also demonstrates how women are challenging the status quo, and this is more fully explored in Chapter 6. Greater social pressures on women to be earners have heightened their work commitment and ambitions to succeed in their careers. All the organizations had equal opportunities (EO) policies which are described in the chapter. Like other studies, my research reveals that formal policies of EO are strictly limited in their effects. However, in a more subtle way they are implicated in a climate of change which has sharpened women's demands for equality and led to increased competition between men and women for promotion chances.

Such competition is taking place, however, in the context of restricted opportunities as organizations strive to become leaner and meaner in a more competitive economic environment, in which market or quasi-market principles are spreading into new arenas, notably the public sector. Chapters 7 and 8 pick up the theme of the capitalist dynamic, exploring its impact on workplace relations. Chapter 7 deals with the employees' experience of class relations in the form of wage labour. It considers the effects of economic restructuring and the resulting changes to jobs and employment conditions. The responses of employees to these changes are discussed, revealing a growing sense of insecurity and work overload. Chapter 8 considers the implications of this in terms of class identities.

The penultimate section of the book extends this discussion, looking more closely at how gender and class relations intertwine. Chapter 9 considers trade unions as a site for both class and gender interests. Differences in women's and men's attitudes and behaviour as union members are outlined and the problems which face women who take on positions of authority within unions are explored. The implications for unions, which need to balance the

demands of female and male members if they are to thrive, are
considered. Chapter 10 then deals in a more general way with the
intersection of structures of capitalist domination and male domination at work, developing the analysis of power which was introduced in Chapter 3. It is concluded that the balance of power is
now slowly shifting towards women, although class divisions at
work persist and have important implications in terms of divisions
among women. Finally, the conclusion seeks to integrate the findings with the theoretical propositions set out in Chapter 3, demonstrating the complexity of class and gender dynamics within
these specific social milieux.

   Three major theoretical endeavours, then, inform this presentation of my research findings. The first is to develop an account of
social relations which deals both with meaning and with material
constraints. Roseneil, in a review of the future prospects for
feminist theory and research, calls for work that combines 'the
insights of feminist post-structuralism regarding the importance
of culture and discourse to the constitution of gender with more
"old-fashioned" attention to the "material"' (1995, p. 200). This
study attempts this task by presenting an account *both* of the 'lived
relations' of gender and class, conceived of in terms of current
economic arrangements and structures of power at work, *and* of
the meanings that working people impute to such lived relations
and utilize to transform them, as exemplified both in the cultures
of the workplace and processes of social identification. The
account of power developed in this book is one that emphasises
both material and cultural aspects. This links to my second theoretical interest, the longstanding sociological quest for integration
of structure and agency. While I offer an account of persisting
constraints of gender and class, I seek also to show how women
and men as collective actors and as individuals are involved in
changing those structures by means of their deployment of various resources of power.

   Finally, in doing this I explore the way in which the dynamics of
class and gender come together in processes of structuration, *both*
in informing the actions of agents *and* in shaping the formation of
workplace hierarchies. Walby in her book *Gender Transformations*
(1997) argues, as I do, that notable changes in gender relations
are under way and that changes in the economy as a whole cannot
be understood without reference to these changes (p. 65). In this

way she demonstrates that gender affects class relations as much as class affects gender. It is above all this interrelation between gender and class that this study seeks to explore. In Walby's words 'the patterns of inequality between women and men have changed...but in complex ways, not simply for better or worse' (p. 1). By applying my model of power to the material provided by the following case studies, I hope to shed some light on the complexities of changing gender relations at the end of the twentieth century.

Chapter 2

The Context of Change: Employment, Class and Gender

'The nature of work and industrial organization is truly changing with unnerving speed' (Kumar, 1995, p. 201). Krishan Kumar's comment on the shift to a postmodern society captures a perception popularly held and reflected in many discussions and representations of work, in the media, in journalistic reportage and in academic publications. But how *is* work really changing? A bewildering array of possibilities is offered. Some have prophesied a major collapse of work, bringing mass unemployment; only by grasping opportunities to rethink radically the link between work and the rest of life, for example by redistributing the limited amount of necessary work fairly among the population, will the threat of a permanently unemployed 'underclass' be averted (Jenkins and Sherman, 1979; Gorz, 1982; Handy, 1984). In contrast, others have presented an idyllic picture of a twenty-first century in which most work is of a professional kind or in which we are all engaged in selling expert services to each other. Some predict continued degradation or deskilling of jobs and the tightening of the bureaucratic organizational hold over the individual, while others suggest that jobs will be enriched and enlarged and that organizations will become more democratic with flattened hierarchies. Management gurus such as Tom Peters (1987; 1992) and theorists of post-Fordism alike present bureaucratic organizational forms as counter-productive, arguing that companies must be formless or at least free-form, continually adapting themselves in order to respond to the vagaries of the market as it reflects new, more specialized and diversified consumer demands.

The consequences for workers are also variously portrayed. We are told that the new generation of workers will have to accustom itself to 'flexibility', both in the way jobs are organized and in the need for individuals to move from job to job as a 'lifetime career' becomes a thing of the past: such changes may be welcomed as liberating and enhancing creativity, or deplored as bringing insecurity both to individuals and society. Managers assure us that their new policies which attempt to 'individualize' the employment relationship will allow more space for people to develop their talents and potentials. But surveys persistently indicate growing levels of stress among all sectors of the workforce. For example, the Institute of Personnel and Development (IPD) estimates that 40 million working days are lost each year as a result of stress, while a TUC survey of health and safety in 7,000 workplaces found that two thirds of union representatives reported stress as the major health and safety issue. This is unsurprising, in light of the revelation of another IPD survey that 50 per cent of workers were working on average an extra nine hours on top of their weekly contractual obligations, while ten per cent were working an extra twenty hours a week. British employees anyway work the longest hours in Europe (47 per cent of the workforce work over 40 hours per week, as compared to 14 per cent in Germany and 10 per cent in France) and have the shortest holidays.[1]

Thus working life eats into leisure and family life. Changes at work, then, have consequences beyond the workplace. Indeed, we may expect radical shifts in the way we view the relationship between employment and the rest of our lives: new technologies of information and communication offer scope for relocation of the site of jobs. Kumar in an earlier text (1978) suggested that this might involve a re-integration of employment into the household, in a kind of return to pre-industrial conditions before capitalist work organization and the factory system brought the familiar split between work and home, the public and the private (Hamilton, 1978; Clark, 1982). Perhaps we are not so far away from E. M. Forster's science-fiction vision of the future in *The Machine Stops* with each of us sealed into our own hermetic bubble and tapped into our computer console to work, play and consume. Forster's futuristic vision is no more extreme than that offered quite seriously by a team of management consultants, Applied Futures, of the world of 2010: suggesting that British workers 'thirsted for post-industrial individuality' they predicted the coming of subterranean shopping centres and factories, the latter operated by robots programmed from employees' homes; of undersea hotels and commercialization of marine-grown products; and interactive videos and computers being used in the home for shopping, financial transactions, education and leisure (Large, 1989).

How do we sift through these competing and often contradictory visions of changes in work and employment? In the following section I suggest that prevailing sociological approaches can be grouped into three broad strands and I place my own research in relation to these. Finally the effects of change on class and gender relations are briefly considered, before a fuller exploration of the theoretical implications in the next chapter.

Change at work: job enrichment, job degradation or 'business as usual'?

Mirroring these differences in popular perceptions, there is considerable disagreement among sociologists about how changes should be understood. Following Lyon (1988), I suggest we can distinguish three strands in the current sociological debates around work.

The postmodernist and post-industrial vision is of striking and revolutionary change in working relations and practices, resulting in improved work conditions. Bell's original account of post-industrialism (1973) proclaimed the coming of a leisure society, the general upgrading of jobs as manual labour gradually became redundant, and the potential for overcoming industrial conflicts as a more co-operative working climate evolved. Giddens (1994) reworks this idea, speculating about a shift from 'productivism' to 'productivity' in a post-scarcity society, and suggesting that Japanese-style lean production occurring within 'a rich social context' (p. 179) may allow for the development of more autonomy and self-esteem within work. Such accounts often emphasize flexibility, but this is viewed positively: 'postmodernist organizations and jobs are highly de-differentiated, de-demarcated and multi-skilled' (Clegg, 1990, p. 181). Lash and Urry speak of economic change freeing individuals from 'the structural rigidity of the Fordist labour process' (1994, p. 5). Workers are consequently upskilled and empowered; the promise is offered of democratization at work.

The radical and marxist position, often associated with the labour process perspective derived from the work of Harry Braverman (1974), presents a diametrically opposed picture. In this view continuities in the arrangement of capitalist organizations are as marked as changes; changes that are occurring are evolutionary rather than revolutionary, since the basic structural parameters of capitalist production remain unchanged. Rather than enskilling and empowerment, capitalist development brings continued task degradation and tightened managerial control. Flexibility is seen as equivalent to intensification and greater squeeze for profits (Garrahan and Stewart, 1992; Roberts, 1997; Danford, 1996). In this scenario, the position of wage labourers is seen as deteriorating. They face casualized forms of employment; they experience greater powerlessness, partly because of the diminished influence of trade unions, partly because new technology and new management techniques offer the chance of increased surveillance of individuals.

An intermediate position, endorsed in much empirical research, such as the nationally based Social Change and Economic Life Initiative (SCELI) and Workplace Industrial Relations Surveys (WIRS), emphasises continuities *and* change, but suggests that change should be seen as piecemeal and incremental, rather than the dramatic transformations suggested in the postmodern scenario. However, the marxist view of increased control and deskilling is also rejected. Change is seen to be pragmatic rather than ideologically motivated, involving negotiation within the framework of existing bargaining relations between managers, established unions, and the workforce. If more radical change is occurring, it is confined to greenfield sites. Compared to the other perspectives, this represents a view of 'business as usual' (Rubery and Wilkinson, 1994; A. Scott, 1994; Martin, 1995). Reviewing the SCELI publications, Martin summarises:

> The 'Thatcher Revolution' wrought less change in Britain in the short run than government spokespeople claimed... The overall message is that academics have exaggerated the extent to which new models were

being introduced ... The overwhelming impression in the SCELI studies is of continuity with previous traditions, not radical restructuring.
(1995, pp. 180–1)

I agree that the pace and extent of change has been exaggerated.
The chapters that follow draw attention to some marked continuities in employment relations, for example the persistence of
gender segregation, the basic conditions of some forms of wage
labour and the continued acceptance of the need for collective
representation. However, I also believe that significant changes
are under way, although they are more fragmentary and complex
than suggested in either the postmodern or radical scenarios, and
affect different groups of workers rather differently. Undoubtedly
the economy of Britain *has* undergone a significant shake-up since
the Thatcher government took over its management, with consequent changes to production systems and employment relations:
the widespread adoption of computer technologies at work,
the 'downsizing' of organizations, bringing consequent job loss
and redundancies, the development of 'new wave management'
(Wood, 1989) with its characteristic package of practices, such as
teamworking, quality control and performance appraisal, have
made their mark on the working lives of most employees.

Such changes are often ascribed to the global expansion of the
capitalist economy. This has forced the nations of the West to face
up to the effects of lower labour costs in less developed nations,
which encourage transnational companies to relocate some parts
of their production processes within them, and also to fiercer
international competition as more nations compete in increasingly
unprotected world markets. These developments, I argue, have
led to three key changes in employment relations in Britain:

1   The gender composition of the labour force has altered, with
    important consequences for the relative fates of women and
    men.
2   There is a climate of increasing employment insecurity, res-
    ulting from job losses and redundancies, and from the demo-
    lition of secure labour market niches; this is linked to
    increased monitoring of individual performance and work
    intensification, which, I argue, constitute a new 'regime of
    control'.

3   These changes have been felt most profoundly in the public
    sector owing to the introduction of market values and object-
    ives. These have replaced what Fulcher describes as 'the nine-
    teenth-century idea of an incorruptible public service with
    distinctive careers, norms and values' (1995, p. 331). These
    developments are discussed further in subsequent chapters.

The recomposition of class and gender?

Despite disagreements about what is happening in the workplace,
most sociologists accept that such changes have been profoundly
disruptive of established class relationships. The rise of service work
and relative decline in manufacturing in most advanced capitalist economies has transformed the class configuration. The
manual working class is declining in number; occupational groups
in the service sector, often consisting largely of female workers,
are swelling, and the spread of long-term unemployment has led
to social preoccupation about the growth of an 'underclass' sub-
sisting largely on state benefits. At the top of the class hierarchy,
the 'ruling' or capitalist class is becoming increasingly internationalized as globalization progresses and multinational companies
achieve greater financial dominance, making it more difficult for
national governments to place effective curbs on the activities of
capitalist entrepreneurs and investors. The old class boundaries
are changing and relationships between classes becoming more
complex.

Some postmodernists go further; they posit the 'decentring' of
work, which will be replaced by leisure and consumerism as the
basis of social identities. Young people, involuntarily exiled from
the world of waged labour by widespread youth unemployment,
are seen by Willis *et al.* (1990) to be pioneering this new way of
living, with its 'New Age' preoccupations and do-it-yourself styles
of culture and entertainment. Such cultural changes are seen as
inimical to class identifications and many postmodernists who
view class primarily in terms of social identity predict its demise
(Beck, 1992).[2] Accordingly Pakulski and Waters (1996) proclaim
that class is already in its death throes.

A more nuanced version of the work decentring thesis is presented by Ray Pahl in *After Success* (1995). He suggests that people

are wearying of the workaholic, materialist world of the Thatcher-
ite eighties and crave a more holistic lifestyle, in which work, leisure and family needs are better balanced and integrated. Such a
shift, argues Pahl, implies an adoption of feminine values and
working patterns, and a break with traditional gender relations in
which long-suffering wives provided the domestic back-up for
their husbands' career ambitions and tolerated their prolonged
absences from home as they proved themselves true 'organizational men'. Pahl, in this and his earlier work (Pahl and Gershuny,
1979; Pahl, 1984), accepts the feminist critique that 'work' is about
more than employment: domestic labour, community services
and voluntary work are also important forms of working. These
have been ignored in the past partly because of their association
with women.

As this discussion indicates, employment changes also disturb
established gender relations. In most advanced capitalist societies
women's economic participation rates are increasing. In Europe
and North America this has been described as a 'feminization' of
the labour force (Jenson *et al.*, 1988; Bradley, 1997). Increase in
the use of female labour also characterizes the 'tiger economies' of
the Pacific rim, while in the less developed countries the cheap
labour of rural women is often the basis for industrial expansion,
used alike by predatory multinationals and by indigenous entrepreneurs setting up production in sweatshop conditions (Mitter,
1986). As Hossfield argues, 'the "new international division of
labour" is increasingly based on gender, as well as class and
nation' (1990, p. 150).

In those economies described as 'post-industrial' the numerical
dominance of service-sector jobs brings gains in female employment while men lose jobs in manufacturing. A post-industrial
economy is also often a 'part-time economy' (Tilly, 1996). Full-
time jobs for life (often 'men's work') are lost; new jobs are often
temporary, part-time, based on various forms of sub-contract.
While these jobs are often designed as 'women's work' men may
be compelled to enter into them as more desirable 'male' alternatives dwindle in number. Moreover, in these new conditions
qualities seen as the 'natural aptitudes' of women (customer care,
communication, catering for people's domestic and personal
needs) are becoming more valued. There is pressure for men to
develop such skills and to 'feminize' their masculine personalities.

As men learn when they go on staff development courses, women are more habituated to giving other people 'strokes'.

Such developments affect the 'traditional' division of labour within families as men can no longer claim to be the sole – or even the major – breadwinners. In Britain as elsewhere 'dual-earner families' are becoming the norm (Harrop and Moss, 1995), with all the implications that brings for power relations between women and men inside and outside the household. The growth of the putative 'underclass' has often been linked by commentators to the increase in female-headed single-parent families and the threat to masculine authority as men's abilities to provide are weakened (Murray, 1990). Indeed, many have linked such developments both to a 'crisis of masculinity' and to the breakdown of family relationships, as young men lose acceptable male role models and drift into lives of violence and street crime (Dennis and Erdos, 1992; Campbell, 1993). As Westwood (1996) argues, a discourse of the 'feckless father' has been added to the canon of folk devils, as men are seen to be abandoning not only the long-established masculine role of breadwinner but also the newer one of caring co-parent. In such ways employment change influences prevailing definitions and identifications of masculinity and femininity, in a shake-up that has been popularly presented as a 'Genderquake'.

This book contributes to these arguments by presenting details of changes at work, as portrayed in the accounts offered by employees, their managers and their union representatives. Before presenting the fieldwork findings, however, I set out a theoretical model which I use to analyse these changes. This deals with the action of dynamics of inequality at the macro-level, but also offers a way to explore their manifestation in everyday interactions at work.

Notes

1 Reported in the *Guardian*, 19 and 25 October 1996; 7 November 1996; 23 June 1997.
2 Problems surrounding the conceptualization of class are discussed in Chapter 8.

Chapter 3

Theorizing Change: Class, Gender and Power

Changes in the organization of work are altering class and gender relations; inevitably this influences the way we theorize them. The study of social divisions has undergone considerable transformation in the past decades. Sociology is no longer so exclusively preoccupied with class. Attention has turned to other forms of inequality, especially those of gender and 'race' or ethnicity, but also those arising from age, disability, sexual orientation, region, religion. While earlier attempts to analyse inequalities of gender and 'race' had attempted to adapt or extend existing class theory, this approach has been criticized for its tendency towards class reductionism. The recent trend has been to view the various forms of social division as autonomous and in need of separate theorization, even though in any given context they are found working in combination.

Approaches to class are themselves in flux. Orthodox neo-Weberian class analysis continues to have its defenders (for example Goldthorpe and Marshall, 1992; J. Scott, 1994). But marxist theorizing on class has fallen into abeyance following the collapse of the Soviet bloc. Moreover postmodern and post-structuralist approaches, now very influential in sociology, pose questions about the analysis of class. Postmodernist rejection of 'grand narratives' throws in question the viability of general theorizing about social structure: preference is given to the study of specific events and interactions in particular contexts and settings. The focus moves from the global to the local. Meanwhile post-structuralist

20

thinking, with its view of reality as linguistically framed and constructed, has turned attention away from material analysis, replacing it with a concern with language and 'discourses'. Class and gender are seen not as material structures which act to constrain individuals, but as discursive constructs used to categorize society's members. Such discourses develop as a result of prevailing power relations and serve as frameworks for the formation of 'subject positions' (as working-class, woman, 'black'). In current sociology there is a distinct drift to the study of culture, meanings and identities and away from economics.

In *Fractured Identities*, I developed a model for the analysis of social differentiation which embraced both meaning and materiality. In this chapter I set out this model, which I shall use as a tool for exploring changing social relations in the workplace. Utilizing the notion of 'dynamics' of class and gender, I distinguish a number of trends operating at a societal level and then develop a model of power which can be used to explore processes of change at the micro-level. The aim is to develop an analytic framework which can link structure and action, the global and the local.

Class and gender as lived relations

Class and gender must be seen as *both* social constructs *and* sets of 'lived relations'. Relationships change as constructs change, but so do constructs change in response to relational change: the link between constructs and relationships is dialectical and it is pointless to speculate as to which is prior.

Thus class and gender, along with other concepts such as ethnicity and age, are terms which we employ to make sense of the way in which members of societies differ from each other. In the jargon, they are various (and different) ways of 'representing the other'. But while many post-structuralists assert that these terms *alone* constitute the 'other' as 'different', I argue that there are indeed 'real' differences 'out there' to which these terms (if crudely and inadequately) correspond. These differences are lived relationships involving different access to social resources and power. Lived relations of class, gender, ethnicity and age are based in different 'existential locations': they relate to a different feature of the way societies are organized in terms of resource allocation and the operation of power.

The concept of class refers to relationships derived from the way we produce, exchange, distribute and consume goods and services. This encompasses the organization of production, the operation of labour markets and the evolution of characteristic patterns of consumption. Economic relations and collective loyalties stemming from these are complex and it is not surprising that sociologists have found it hard to agree about class. Though a common strategy has been to define social classes in terms of clusters of occupations sharing common conditions or 'life chances', I am suggesting a broader view of what class encompasses: not just occupation, but ownership and control of production resources; the distribution of social resources derived from production (wealth, income, state benefits financed by taxation) and from the operation of markets and circulation of money (shares, investments, pension schemes); and consumption arrangements (including housing arrangements, differing lifestyles).

The concept of gender refers to relations between 'men' and 'women', that is, the way we divide society's members up into two (or more) biologically-distinguished sexes and allocate to them different social roles and attributes. It covers, then, *both* the sexual division of labour *and* cultural definitions and ascriptions concerning femininity and masculinity. Gender differences are particularly diffuse: they include economic inequalities which derive from the organization of the sexual division of labour both within the household and within employment, and from the organization of reproductive relationships, which restricts women's entry into economic life. Reproductive relationships are a crucial part of gender differentiation and it should be emphasised that, while these may be predicated on genuine *biological* differences, it is the *social* arrangements around pregnancy and childbirth, and their effects on other aspects of social life, that create inequalities. Such inequalities have often been linked to men's historical control over female fertility and sexuality. But gender allocations and ascriptions are found in all aspects of social life, from sport to artistic production.

Age and ethnicity are also important forms of social difference. which are touched on in this study. Age refers to relations derived from the social arrangement of the life course. Characteristically, societies divide their members into age bands, designating particular forms of behaviour as suitable for each group and assigning them to different social functions. The social positions of different age-groups are historically variable. It is important to stress this as age, like gender, has a biological referent in terms of the bodily processes of ageing, and this may lead to age differences being seen as 'natural'. Chronological age, however, has relatively little significance in itself; it is the social categories we employ (such as childhood, youth, old age) to distinguish age-groups and the rules and meanings associated with membership of them which act as constraints. In contemporary western societies, the young and the old are characteristically disadvantaged, with middle groupings forming an 'age elite'.

'Race' and the now more favoured and broader term 'ethnicity' are part of a package of concepts referring to a very complex set of relationships which derive from territorial arrangements and from the migration of people from different territorially based groups (nowadays normally described as 'nations' or sometimes the smaller 'ethnic groups') around the globe. Such movements, often involving invasions and conquests, have led to the development of ethnic hierarchies. Ethnic inequalities have been justified in terms of ideologies of 'race' which suggest that humanity can be divided up into groups with distinct genetic origins. Since the discrediting of these purportedly scientific theories, sociologists are wary of the term 'race'. Indeed Fenton suggests we should avoid the term altogether because of its roots in theoretical error (Fenton, forthcoming). The broader term ethnicity is used to refer to the designation of groups not just on the basis of differing 'racial' origins, but in terms of a common territorial origin, a shared ancestry, culture, language or religion.

All these types of 'lived relations' involve both 'material' and 'cultural' aspects (Bradley and Fenton, 1999). They encompass material factors, such as the distribution of power, wealth and income and other social resources (for instance, healthcare, education, citizenship rights). But they also have 'meaningful' or symbolic aspects in terms of how we identify ourselves as members of the social whole and of particular collectivities within it; how individuals and groups are represented in social and cultural imagery; and how particular ways of living are associated with particular groups. Classes, age-groups, ethnic communities develop their own distinctive 'subcultures' and practices (although not everybody located within that particular class, age-group or ethnic community may subscribe to them); while women and men in employment often develop distinctively 'gendered' work cultures (Westwood, 1984; Cockburn, 1985). More broadly, women and men are subject to prevailing cultural definitions of the appropriate ways to practise femininity and masculinity (although, again, not every woman or man will choose to conform). Similarly, classes, age-groups and ethnic communities lay down rules for class-appropriate, age-appropriate and ethnically specific forms of behaviour. How we as individuals exist in the world is, then, influenced by our position at the conjuncture of meanings of gender, class, age and ethnicity – and by the material con-straints that membership of a particular gender, class, age-group, ethnic origin impose upon us.

In *Fractured Identities* I referred to these various sets of lived relationships as 'dynamics' rather than 'structures' to indicate that they are fluid and changing, and to distance myself from the types of structural theory which conceptualize class and gender in terms of self-sustaining systems (which may be described as 'capit-alism' and 'patriarchy'). Such theories present social relationships in too static a fashion, which leads to inadequate explanations of change and variety. Another problem with systemic theories is that they present whichever form of relationship they hinge on (class in marxist theory, gender in feminist theory) as prior. The well-known attempt within feminist theory to combine a class and gender analysis as 'dual systems' theory failed to solve this dilemma (with the various versions tending to slide one way or another). Also, as non-white feminists pointed out, dual systems analysis was ethnocentric and contributed to the marginalization of minority groups by failing to offer an account of a 'system' of ethnic inequality. Systemic theory presents real difficulties in developing a multi-dimensional account of social differentiation.

While eschewing systems theory, I differ from the postmodern-ists in believing that an adequate account of social differentiation must deal with the global as well as the local. The global dimension of gender and class dynamics is demonstrated in large-scale survey findings which show regular patterns of gender and class differences (for example, the regularities in pay differ-entials between women and men, or in women's responsibility for domestic labour). Such regularities are not only replicated throughout any given society but often operate across societies as comparative research has demonstrated (for example, Jenson *et al.*, 1988; Bottomore and Brym, 1989; Bailey, 1992).[1]

However, nationwide statistical data which underpin analysis of global trends mask important variations of region and locality and gloss over the way social divisions take different forms in different settings. It is unwise, if not impossible, simply to 'read off' local effects either from national statistics or from macro-theories of social change. There is certainly, as postmodernist accounts of 'difference' have emphasized, a need for careful study of lived relations in specific contexts to reveal the complexities and variations of gender and class, and the diverse ways that global tendencies such as globalization or feminization manifest themselves at the local level. This is the task that I have undertaken in this piece of research.

The dynamics of gender and class: continuities and change

How then do class and gender dynamics operate at the global level? Here I distinguish a number of tendencies characteristic of class and gender relations in contemporary industrialized or indeed 'post-industrial' societies. These tendencies form the global context for developments in specific locations.

Class

As discussed in Chapter 2, class relations are altering in reponse to economic development. The typical class configuration of those societies which are evolving a 'post-industrial' economy consists of: an increasingly internationalized capitalist elite; a large and heterogeneous service class or 'new middle class'; a service proletariat; a shrinking manual proletariat; and an excluded or labour surplus class at the bottom who are dependent on state benefits, crime or the black economy (Esping-Andersen, 1993). This configuration arises from the interplay of a number of tendencies:

1 *Polarization and proletarianization.* The notion of class polarization derives from Marx's theory of capitalist development.
   Competition and the drive for capital accumulation compels
   the capitalist class to squeeze more surplus out of the proletariat so that the gap between the two groups increases, with the
   former becoming ever more wealthy and the latter relatively
   impoverished. The logic of competition also pushes the middle
   groupings towards one of the two major classes. Marx's theory
   has been comprehensively attacked, not least because the middle
   classes rather than shrinking have expanded to become the
   most numerous group. Yet there is much evidence to support
   the notion of polarization, although within the context of a
   more generally fragmented class structure. In Britain the gap
   in income and wealth between the richest and poorest has
   been steadily increasing. In Chapter 8, I explore the possibility
   that certain sections of the middle class are being proletarianized.

2 *Globalization.* At a very general level, Marx's analysis of the
   dynamic of the labour/capital relationship still applies: the
   drive for capital accumulation through greater appropriation
   of surplus is still the major factor in shaping employment relations. This persistent search for greater profit and for new
   forms of investment is currently manifested in the process of
   globalization. Structures of production have been reorganized
   on a more international basis to allow for the most productive
   and profitable use of the various factors of production (technology, raw materials, labour). There has always been an
   international aspect to capitalist production: for example, in the
   imperialist phase colonial relations supplied it with cheap raw
   material and labour, while the colonizing nations carved up
   world markets between them. But globalization theorists point
   out that the recent decades have seen an intensification of
   these international links, which has been facilitated by
   improvements in communications and transport.

   In the post-colonial context, world markets have been
   opened up further. Large corporations have exploited this
   and increasingly transferred their operations to a transnational
   basis. This transnational strategy has been facilitated first by
   the liberating of financial markets, which allows the unchecked
   flow of capital around the globe, and by new productive and

information technologies based on the micro-chip. These make it easier physically to relocate certain production processes (near to targeted markets, in locations where cheap land and labour are readily available) and allow for near instantaneous communication between the scattered parts of multinational enterprises, their clients and their customers. The importance of this for class relations is that the employment of cheap labour in less developed societies has squeezed labour costs in the West, leading firms to shed labour or reconstruct employment relations to use cheaper forms of labour; national enterprises must become 'leaner and fitter' to survive in this context of global competition.

3   *Fragmentation*. Weberian theorists have long opposed to marxian analysis an account of a counter-process of fragmentation which is caused by the complexities of bureaucratic capitalist organization and by the operation of markets. By such processes the 'propertyless' are divided up into a number of groupings with different market assets. Current forms of fragmentation involve the old division between manufacturing and service-sector workers; and the splitting of the latter into different groups (such as managers, professionals, public-sector bureaucrats, the self-employed) with different cultural and economic assets and characteristic patterns of consumption (Savage *et al.*, 1992). Fragmentation is also caused by the interaction of class with the dynamics of ethnicity and gender, so that, for example, the situation of women as wage labourers is markedly different from that of men, as will be seen in subsequent chapters.

4   *Exclusion*. Certain groupings are pushed out of employment altogether. Two manifestations of this are particularly relevant at present. Class and age dynamics together have operated to push older employees (often stereotyped as less 'flexible' and productive) out of their jobs. Redundancy and the increasingly significant phenomenon of early retirement cause hardship for many older workers. The other major excluded group consists of those of working age who do not find employment and are often described as an 'underclass'. The existence of such a class in areas like the North East is a significant social fact which has implications for the behaviour, attitudes and class identification of the employed.

5   *Individuation.* As we saw in Chapter 2, some postmodern
    accounts predict a collapse of social collectivities, as new con-
    sumption patterns and liberal pluralist ideologies promote
    individualist attitudes and behaviours in a 'surge of individu-
    ation' (Beck, 1992, p. 87). I reject this idea on the grounds that
    it confuses class relations with class identifications, and this is
    discussed fully in Chapter 8. However, the cult of individual
    responsibility promoted by the ideology of the New Right
    does affect employment relations. This can be seen in the weak-
    ening of trade unions and therefore of workers' capacity to
    take collective action; while deliberate use of individualizing
    strategies by employers (performance appraisal, performance-
    related pay, staff development programmes) further blocks
    the development of class solidarity. Individualism does not des-
    troy the class dynamic but limits processes of class identifica-
    tion and action: the end result is the spread of feelings of
    powerlessness which is discussed in Chapters 8 and 9.

Gender

Gender relations affect all aspects of social and cultural life. Here I
deal only with tendencies in the gender dynamic which relate to
employment.[2]

1   *Segmentation.* Attribution of different characteristics to men and
    women characteristically leads to the segmentation of social
    roles and tasks and their assignment to either women or men.
    Historically this has involved men taking superior positions:
    whatever functions are defined as masculine receive higher
    social evaluation. In contemporary employment relations this
    takes the form of vertical and horizontal segregation in which
    jobs are designated as men's work or women's work. Men have
    employed strategies of social closure, such as exclusion, inclu-
    sion and marginalization, to keep the best jobs for themselves
    (Witz, 1992). At times, such as during early industrialization,
    the pattern of segregation is disrupted and becomes unstable,
    but normally this is followed by a period of resegmentation.
    Arguably such a period of disruption is occurring at the
    moment, as we see in the notion of the 'genderquake'.

Segmentation is also manifested in the domestic sphere where there has been more stability. The link to biological reproductive function has for many centuries legitimated the assignment to women of the major responsibility for childcare and domestic labour. Despite claims about 'symmetrical families' and 'new men', surveys continue to show that women in Britain carry out about three quarters of domestic work (Henwood *et al.*, 1987; Jowell *et al.*, 1992). Warde and Hetherington studying the domestic division of labour in households in Greater Manchester found that gender stereotyping of tasks remained strong, noting the 'persistence of a strong sense of what are men's, what women's tasks' (Warde and Hetherington, 1993, p. 42).

2   *Fragmentation.* As in the case of class, fragmentation occurs because of the interaction of gender with other dynamics such as those of ethnicity and age. Women and men of different ethnic origin or in different age-groups, are subject to different rules of femininity and masculinity. Fragmentation may also derive from the contradictions within socially-dictated gender roles. The tension between domestic and employment roles is one such contradiction. Thus, for example, Hakim (1991) suggests a division among women between those who follow careers in a way similar to men and 'family-oriented' women who enter employment reluctantly, often in part-time jobs. This theme of differentiated experience is currently a preoccupation within feminism and is explored in subsequent chapters.

3   *Feminization of employment.* This tendency arises from the interaction of gender with class dynamics. Taking advantage of the structure of segregation, which puts a lower value on 'women's work', capitalist employers draw in female labour to cheapen costs. This is not a new phenomenon. In a well-known paper, Jane Humphries (1983) suggested that women formed an ideal proletariat and that capitalist development was likely to see a long-term tendency to female proletarianization. Although male workers through their unions have managed at times to resist such a strategy, the last decades have witnessed a new wave of feminization in many advanced economies. It is encouraged by the shift from manufacturing to service employment, since service jobs are commonly designated as 'women's

work'; and by women's increasing use of the 'qualifications
lever' (Crompton and Sanderson, 1990) which enables them
to compete with men for managerial and professional jobs.
Feminization is also linked to globalization: 'the growth in the
number of informal-sector and women workers is the centre-
piece of global restructuring' (Ward, 1990, p. 2).

4   *Polarization.* This, too, rises from the interaction with the class
    dynamic. Women from the upper and middle classes have
    advantages, in the form of economic and cultural capital,
    which help them overcome the effects of gender segregation.
    In Britain up to the 1960s it could be said that the effects of
    stereotyping, sexism and the association of women and dom-
    esticity was so strong that gender overrode class in the con-
    struction of employment hierarchies. This has apparently
    been reversed: there is a growing separation in the fates of
    middle- and working-class women. At the top of the employ-
    ment hierarchy gender segregation is less rigid, and profes-
    sional and managerial women have been the beneficiaries of
    equal opportunities programmes. Among manual workers
    and in the lower levels of service work, segregation remains
    strong. These developments are explored in Chapters 5 and 6.

5   *Gender homogenization: the 'blurring' of gendered boundaries.* The
    postmodern accounts of individuation discussed in relation to
    class also suggest a breaking down of gender divisions. Thus
    Pahl speaks of the 'collapse of both traditional work identities
    and of gender identities' (1995, p. 192). Again, the same theoret-
    ical objections can be raised; that gender relations (which
    remain unequal) are not the same as gender identifications.
    However, there is evidence to suggest some weakening of
    segregation. For example, there are signs of convergence
    between men and women in patterns of employment and work
    histories (Bradley, 1997). The greater involvement of women
    in the labour market leads some couples to renegotiate the
    domestic division of labour. These changes are discussed in
    Chapter 6.

The current operation of the gender dynamic is one
in which countervailing tendencies are delicately poised, as
the case studies will demonstrate; pressures to segmentation
persist obstinately, but are shaken by processes of feminization
and homogenization. At home and at work, gender roles are

contested and the balance of power is subtly shifting. To study how exactly this is occurring requires a theory of gendered power.

Gendered power: a multi-dimensional approach

The account offered above provides the base for a societal theory of power relations, that is power operations that act generally across a given society, placing some groups in a superior, others in a subordinate position. Such power relations can accurately be described as 'capitalist' or 'patriarchal'. However, I have suggested that we abandon system theories which equate 'society' with 'patriarchy' or 'capitalism', thereby implying that 'patriarchal' or 'capitalist' relations are all-encompassing, self-reproducing and determinant of other aspects of social life. Janet Siltanen (1994) rightly warns against assuming that gender is a relevant category in all circumstances. It must be empirically established. In fact, owing to the pervasiveness of gender difference in social and cultural life, empirical research usually *has* succeeded in substantiating the claim that, in Joan Scott's words (1988), gender is indeed a 'useful category of analysis'. But systems theories by definition take that relevance for granted and thus lay themselves open to the charge of essentialism levelled by Siltanen.

Moreover, the macro-level approach that I am advocating must be seen as limited. It only offers a generalized and abstract account of power which conceals variations, complexities and irregularities. For example, while at a societal level power may generally take the form of male dominance over women, it is possible (and empirically observable) that in certain contexts some women exercise domination over some men. We need, therefore, a micro-level analysis of power which can cope elastically with these complexities.

Currently the most influential approach to power at the micro-level is derived from the work of Michel Foucault. The Foucault-ian approach has many appeals in its account of how we are all involved in relations of power as we engage in everyday practices. It highlights the way in which the experience of power can encompass enablement and pleasure as well as repression; it avoids crude and over-generalized accounts of the state and the capitalist class as the sole exercisers of power, by showing how power can operate from below and is 'capillary', that is diffused to the extremities of society, rather than centralized; it demonstrates the way in which power acts upon our bodies to categorize, normalize and control us as citizens, a theme that has proved especially popular with feminists (see Sawicki, 1991; Bordo, 1993); and it shows how power operates through various discourses, which often enshrine ideas of expert knowledge.

But in common with some other feminists (Fraser, 1989; McNay, 1992) I find Foucault's account of power an unhelpful one for the analysis of social divisions. This is because Foucault refuses to accept that power has a subject (instead it is carried by discourses) or that it operates to further the interests of particular individuals or groups (we are all equally implicated in power relations). Like the account of power offered by Talcott Parsons (to which the Foucaultian account bears strong resemblances) this is a curiously egalitarian view. Power, for Parsons, is a benign and enabling social resource. For Foucault power seems more malign, but also appears as a resource for the social totality. Sophisticated as such an account may be, it has little purchase in explaining regular disparities of power between women and men, capital and labour

Feminists have looked elsewhere for a theory of power which can deal with agency. Currently the ideas of Lukes, Bourdieu and Giddens are all being explored (see, for example, Davis *et al.*, 1991; Skeggs, 1997a[3]). The work of Giddens or Bourdieu can be the basis for theorizing power in terms of different forms of resources (Giddens) or capitals (Bourdieu). Thus we can conceive of power, following Giddens' theory of structuration, in terms of differential access to and control of rules and resources: 'power involves the skills and resources which members bring to and mobilize in the production of interaction, thereby directing or influencing its course' (Davis, 1991, p. 72).

Neither Giddens nor Bourdieu apply their ideas to the empirical study of gender. I have therefore developed my own empirically-grounded account of a range of power resources which are involved in relations between men and women. This enables me to explain variations in power, by showing how women and men have control of and access to different forms of power resource, and to differing amounts of each resource at different times. Thus we can grasp power relations as complex and fluid; and, since power resources are not seen as finite, it is not a zero-sum approach (i.e., one in which power *is* finite and more power for men means less for women). This approach avoids the problems associated with the concept of patriarchy: a universalistic view of power, the suggestion that men are inevitably the power-holders, the presentation of all men as powerful and all women as oppressed victims. We can show how power operates differently in different sites (for example, women may control more resources in the home than they do in the workplace). This approach avoids the vagueness and generality of the Foucaultian approach, and can explain asymmetries of power, and allow for the identification of power-holders and the interests they protect. Power, then, has agents, both subjects and objects. As Davis says, advocating a similar adaptation of Giddens' work,

> Giddens' notions of power, as well as his theory of structuration as a whole, are urgently in need of both empirical and theoretical grounding. When this is done...the result is a grounded theory of gender relations as power relations in a specific context. Using both structural and individual approaches to power, it becomes possible to show how power works without losing women as subjects. (Davis, 1991, p. 83)

In this book I offer such a grounded account. I define power very broadly as the capacity to control patterns of social interaction. This may take many forms (class power, racial power, state power, for example). Gendered power refers to the capacity of one sex to control the behaviour of the other. Patriarchal power refers to the capacity of men to control women. Gendered power, then, is a broader concept which allows for variable relations between men and women, but does not rule out the possibility that power relations may be patriarchal.

I distinguish a number of dimensions of gendered power relating to different resources. While typically men have monopolized many of these, some have been deployed by women to resist male dominance. I shall show how women are now gaining greater access to some of these resources, causing a shift in the power balance in the workplace. Here I distinguish nine different types of resource, although this list is not exhaustive.

1 *Economic power* refers to the control of economic resources, notably property, income, earnings and other rewards from work. In the context of employment relations, men almost always control capital. However, more relevant to this study of employees, men have characteristically earned the greater share of income, acting as the major breadwinners, and use this as a lever both for financial decision-making and as a way to maintain dominance in the household.

2 *Positional power* relates to power and authority gained by virtue of holding positions, such as employer, manager, supervisor, trade union leader or head of household. Men have historically dominated in authority positions in the workplace.

3 *Technical power* involves the deployment of technical expertise and mechanical competence. Cockburn in a series of studies has shown that men monopolize technical skills and use this to legitimate their dominance at work and to portray women as technically incompetent. She sees technical power as a vital part of 'the material of male power' (Cockburn, 1981, 1983, 1985). Men's ability to claim that what they do is 'skilled' has been an important prop for gender segregation and gendered pay differentials.

4 *Physical power* relates to the deployment of physical strength. In terms of muscularity and body shape men are held to possess natural advantages. Historically this helped them establish their claim to dominance at work, but the advance of technology makes this more difficult to sustain, as we shall see. However, in other spheres of life, male physical power remains a potent source of male domination through the threat of violence, especially in the domestic context.

5 *Symbolic power* relates to the ability to impose one's own definitions, meanings, values and rules on a situation, to give one's own experience primacy. Symbolic power involves access to and control of the apparatus needed to determine meanings, including the various media of communication. As I shall argue, men retain symbolic power in the workplace, because of their historical ability to define what work consists of and their manipulation of the textual presentation of employment relations, both through image and word. Carson's (1997) research on trade unions shows how 'talk' can be an important adjunct to symbolic power as men in meetings deploy various

conversational devices to manipulate the agenda and marginalize women's contributions.

6 *Collective power* involves the mobilization of collective resources: the ability to organize groups of people to pursue common goals, for example within trade unions, pressure groups or networks. Male domination of the major institutions of collective action in the workplace, trade unions, is well documented. Collective power may also involve mobilizing smaller groups or networks which organize to promote more specific interests or help individuals to gain access to other power resources. Judi Marshall's work on women managers (1984; 1995) shows how powerful men within organizations form networks of this kind, often bolstered by shared social activities such as drinking and sport; but women too are beginning to construct their own networks to defend themselves against male discrimination and challenge prevailing organizational practices.

7 *Personal power* involves the utilization of a multitude of personal resources, such as strength of character, knowledge, ability to get on with people, charisma, experience, articulacy, the range of stratagems which people use in handling interpersonal relations. This aspect of power is often overlooked in theories of power which hinge on the public sphere but is very important in gender relations, especially in the family, where women may use these resources to establish their influence over men, other women and children. To a lesser, but still important degree individual women use such resources in the workplace to counter male domination and to achieve positional power.

8 *Sexual power* is an aspect of the above, but the control of sexual resources is such an important way in which women can assert themselves against men and also gain economic advantages that I list it separately. However, men can also use sexual power against women and do habitually in the workplace in the form of sexual harassment (although women can harass men, too). As many studies have shown, sexuality is a potent force in the workplace and can be used by individual men and women either as a weapon of self-advancement or a way to intimidate and exclude others.

9 *Domestic power* derives from control of household goods and materials (including money once it has been put into the household 'pool') and the use of domestic skills and expertise

to fulfil household subsistence needs. Together with personal resources, control of domestic resources can give women considerable power in the home, with men dependent on them for subsistence and comfort.

Within workplaces, power manifests itself through processes of interaction in which these various resources are at play. It must be noted that the use of such resources to achieve male (or female) domination is occurring simultaneously with other forms of interaction; towards the end of the book I explore how gendered power relates to the changing power relations of the class dynamic.

Conclusion

This chapter has set out a model for the analysis of gender and class along with a resource-based account of power. These facilitate the exploration of both material and cultural elements and offer a way to link structure and action, the global and the local. In developing this conceptual framework I have been attentive to the criticisms made by postmodernists and post-structuralists of modernist theories. Yet I have wished to retain a key aspect of modernist thought, its insistence that social phenomena are manifested at the level of the social totality.

A full understanding of gender and class relations requires analysis at *both* the macro *and* the micro level. Such an analysis can be sensitive to difference (best observed in local and specific contexts) and to similarities (manifested at the global level): to capture what Ken Plummer calls 'international connectedness, yet local uniqueness' (1992, p. 19) As Crompton and Le Feuvre state, 'there is no single category, "gender", which can be applied across a range of societies' (1992, p. 105). Gender relations operate differently in different contexts and must be accessed empirically. However, as they also argue 'there are no empirical instances available where the labour force is not "gendered" in some fashion, and the consequences of that gendering usually mean that women will be found occupying the lower positions' (1992, p. 105).

This approach requires the deployment of varied methodological strategies. National survey research and statistical analysis of macro-data give indications of the homogenizing and unifying dynamics of gender and class in contemporary societies. How these are specifically manifested in local settings demands more qualitative techniques, ethnography, in-depth interviewing, observation and case studies. The remainder of this book explores the dynamics of gender and class in a particular site (the workplace) and specific locations: five organizations in the North East of England.

Notes

1 See discussion in Bradley, 1996, Chapter 7.
2 For example, there is no place here for the discussion of the persistence of certain psychic structures of masculinity and femininity; psychoanalytic theories such as those of Lacan and Chodorow are used within contemporary feminism to explain these.
3 Skeggs has used Bourdieu's notion of different forms of capital to build a compelling account of how working-class women deploy their femininity and caring skills to gain respectability. There are obvious similarities with my analysis. However, since Bourdieu's conceptualization in terms of 'capitals' rather than 'resources' ultimately stems from his marxist roots, this theoretical framework, as I think Skeggs' discussion also demonstrates (p. 16), tends to relegate gender and ethnicity as secondary features in a primary dynamic of class. The notion of resources offers more flexibility.

Chapter 4

Workplaces in a State of Change: The Research Organizations and their Employees

Tyne and Wear, where my research was carried out, is an area long associated with heavy manufacturing industry: coalmining, shipbuilding, armaments, engineering and steel. But Tyne and Wear, and the Northern region more generally, have experienced savage attacks on their traditional forms of employment over the past two decades. The steelworks of Consett are gone; the pitheads are still; the shipyards of the Tyne and Wear rivers are shut. During the period of my research, in 1994, the last deep pit in the area (Wearmouth in Sunderland) closed down, as did the last shipyard on the Tyne (Swan Hunter).

The newer industries and occupations that have taken their place as employers of local people are radically different in the forms of employment they offer, the work cultures they generate and the types of labour they employ. Not all manufacturing industry has disappeared. Down the coast at Billingham the giant ICI chemicals plant broods and steams sullenly over the marshlands; and Teesside also houses one of the most modern steel plants in Britain. At Washington, halfway between Newcastle and Sunderland, the Nissan plant turns out its endless stream of just-in-time cars; the most notable of the region's batch of Japanese implants (others include Komatsu, Sanyo and Fujitsu). These firms, and others like them, continue to offer sought-after jobs

38

to the region's male workers: in 1995–6, 6,066 jobs were created in the Northern region as a result of overseas inward investment. But the most characteristic feature of the region's development has been the switch to service-sector employment.

Between 1979 and 1993 the number of employees in manufacturing in the Northern region fell from 410,000 to 241,000, from 33 per cent to 23 per cent of the total employed workforce (Robinson, 1994). The manufacturing loss in the early 1980s was greater than in any part of the UK apart from Wales (Stephenson, 1994). Between 1978 and 1989 there was a 54 per cent loss of manufacturing jobs in Wearside (Robinson, 1994). According to *Regional Trends*, in 1994, 53 per cent of male employees and 82 per cent of female employees were in service industries, with a massive 49 per cent of women's employment in public administration and other services (CSO, 1995). Over the period there has been growth in retail, in banking and insurance, in distribution, hotels and catering, in professional work and most strikingly of all in public sector employment. This has arisen from the expansion of local government and the health and education sectors (the region boasts five universities alone) and also from the relocation of some civil service agencies, such as the huge DHSS complex at Long Benton (Williams, 1996), as part of government regional development policy.

But the expansion of private services is what meets the eye more markedly in Tyne and Wear: the steady growth of retail, leisure and entertainment facilities as part of the spread of consumerist capitalism. The massive Metrocentre in Gateshead, with its 6,000 plus jobs, has become a symbol, both national and local, for the regeneration of the 'Great North'. The largest retail centre in Europe, it is the archetypal shopping mall. Planted beside a motorway, it offers corridors of glitzy shops, food courts, potted plants and fountains, a multi-screen cinema, a funfair, endless rows of cars packed in sprawling parks (there is space for 10,000 vehicles), and the Marriott Hotel located next door to house the parties of tourists who come to marvel and to shop seven days a week. As Chaney argues (1990), the Metrocentre is more than just a place to shop; it is a leisure experience, a celebration of consumerism that is at once spectacular and reassuringly commonplace, providing imagery of neighbourhood and community in an area where neighbourhoods and communities have been ravaged by economic change.

One aspect of this change has been the shift in the gender composition of the workforce. The growth of the service sector is, of course, linked to the feminization of the labour force discussed in earlier chapters. Service-sector jobs have traditionally been seen as women's work and new jobs, especially part-time ones, tend to be targeted at women. As Garrahan and Stewart report in their study of Tyne and Wear, 'increasingly the gender composition of the workforce indicates a trend for well-paid jobs for skilled workers to be replaced by low-paid and insecure work for women' (1994, p. 3). By 1987, around a quarter of jobs in Wearside were part-time (Hollands, 1994).

It can be argued that feminization has been even more notable in the region than in other parts of the country. Northumberland and Durham historically offered limited employment opportunities for women. Wives in mining communities did not work outside the home because of the burden of housework created by mining husbands and sons (Williamson, 1982). There was no major textile production in the area and the main jobs for women were in domestic service, agriculture or shopwork. However, the decline in traditional industries and the rise of male unemployment has brought change that really can be called startling. The unemployment rate in the region has been the highest in mainland Britain, running at 17 per cent through the mid 1980s (Darnell and Evans, 1995). Male unemployment has been higher than the national average: it was 18 per cent in 1991 (OPCS, 1991). By 1981, 41 per cent of employees in the region were women. In 1993, the situation was approaching parity. Women now made up 49 per cent of employees. However, as will be discussed in subsequent chapters, gender segregation in employment remains strong: feminization does not mean an end to 'women's work' and 'men's work' (R. Brown, 1995; Bradley, 1997).

The five organizations I chose for my research could be considered crucial if not entirely typical providers of employment within this evolving and feminized Northern economy. Four of them are service organizations (two public, two private), and the manufacturing company was in a sector which has fared quite well during the last two turbulent and depressed decades, pharmaceuticals production. All the organizations employ considerable proportions of women workers, between 60 and 80 per cent, which was a necessary condition for my study. Less typically, they are organizations in which women and men work together performing tasks which, if not identical, are similar. This was a deliberate part of my research design. I wanted to screen out the sharpest effects of gender segregation in order to be able to compare more directly the experiences of women and men as employees and as trade union members. It was also necessary that the organizations recognized unions and had high levels of union membership, estimated at 70 per cent or more (which is not typical of organizations in the economy as a whole). They were all committed to equal opportunities and four were members of Opportunity 2000.

These were well-established large or middle-sized organizations, and display very different work conditions from the small firms which are also typical of Britain's new 'flexible economy'. Yet all organizations could be described as 'flagship enterprises' in the regional economy, in that they continued to provide reasonable levels of full-time permanent jobs, were considered good employers whose jobs were sought after, while at the same time they were committed to the changes in work culture and employment practices which have been described in Chapter 2. Most importantly for my research, the types of job they offer are those which Britain's women employees characteristically occupy. In the Northern region, as elsewhere, women are concentrated into four of the occupational orders distinguished in government census data: clerical and related (26 per cent); catering, cleaning and other personal services (24 per cent); professional and related, in education, welfare and health (14 per cent); and selling (12 per cent) (R. Brown, 1995).

The remainder of this chapter introduces the five organizations and offers some details of the groups of employees chosen for interview. These details set the scene for the chapters which follow and their account of the changing dynamics of gender, class and power in these organizations.

The research settings

The five organizations which fitted my specifications and agreed to participate in the research were a clearing bank 'Albion Bank'; a supermarket chain 'TradeFare'; a chemical firm 'Pillco'; a group of linked hospitals which now have formed a trust 'Northtown District Hospitals'; and a regional branch of a civil service agency 'the Bureau'.[1] The organizations were all located in Tyne and Wear, which includes the cities of Newcastle, Gateshead and Sunderland and the new town of Washington.

In each of these organizations I conducted structured interviews with a sample of female and male employees in matched occupations. The interviews were carried out between January 1992 and March 1993. I also interviewed personnel managers and line managers, sometimes as part of the initial procedure of negotiating access, sometimes to gather additional information about the organization and its employment practices. To ease the burden on heavily pressed managers, since I was conducting interviews in work time, in four of these organizations I interviewed in two or more different work sites. This also helped me to obtain a sufficient pool of male employees from which to draw my samples, since I had selected occupations in which women predominated.

Albion Bank

Albion, in common with other high street banks, had enjoyed a financial boom in the 1980s, but was now in some difficulties after a period of rather unchecked expansion, particularly as a result of bad debts. The bank was known to be attempting to rationalize and streamline its organization, closing down unprofitable branches and reorganizing its regional operations. Like all banks, it was also steadily innovating with computer technologies designed to cut down on direct employment. These developments contributed to rumours of redundancies.

In the past, however, Albion had provided stable employment with predictable promotion structures and pension rights. This had made it a desired working environment. The majority of the employees I interviewed (65 per cent) had joined Albion straight from school and had spent their working lives at the bank, in the case of the men moving from branch to branch around the region to achieve career mobility. It appeared to be the norm among male workers to retire in one's mid-fifties, making use of the pension accumulated over a lifetime's service to the bank.

I interviewed employees at two medium-sized city-centre branches providing customer services. One employed 87 staff, of whom 66 worked full-time, the other branch 53, 41 being full-time.[2] Two thirds of the employees were women. Both buildings were old-fashioned, rather grandiose, with stately facades looking on to busy shopping streets. The space for dealing with customers was cramped compared to more modern branches. At peak times uncomfortable queues tended to build up. However, the office spaces which were located on the first and second floors above the public area were quite spacious, and the bank provided good facilities for its workforce: there were large rest rooms, with comfortable chairs, TV, kitchen facilities, drinks machines and pool tables. In the larger branch I interviewed in the rest room, sharing the space with employees chatting over cups of coffee, men (never women) playing pool, and a seminar group listening to an account of the pension scheme.

Certainly, Albion was considered a good employer and had won national recognition for its EO policies. Employees had access to creche facilities (none of the other organizations had childcare provision). There was an established job share scheme, along with good maternity leave and career-break arrangements. Predictably, however, all the part-time staff in these branches were women and all top managers were men. Almost all employees, including the branch managers, were members of the banking, insurance and finance union, BIFU.

TradeFare

TradeFare was another success story of the 1980s. A leading supermarket chain, it had experienced considerable expansion and was still busily planning new stores during the research period in the early 1990s. Its success was linked to a company shake-up in the mid 1980s, involving substantial restructuring and the development of a new corporate culture, along with an updated image. This had brought some job loss, though while I was carrying out my research the situation had stabilized. This was the only organization where the employees seemed to have no fear of redundancy. The workforce here, however, was rather different from those at the other organizations and perhaps job security was less of an issue for them. There was a high proportion of married women with children along with many student workers. Among those I

interviewed many of the older employees had previously worked
in manufacturing and most had held many other jobs before coming to TradeFare.

I interviewed in two sites, an older inner-city shop and a new
'state-of-the-art' store situated in a housing and industrial estate
on the fringe of a city. The older store employed 218 staff, 151 of
these being part-timers; the new store 294, of whom 204 worked
part-time. Sixty-five and 62 per cent respectively were women.
The older store was in the middle of a dejected, run-down older
shopping centre and the building was barn-like, functional. The
new store is a market leader, luxurious, glossy, enticing customers
with an enormous range of beautifully displayed products. It provided good staff facilities, including a large and pleasant restaurant, brightly decorated and light, with palatable cheap food (I ate
there during the days I was interviewing), a coffee room and a
pool table. The atmosphere in the restaurant was cheerful and
friendly, with employees from different grades mixing to chat.
Workers here were envied by those at other stores.

Part of the new corporate culture involved reinforcing the
package of benefits for the workforce: these included a good dis-
count on purchases from the store, a profit scheme and various
insurance deals. TradeFare claimed that their pay rate was better
than that of competitors. They had a long-standing agreement
with the shopworkers' union, USDAW, and a recently initiated
EO policy, linked to Opportunity 2000. Having formerly worked
in shops myself, my impression was that the conditions of employment were indeed good for the retail sector, despite the fact that
the work tasks, especially for cashiers, were carried out under
pressure. This might account for the fact that full-time jobs, when
they came up, were normally snapped up by part-time staff. The
staff I interviewed generally appeared contented with their jobs
and there were few grumbles.

Pillco

The Pillco factory is in the large estate where the new TradeFare
store was built. Like TradeFare it draws on the estate for its labour
and I met several people who had been employed by both firms.
Pillco was a long-established producer of proprietary medicines

which had experienced a number of takeovers and mergers, and had recently become a subsidiary of a British company which had formed an alliance with a large successful European petrochemicals company, although it continued to produce medical products for the British market. The alliance allowed what was a smallish concern to compete more successfully in the international market; the group now ranks as one of the top ten pharmaceuticals companies in Europe in terms of expenditure on research and design.

Pillco is a medium-sized factory employing about 560 full-time production workers, with about 80 part-timers and 74 managerial staff. Around 60 per cent of employees were women. Pillco produces a range of pills of various types and liquid medicines, which must be manufactured under strictly controlled hygienic conditions. Visiting the production side of the factory is thus a strange experience for a newcomer, who must don protective clothing covering not only body but face, hair and shoes. I was escorted round the factory at the beginning of the interview period, getting a tantalizing glimpse of processes which still remain slightly mysterious. The factory is modernized, consisting of numbers of smallish spaces and rooms designed for particular processes. Certain products must be produced under particularly delicate 'sterile' conditions and involve the use of chemicals which can trigger side effects such as skin rashes: I was not allowed into these rooms. Chemicals from huge cans are put into large machines which mix, compress and shape them into pills; some are then coated with an outer shell to make them easier to swallow. Male operatives oversee the operations of these machines, often working on their own in a small cell with one or two computerized machines. The process stage is highly automated and replaces the old skilled work of chemicals mixing.

Pills are then put into plastic containers, tagged and sent to packaging where they are packed in various forms, into boxes, tinfoil, sachets, tear-off strips, sheets with polystyrene bubbles (blisters), on assembly lines which are mainly operated by women. There are numerous short lines, most of which are highly automated, while others involve a certain amount of human intervention, including some hand-packing. The goods are then crated and warehoused: warehouse work and stock control are carried out by both women and men, as will be explained in Chapter 5.

Workers in the factory move around quite freely, appearing
simultaneously relaxed and purposeful. They chatted and joked
with the personnel manager who escorted me around and who
knew them all by name. At a casual glance they do not appear
tightly controlled, seemingly operating under the sort of conditions that Friedman has labelled 'responsible autonomy' (Friedman, 1977)

Production on most lines is carried out on a shift system with
shifts from 6 to 1.30, 1.30 to 9 and a night shift of 9 to 6. Most
operatives work alternative shifts, with a few (envied) lines running
a single day shift. The complexity of the shift system poses some
problems for management and many for the Transport and General Workers Union (TGWU) which organizes the plant; it made
the work of scheduling interviews quite a task for the personnel
manager and his assistants who arranged access for me. Shift
work was unpopular with many of those I interviewed, who complained that it disrupted social and family life and left them
exhausted.

The interviews were conducted in the office section of the factory which is sharply discrete from the mysteries of the 'production
side'. The production section is full of strange noises, windowless
and stark if extremely clean, strictly functional, full of ceaseless
activity. The offices, also very modern, were in contrast comfortable, roomy, quiet and relaxed. But production workers, office
workers and managers meet in the staff canteen where I ate my
lunches during the week I spent at Pillco. Food here, as at Trade-
Fare, beat university canteen fare for price and quality and the
environment exemplified the ethos of Pillco: quiet and efficient,
business-like, male-dominated, clinical and relentlessly exempli-
fying the spirit of the 1990s.

Northtown District Hospitals (NDH)

Nothing could have been less like the Pillco ethos than that of
the two Northtown hospitals where I spent a month doing interviews. Both sites are located centrally in the city they serve. The
smaller, Victoria Hospital, is an imposing early twentieth century
construction which must have been impressive when it was
opened, though now its long corridors, wood-panelled offices and

bleak high-ceilinged rooms are out of line with current trends in health care accommodation. A huge entrance hall with marble pavements welcomes the visitor and in the corridors photographs of redoubtable matrons and superintendents, relics of an earlier epoch of nursing, gaze sternly at passers-by. The wards are large and rather gloomy, although many have been subdivided into the smaller units which are now fashionable, and there appears plenty of space for patients. There was talk of closing the building once new accommodation at the larger site was complete, but currently it was housing some specialist units, such as the renal unit where I conducted several interviews. The Victoria employed 844 staff, 262 of whom were classified as nursing and medical, 155 professional and technical. Seventy-seven per cent of employees were women, of whom 43 per cent were part-timers. Only two per cent of men worked part-time.

Civic Local, the other much larger site, employed 2,024 staff, of whom 967 were nursing and medical and 74 professional and technical; 83 per cent here were women, with 46 per cent working part-time as against one per cent of men. The hospital, where the bulk of residential patient care for the area was carried out, was an agglomeration of Victorian, Edwardian and postwar buildings, prefabs, portakabins and wooden huts. The central building, sixties-style in design, holds casualty, the operating theatres and surgical wards. These more modern parts, including some of the labs where I did a number of interviews, were pleasant and comfortable, with drinks machines, armchairs, pictures and reading materials (stylistically reminiscent of Pillco or the out-of-town Trade-Fare). In contrast the geriatric wards, where I interviewed a number of nurses, formed a bizarre warren of odd huts and rambling old buildings, where wards shaded into corridors and storage spaces.

As this implies, standards of accommodation and facilities were greatly varied between wards and departments in the two sites. Some were modern and well equipped, some ramshackle and lacking in rest facilities for staff. One of my interviews was carried out in a room with settee, television and soft chairs, nice enough to be anyone's lounge; another, in a very overcrowded ward, took place in the lavatory! Bits of both buildings seemed to be constituted mainly of dingy corridors and endlessly confusing stairs. It was easy to get lost: and on several occasions I did.

But Northtown also exemplified the romance and excitement of hospital life which has so endlessly captivated TV audiences. Hospitals are not merely workplaces: they are social organisms, sites of human drama, communities; and, in contrast to the calm efficiency of Pillco, Northtown was always abuzz with activity, events, excitement. Patients and visitors drifted in and out, medical crises loomed for the over-stretched staff and disrupted my interview schedule. The routine of the hospital day was interrupted by ward parties, prize draws, fund-raising events, competitions, bingo sessions. Cards from grateful patients decorated ward walls. The coffee bars and canteens, though the food and drink they offered was at the Spartan end of catering, were more lively than those of the private-sector companies. Porters, nurses and administrative staff smiled at me in the corridors and as I wandered around seeking the nurses I wanted to interview, people would frequently ask if they could help me. The hospitals pushed the social side of working to the fore: more than any of the other organizations, it was positively fun to be researching there; and, since these were buildings with public access, I was able, within the normal constraints, to wander where I wanted and to observe what I wished.

But life at Northtown was not, of course, all fun. During the interview period, NDH was undergoing difficulties as a result of the NHS 'reforms'. It had to balance its budget to facilitate its bid for trust status (a previous bid having been rejected). The resultant freeze on expenditure had involved ward closures and cutbacks on staff recruitment. The hospital unions (RCN, COHSE, NUPE, MSF)[3] were opposed to trust status and so were the majority of employees to whom I talked. Trust status was also linked in the minds of many staff with potential redundancies, increases in workloads, declining promotion chances and impaired work conditions. Despite this climate of discontent, which, I suspect, was greatly fostered by the social, gossipy nature of the hospital culture, Northtown was seen as a good place to work and staff turnover was low. There was a real sense of teamwork, and relations between the various groups, especially with patients, were clearly good. Northtown District Hospitals had an extended EO programme worked out as part of its affiliation to Opportunity 2000 and promoted by the head of personnel, a woman strongly committed to gender equality.

The Bureau

The Bureau was considered something of an elite corps within the Civil Service. Like banking, Civil Service work has long been viewed as a good career option for school-leavers, offering 'a job for life' and promotion pathways. The Bureau has a number of offices around the region, processing local information and documentation. In the 1980s shortages of labour and high turnover in London and the South East meant that the Bureau transported some of its specialist work to the Northern region. New offices were built to house these units and more jobs became available. Some of the work carried out by the Bureau requires considerable technical expertise and the higher-grade employees took pride in their accomplishments. There was a sense of professional achievement and trust.

My interviews were carried out at three Bureau offices, one in a central city location, the other two on a suburban site. Each employed about 200 workers, of whom 10 to 20 per cent were part-time. Taken together the three offices employed 634 staff, 70 per cent being women. The city centre office was housed in a new postmodern style building in a part of the city undergoing regeneration: once the visitor passed in through its daunting security systems, it proved roomy, carpeted, luxurious, its space seemingly under-utilized with long empty corridors and large modern offices. The other two offices were in older, tattier tower blocks, looming like megaliths over a bleak landscape incorporating a shopping centre and large car-parks. Inside, the buildings were cramped, facing managers with problems of accommodating staff, work-stations and storage space for documents. However, relations within the offices and between grades were informal and friendly, and this was mentioned as a good feature of the job by many of those I interviewed.

The pressures felt at Albion and at NDH were mirrored here; the interviewees were concerned about possible redundancies, diminishing promotion chances and increased workloads. These anxieties were linked to government policies on public-sector restructuring. New staff quotas laid down by the government implied possible job losses, or even closure of some offices with consequent relocation of staff. The Bureau was subject to the policy of 'market-testing' which involves contracting out of some of

its operation to tender by private firms (and with no chance, as
has happened with competitive contract tendering in the NHS, of
in-house bids securing these functions for the existing section).
Employees feared this was that this was a first step on the road to
privatization of the entire agency.

The Bureau is highly unionized with its own specialist union,
BWU (Bureau Workers' Union).[4] It shares in the progressive
equal opportunities climate for which the Civil Service, like the
banks, has established a reputation. For the women in my interview samples, this was another reason why the Bureau was seen as
a good place to work, despite the current upheavals.

The samples

The core of my research design was the set of interviews carried
out in each of these organizations. In each I sought to interview
twenty women and twenty men working in similar jobs. The
targets were achieved in all the organizations except the factory,
where I interviewed twenty-one women and seventeen men. The
samples were chosen in most cases by random sampling procedures using lists of employees in the selected jobs. Where people
declined to be interviewed or were unattainable because of
absence or sickness substitutes were found from a second random
sample. In a few cases substitutes were volunteers chosen by management. It was more important to me to achieve target numbers
than to maintain the purity of the sampling methods. At Trade-
Fare I could not use a random sample and here employees were
selected for me by management on a quota basis. All the interviews were carried out within the workplaces, most in private
rooms. Time pressures at Albion meant that I had to ask nine people
to fill in the interview schedule themselves. The rest were all
interviewed face-to-face: interviews lasted from half an hour to an
hour and contained a mix of closed and open-ended questions.
Further details of the sampling procedures can be found in the
Appendix, along with the interview schedule.

At Albion I interviewed employees drawn from Grades 1 to 5
(below management level) including a couple of entrants to the
bank's 'fast-track' accelerated promotion scheme for management trainees. Similarly at the Bureau the bulk of my respondents

came from the three non-management tiers (assistant, administrative and executive grades), but also included five top specialist executives who perform some managerial functions. The lower grade jobs at both organizations were repetitive, involving routine tasks like data-entry and filing; but higher grades involved specialist work and expertise, dealing with individual clients and their problems and with the co-ordination of office activities.

TradeFare's corporate restructuring had involved a process of 'de-layering' or flattening of the hierarchy so that there were now formally only three employment grades: assistant, supervisor and manager. My sample consisted mainly of assistants, who were selected to cover the mix of jobs in the store: these jobs included cashier (on the automatic till), stock control, shelf-filling, specialist counter assistants (such as delicatessen, meat, wines and spirits), cafe attendant, security guard, car park attendant, trolley collector. People filling all these jobs were described as 'general assistants'. They were said to be trained to do any job in the store to achieve flexibility, but in fact almost all those I spoke to identified themselves with a particular task. Jobs of this kind are described by Du Gay (1996) as repetitive, routine and involving easily acquired skills. I also interviewed seven supervisors.

This was the only organization where I interviewed part-time workers, largely because the managers felt it would be difficult to find enough full-time men for me to interview. The necessity to include the part-timers involved some difficulties concerning comparability (the female part-timers were virtually all married women, while most of the part-time men turned out to be students); but the positive side is that it did provide insight into the conditions and attitudes of women in part-time employment who are otherwise absent from the project.[5]

Northtown, like most hospitals, displays a traditional pattern of gender segregation. I chose to interview two occupations where I could find both women and men employed together, although one or other sex was likely to be in a minority: nursing and professional and technical staff (P and T). The nurses covered grades A to G, that is from auxiliary nurse up to sister or charge nurse level. Most worked on the medical or geriatric wards or in the renal unit. The P and T staff were all classified as MLSO (Medical Laboratory Science Officer) or MTO (Medical Technical Officer). They were drawn from a number of specialisms: microbiology, haematology,

audiology, cardiography, speech therapy and renal unit technology. All but one were in non-management grades 1 and 2 or were
trainees.

Finally, at Pillco I interviewed production workers covering the
range of departments. These were mainly process operators or
assembly line workers on packaging. I also interviewed a number
of women and men who worked in the warehouses as stock con-
trollers and fork-lift truck drivers.

The sample as a whole is thus quite mixed occupationally, but
can be seen to cover a range of jobs in which women are commonly
found working (clerical, retail, nursing, unskilled or semi-skilled
factory work). The sample over-represents service workers as against
manufacturing (80 per cent as against an estimated 70 per cent
in the region); but if I had included a second manufacturing
organization the bias would have been the other way. The choice
of four service-sector organizations was made to reflect the concentration of women in the sector (82 per cent of the region's
female employees), the trend in the economy towards service
work, and my conviction that developments in the service sector
will set the tone for gender and class relations in future decades, as
capitalism in the more advanced economies takes a post-industrial,
service-based form.

Only 2 of the 198 employees (one per cent of the sample) were
non-white: a Filipino factory operative (who had trained for medical work in London before ending up in a chemical factory in the
North East) and a young female Asian bank clerk. The fact is significant in itself, since the organizations were seen as providing
'plum' jobs and had traditionally offered secure employment. The
ethnic minorities of the North East region were being excluded from
these coveted jobs, despite the fact that some of the organizations
claimed equal opportunities on 'race'. The Bureau, for example,
had a racial equality policy, as did NDH. The latter was carrying
out ethnic monitoring, but figures showed very low proportions of
minority employees, a striking fact in view of the strong postwar
association between the NHS and the utilization of migrant labour.
At both Victoria Hospital and Civic Local only one per cent of the
workforce was classified as 'Black' with a considerable minority
(19 per cent and 10 per cent respectively) described as 'unknown'.
During the month I visited the sites I did not see any non-white
nurses or laboratory staff. At Albion bank, the regional personnel

officer professed concern about the lack of minority employees, but imputed it to the fact that recruitment was virtually at a standstill which impeded attempts to implement EO on race. Moreover, these organizations had developed marked internal labour markets (including Pillco and TradeFare). As John Carter has pointed out in his study of racial segregation in the NHS in 'Bridgetown' (Carter, 1997), the development of an internal labour market for job allocation and promotion favours the perpetuation of existing ethnic hierarchies and effectively acts as a mechanism of social closure to exclude and marginalize minority members.

I also carried out a number of other interviews within the organizations or at the headquarters of the trade unions linked to them. I interviewed a total of seventeen managers (regional and plant personnel directors, line and branch managers, section heads and operations managers). These interviews varied from brief chats about arrangements to lengthy discussions; in some cases I spoke to key managers more than once.

Trade unions were involved in the project from the start since I was reliant on union co-operation to cover some aspects of the research. I used local union officers to help me identify organizations that would fulfil the research requirements and which were likely to be prepared to participate in the research. Consequently, I interviewed officers of all the unions which covered my case-study firms, plus some others I thought might be helpful. Where there were specialist women's officers I spoke to them. Subsequently, I interviewed shopfloor representatives or stewards of all the workplace unions. In all I spoke to fifteen officers and eighteen workplace representatives.

A further set of interviews was carried out in a city comprehensive school, Beechgrove Middle School. I had originally hoped to include an educational establishment among the five organizations, given the importance of the education sector as an employer in Tyne and Wear. However, although I gained the co-operation of the teachers' unions (NUT and NAS/UWT) with the project, I was unable to persuade enough people to participate to include the school in the study. However, I interviewed 10 women and 3 men at Beechgrove. Although these two sets of interviews do not constitute a major part of my study, they yielded interesting information and a few quotations from the interviews have been used to illustrate points made in the book.

Summary

This chapter was designed to provide a background to the case-study material presented in subsequent chapters, offering a brief account of the Northern region economy in which the workplaces are located (although it should be recalled that all five are nationally-based organizations, so that policies and practices rest upon national as well as local considerations). The discussion highlighted the decline of manufacturing and its effects on male employment, the proportional rise of service employment and the feminization of the region's labour force which form the context of employment relations in the region. In introducing the organizations, I have emphasized both their unique features and the things they had in common with the others. Such differences and commonalities will be explored further in the chapters to come.

It should be emphasized that, while the interviews were planned to yield some quantitative material of a descriptive nature, the research was conceived as five distinct case studies, which would produce data of a more qualitative nature. Inevitably, a case-study approach raises issues about the representativeness of the findings. I could not claim that my sample of employees was typical of the national workforce as a whole, for reasons which have already been touched on. First, the study was located within a very specific labour market (although I would argue an indicative one). The various Social Change and Economic Life Initiative publications have shown how every regional labour market has its distinctive features, while also emphasizing how important the study of local labour markets is for the understanding of social change (A. M. Scott, 1994; Gallie *et al.*, 1996). Secondly, my sample was drawn from large, well-established, highly unionized organizations which do not represent the whole spectrum of enterprises in the UK economy. Thirdly, the sample was ethnically homogeneous, which reflects the population of the region but not that of the UK as a whole. Only one per cent of the sample was from minority ethnic backgrounds, as against 1.8 per cent of the total Tyne and Wear population (OPCS, 1991). Finally, the samples mainly consisted of full-time employees and were deliberately selected to minimize the effects of gender segregation, so that two major characteristics of women's current employment are marginalized in the study. However, because of the importance and influence of these organizations and the forms of employment they represent (the NHS, for example, is Britain's largest employer), I contend that studying developments within them can teach us a great deal about the direction of the evolving service-based economy and the gender and class relations it is generating. These organizations show us the future within the present.

Moreover, the case study approach, despite problems of representativeness, has some important advantages. Large-scale surveys, though providing useful and reliable data, can often give a misleading impression in terms of the complexities and variations which they cover up (Siltanen, 1994; A. M. Scott, 1994; McCarthy, 1994; West, 1996). For example, it is well known that occupational data conceal the true extent of gender segregation in employment, which is manifested more sharply at workplace level and also in the allocation of specific tasks within an identical job category. Also, as Siltanen argues (1994), aggregate data from surveys or government statistical sources show outcomes but not processes. The case-study approach, by digging deeper into particularities, can throw more light on the subtleties and contradictions of relationships within institutions, teasing out the complexities by which existing hierarchies are both challenged and maintained. Another important function of case and locality studies, as emphasized in an account of nearby Teesside, is to trace out the consequences of world-wide and national trends at the local level, showing how 'processes of globalization are made real in everyday life' (Beynon *et al.*, 1994, p. 198). In the chapters which follow I explore the complex and varied processes by which established relationships of gender and class within these workplaces are simultaneously being recreated and transformed.

Notes

1 The names of all these organizations have been disguised in order to protect the identity of participants and the confidentiality of the statements they offered me.
2 All figures for numbers of employees relate to information given to me at the time of the interviews (1992–3).
3 At the time of the research COHSE and NUPE had not yet joined together with NALGO to form the 'super-union' UNISON, although the officers were preoccupied with the impending merger.

4   This particular union has been given a pseudonym, again to protect
    the identity of the organization. All other unions have been given
    their true names. The pseudonym is not used to protect the identity
    of the union itself. Indeed, the BWU deserves recognition for its
    work. Of all the unions covered by the study it seemed to me to have
    the most effective and comprehensive organizational structure; it
    served its members particularly well.

5   Because of the problem of the lack of comparability between young
    male students and older married women, where data for the whole
    sample is presented and comparisons between men and women are
    offered, I have frequently omitted the twenty part-timers. The total
    sample number then becomes 178.

Chapter 5

Women and Men at Work: Gender, Inequality and Jobs

Chris[1] is 30 and works in the computerized stock control department at Pillco. Her father was a factory worker and her mother she described as a housewife who did 'bits of cleaning'. She left school at 18, having previously worked part-time at Woolworths and in a record store. After several months' unemployment she succeeded in getting a job on the line at Pillco and has worked there ever since, recently moving to her new job in the warehouse, which she likes: 'I'm much happier with it because, a, I'm working by myself which I enjoy and, b, it's more interesting. I have to think about what I'm doing. I'm more mentally stimulated.' The warehouse was at that time a male domain and Chris had to fight the men to get accepted: 'I've shouted them down. I had to put up with them saying darling all the time at first.'

Chris is a single woman, independent, intelligent and ambitious. She would like to get on, achieve what she describes as a 'middle job' but can't quite see how to do so and fears 'being stuck and not being able to find the way out'. She dreams that perhaps the company might support her in doing some kind of college course which would help her progress, perhaps in language, or in management. She has a feminist commitment to women's careers and believes her trade union should do more to help women and counter the gender inequality she perceives in the factory:

'When it's put down on paper in management-speak it's equal, but when it comes down to the nitty-gritty you still have to be twice as good, as a woman...We don't seem to be regarded very highly for promotion. What seems to be the trouble is the idea that she's going to get married and have children and run off.'

Peggy is also frustrated about her prospects, though she tends to see her problems in terms of class and age, not gender. She is 47, divorced, with three children. She comes from a classic working-class background: her father was a steel worker who was killed in the Second World War, her grandfather a union officer. Her mother brought up her children on a war widow's pension, supplemented by cleaning and childminding. Peggy left school at 15 and worked in shops and offices until she had her children. After six years out of the labour force she returned to part-time shopwork, and then got a job she really liked at the Electricity Board, but after 9 years' service she was made redundant. She was taken on as a temporary worker at Pillco and made permanent a year later. She works as a trainer on one of the lines. The way she views her job was typical of the women at Pillco:

'The good thing is that the salary's good. The people I work with are nice, you know, I like the company. On the bad side it's very boring. The job's not taxing in any way. But when you get to my age the jobs are not there.'

Peggy would like a job which utilizes her mental abilities, her skills in communicating with people and her love of figures and accounting, but the clerical jobs in the factory are closed to her. She regrets her limited education: 'They ask for so many qualifications, sometimes I think experience doesn't count. When I left school you didn't sit the GCSEs. I wish I had.' She has tried to get clerical jobs elsewhere, but failed, she believes because of her age and also because of prejudice against single mothers. Ironically, she is also trapped by the better pay which women manual workers have often traded for the status of 'clean' service jobs. At Pillco women can earn £145 per week take home pay and prospective employers were suspicious as to why she would wish to take a cut in salary.

Peggy describes herself as very independent: 'I won't ask anyone for help. I've been on my own so long, I've had to do everything for myself. Perhaps it's silly, my mother always says you shouldn't be so independent.' Her spirit, she believes, has rubbed off on her younger daughter who is determined to be a doctor. But Peggy's two grown-up children have followed working-class routes: her son trained as a motor mechanic, but couldn't find a job, so he now works as a taxi-driver. Her older daughter is a beautician.

Jennie, too, feels herself stuck. She has made it up through the shopfloor hierarchy to be team leader on her line, but now faces a 'glass ceiling': there is no route for unqualified people into management. She left school at 15 and took a secretarial course which led to a string of office jobs, but she found the conditions uncongenial and did not stick in any of them: 'They were all older women, the last thing they wanted was a young girl, unless she was willing to be a general dogsbody and run around all day for them. And I wasn't.' Jennie then tried factory work but did not settle there either and left to have a baby. After three years, aged 20, she took a job at Pillco and has been there ever since. The break-up of her marriage contributed to her desire to settle into the job and become self-sufficient, although subsequently she remarried.

Jennie is a forthright, strongly militant woman, with a history of union activism. In her account, age, class and gender have combined to disadvantage her. At 38 she feels herself 'too old' to take a degree and start again, though she would like more stimulating work. Her job she describes negatively: 'It's boring as hell. It's just totally repetitive. You make sure the machines are set up, you look at the line, you do your stats, it's the exact same thing, day in, day out.'

Like many women in the factory Jennie has a strong sense of self-esteem. These are no passive victims: 'I often say I'm worth twice what I'm paid.' But her age and lack of qualifications are blocks to moving elsewhere: 'Realistically at my age if I wanted to go to another company, they can take a younger person on. Let's face it, they're going to take degrees first.' For Jennie, education is the only way for people to escape their class fate, otherwise 'you don't get above what you were born into'. Her father worked for British Rail, her mother ran a shop, and she describes herself as not lower class or upper class, 'middling really, working class'. Jennie also has very strong opinions on gender relations in the factory:

'The women work harder. The men might do an equal job on the line... but throughout the plant, the jobs that are totally male jobs, they get away with murder. It's as if management are too frightened to tell them what to do. I don't think women get a fair crack of the whip in this company.'

Describing being stuck as home as 'mind-numbingly boring' and herself as being determined to avoid domesticity and achieve independence, Jennie offers a radical critique of men's social power:

'It begins for them when they're born, their mothers take care of them, when they get older their girlfriends look after them, then their wives take care of them. Women are the independent ones, work harder. We are trying to prove in most cases we're better than men. I still think in this country it's a lot harder for women to go on, because there's an old boys' network. In the factory, rugby is the way on.'

This chapter explores inequalities between men and women at work, focusing on the sexual division of labour in the workplaces. Although all the organizations were developing promising equal opportunities policies, patterns of gender segregation persisted. But rather than accept these as inevitable, as women seemed to have done in the past, many of the women I spoke to were aware of gender disadvantage and some were challenging it.

The stories of Chris, Peggy and Jennie are typical, although these women responded more militantly to their circumstances than some others I spoke to. These women are experiencing the contradictions of a feminizing workforce and the fierce competition of the global economy. Feminization, as I shall argue, seems to have raised the expectations of female employees in the North East. Many of them are part of a dual-earning partnership. Others, single, separated or divorced, or coping with sick partners, are the main breadwinners. Women now expect to have to work for much of their lives and are becoming more ambitious to develop careers. But at the same time, many find themselves facing stereotyping and discrimination from some managers and male colleagues. Moreover, the restructuring of organizations to be 'leaner and fitter' has restricted promotion opportunities and the chances of finding new employment at the very time when progressive employers are developing EO programmes for women.

While the case studies reveal the obstacles to achievement of gender equality, the picture is not hopeless. Things are slowly improving, partly as a result of EO policies. Such developments are explored in Chapter 5, which also links changes within the workplace to broader shifts in the social division of labour. I start the discussion, though, with a brief account of feminist analyses of gender segregation.

Gender segregation and change

Gender segregation became a key concept in the study of women's employment as feminists attempted to explore inequality in the workplace in a way that would highlight the specificity of women's disadvantage and not reduce it to class. In a now classic article, Catherine Hakim (1979) analysed the overall pattern of gender segregation in Britain this century, arguing that there had been little breakdown of segregation between 1900 and 1980. Hakim distinguished between vertical forms of segregation, the concentration of men in the higher tiers and women in the lower tiers in any occupational pyramid, and horizontal segregation, the clustering of women and men in different types of occupation. It now seems doubtful whether this distinction is really valid, since there tends always to be a vertical dimension in any ordering of different occupations: thus, in hospitals, when men work as porters, women as ward domestics, the male job is better paid and accorded more status. A true situation of horizontal segregation would be one in which women and men worked in different jobs but were rated economically and socially equal – and such cases are rarely found. However, I retain these terms in the discussion as they are now so familiar.

Macro-data such as those analysed by Hakim are significant but cover up a more complex set of processes. It is accepted that gender segregation is more extensive if one moves from the occupational level to the level of jobs. Moreover, the structure of gender segregation, though persistent, should not be seen as fixed but as fluid. Jobs change from being men's to women's jobs and vice versa. Old gendered jobs disappear and new jobs emerge, some immediately assigned to either men or women, others occupied by both sexes for a time. The process of gendering, therefore, is pervasive and continuous, and the precise form of sex-typing is variable, specific to particular times and places. Nevertheless, it can be argued that something approximating the currently pre-vailing pattern of gender segregation in Britain was consolidated in the latter part of the nineteenth century.

Various factors contributed to this: the desire of employers for cheap labour encouraging them to designate some jobs as 'wo-men's work' and pay them at a lower rate; men's desire to retain the best jobs for themselves; the campaigns by male-dominated trade unions to maintain gender differentials and exclude women from male specialisms; prevalent definitions of masculinity and fem-ininity which decreed which types of work were suitable for women and for men; workers' preferences for working in groups with their own sex; the formation of strongly gendered work cultures which make it difficult for individual women and men to cross over into the employment territory of the opposite sex; and women's domestic responsibilities which put limitations on the type of employment they are able to undertake (Bradley, 1989).

Commentators currently disagree about the persistence of gen-der segregation in Britain, following two and a half decades of fem-inist campaigning and the passing of EO legislation. Several analyses suggest that there has been some diminution in the degree of se-gregation since 1980 (Mallier and Rosser, 1987; Hakim, 1992; Walby, 1997), although this has occurred chiefly in professional and managerial jobs and there is less change in the manual sector. Crompton and Sanderson (1990) argued that women were pushing their way into men's jobs by using the 'credentials card'. Women are catching up with men in their educational achievements and can compete more equally for professional and managerial jobs. Walby (1997) endorses this position with reference to younger women.

However, Blackburn *et al.* (1993) in their analysis of national data argued that the breakdown of segregation discerned by Hakim and others is largely an effect of the particular statistical methods used. The results were distorted by the increased numbers of women entering the labour force. Using a technique called mar-ginal matching, they claim that there has been virtually no change in the levels of gender segregation in Britain. West (1996) points out the problems involved in all the indices used to measure segregation at the macro-level, and suggests that statistical surveys tend to cover up significant aspects of inequality. Certainly the

SCELI studies of particular workplaces revealed that gender segregation was still very marked (A. M. Scott, 1994). So what is really happening? Is segregation persisting despite the prevalence of EO? Are better qualified women breaking the barriers and entering jobs previously assigned to men? Are glass ceilings being shattered? And, contrariwise, are men moving over into female specialisms? My case-study materials throw light on these questions and reveal the processes which contribute to the persistence of existing structures and others which weaken them.

Women's and men's jobs: segregation in the five organizations

To get a general measure of segregation I asked both men and women whether they worked mainly with their own sex, mainly with the other sex or equally with both. The answers are summarised in Table 5.1. The table shows that there are considerable variations between the organizations, with Pillco and Northtown Hospitals displaying the strongest pattern of segregation and Trade-Fare being the least segregated. Overall, though, the general level of segregation is strong with nearly half the sample reporting working in same-sex groups. The high figures for people working mainly with the other sex at NDH, Albion and the Bureau reflect the numerical dominance of women in these organizations, where men are in a minority. The crucial figures, however, are those on the bottom line. In a completely desegregated workplace, 100 per cent of employees should report working equally with both sexes. Here the overall average figure was 27 per cent.

TABLE 5.1 **Levels of reported gender segregation (percentages)**

	Pillco	NDH	Albion	Bureau	Trade Fare	Totals
Work mainly with own sex	66	42.5	37.5	32.5	42.5	**44**
Work mainly with other sex	16	50	35	35	7.5	**29**
Work about equally with both	18	7.5	27.5	32.5	50	**27**

This figure is the more surprising since my organizations were deliberately chosen because women and men were to be found working in the same or similar occupations: these are organizations which display considerably less than national levels of gender segregation. Moreover, this particular question reveals horizontal segregation rather than vertical segregation and, as I shall show, vertical segregation was marked in all the workplaces. Thus the table tends to under-represent the degree of difference between women and men. These responses, then, confirm that gender segregation in the British labour market remains at a high level.

The strongest patterns of segregation were found at Pillco and Northtown Hospitals, where what we might call a 'traditional' division of labour was still in existence. In the clerical workplaces, the Bureau and Albion Bank, there was little evident horizontal segregation, but vertical segregation persisted. TradeFare had the highest proportion of employees (50 per cent) reporting working with both sexes, reflecting the mixing of men and women in many shopfloor jobs. But digging beneath the surface, even here considerable elements of horizontal segregation remained.

At Pillco there had been a longstanding tradition of sex-typing of jobs. Men had been process operators, seeing to the initial handling and mixing of chemicals. This involved overseeing complex but highly computerized machinery and required the men to lift heavy cans of chemicals weighing up to 50 kilos. Men also worked as fitters and in the warehousing jobs (fork lift driving and stock control). Women carried out the rest of production work, mostly on the automated packaging lines: clerical and secretarial staff on the office side were women. This extremely typical sexual division of labour was defended by the men on the grounds of differences of strength and temperament:

> 'The way I would describe it is the men do most of the hard work, the physical side, and the women mostly try to do a job sitting on the line.' (process operator)

> 'Well really speaking it's like it's based on two sides, I would say that the male side is heavyish and women would do the lighter work where there's not so much lifting...One woman tried to do my job and she couldn't stick it...On the packaging side it would be best for a woman and I don't think you'd get too many men.' (process operator)

Vertical segregation was also very strong. Almost all managers and group leaders were men. While there was mixing of women and men at the supervisory level of team leaders and trainers, women could not pass upwards into management, as the stories of Peggy and Jennie indicated, since graduate qualifications were required for managerial staff. Many of the women described the firm as male-dominated:

> 'It's a male-dominated firm. The main man's job is management and naturally the fitters...They've got this policy now of starting men on women's jobs like packing. Women can't go no further.'

> 'Men get favoured more...Men get the prime jobs.'

Northtown, too, displayed a well-established division of labour typical of hospitals. Traditionally in the health service, women have fulfilled caring and domestic roles and men curing, managerial and technical ones, and NDH was no exception. Women dominated numerically in nursing and in laboratory work, although in both areas higher grades were held by men. Cardiology and speech therapy were female P and T specialisms and within them women could rise to hold the top posts: but by tradition these were seen as lower-status areas. In the hospital women were employed as receptionists and telephonists, clerks and ward domestics. The renal technologists were men, as were the porters. The only evenly mixed occupational group in my sample was the audiologists, but from observation there was a reasonable gender balance among the doctors.

Among medical staff, however, a strong vertical division of labour is likely and this was the case among the nursing and P and T staff at NDH. Thus 95 per cent of the lowest grade A (auxiliary) nurses were women, as opposed to 76 per cent at the high grade G. Of the tiny minority of male nurses (21, as opposed to 215 full-time and 139 part-time women), 43 per cent had reached grades F, G and H, as opposed to only 11 per cent of full-time and 4 per cent of part-time women. Similarly among the MLSOs and MTOs men were at the top. All the laboratory chiefs were men and a man headed the audiology unit. There were no men working in the lowest laboratory grade (assistant) while 21 per cent of men had reached top grades 3 and 4, compared to 2 per cent of women. A male MLSO suggested the pay was too low for men to take the jobs:

> 'Generally speaking, the money isn't enough to support a family. Young men won't come into the job. It's all right for a second income.'

A different pattern could be found at the Bureau and Albion Bank. These were feminized workplaces with less horizontal segregation. Men and women worked side by side in clerical and administrative jobs. There was a slight tendency towards gendered specialisms at Albion, with women being student advisers (a job requiring caring and communications skills) and men dominating in the foreign department and securities (requiring technical expertise). One woman described this more insidious form of gendering:

> 'They seem to go, like, not into the administrative side of jobs, but into the decision-making posts like the lending. Men take the exams and make the career moves.'

In both organizations there was marked vertical segregation: all managers were men. At Albion the concentration of men in higher posts could be traced back, as the above comment indicates, to the old two-tier system in banking, in which men took exams and followed careers, while women acted as a 'white-collar proletariat' filling subsidiary 'dead-end' clerical slots (Crompton and Jones, 1984; Savage, 1992). Men at Albion had conformed to this pattern, taking exams and moving from branch to branch in a steady trail of promotions. One man had moved fourteen times between the cities of the Northern region! Only recently had women also begun to enter the career arena.

At the Bureau, women and men could be found in all four tiers; but men dominated in the top tier and women were concentrated in lower grades, as shown in Table 5.2. Half the men were in management or the top two grades compared with only 18 per cent of the women. Horizontal segregation also prevailed at the Bureau in two respects: all secretaries were women, and all part-timers were women, as was also the case at Albion. As Walby (1988) and Robinson (1988) have pointed out, the concentration of women in part-time work is a major form of gender segregation.

TABLE 5.2   Gender and job hierarchy at the Bureau: numbers and percentages of women and men in each occupational category

	Men	Women
Manager	3 (1.5%)	0 (0%)
Grade 4	19 (10%)	9 (2%)
Grade 3	73 (38%)	70 (16%)
Grade 2	58 (30%)	138 (31%)
Grade 1	35 (18%)	103 (23%)
Typist/secretarial	0 (0%)	29 (6%)
Messenger	2 (1%)	0 (0%)
Part-time staff	0 (0%)	95 (21%)

TradeFare displayed the least segregation. I was told that all jobs were open to all sexes. The use of pallets for lifting made warehouse work, once a male preserve, feasible for women. Certainly on first sight looking around the store women and men seemed to be deployed in all areas. None the less, more careful study revealed gender biases. Work on the checkouts was still an area dominated by women though some of the part-time males (school and university students) helped out on them especially in the evenings and on Saturdays (times less compatible with women's household responsibilities). Wages clerks were female. The job of 'trolleyboy' was a male one, as was security guard and car-park attendant. It may be argued that such tough, physical and possibly dangerous jobs are better filled by men. But what was interesting was that nobody commented on this aspect of segregation, any more than they did about the all-female secretarial group at the Bureau. Some forms of gender segregation, it seems, are so taken-for-granted, so much seen as 'natural', as to be invisible.

The mixed jobs at TradeFare were counter assistance and stock control. But there was some channeling of women and men in different sectors of the shop. Women worked as attendants in the coffee shop and in the household goods section, men in wines and spirits. While there was no formal segregation at play here, there is a more subtle drift of staff towards areas seen as sex appropriate. This principle operates at higher levels, too. As Chapter 6 will show, women have benefited from recent changes to the job hierarchy, but while team leaders are drawn from both sexes, women are more likely to head teams of cashiers. Similarly, all the managerial staff in the two stores were men, except for the personnel managers who were all women. TradeFare made a big issue about encouraging women into management, but women are apparently steered into the personnel function, with its connotations of dealing with and looking after people, as opposed to store management and marketing, posts seen as requiring authority and expertise. Thus horizontal segregation lingers, if in concealed form, as one woman reflected:

> 'Well, I think, like, high management is all based on men. There's not many store managers, trading managers who are women ... The checkout has always been a woman's job. There seem to be certain jobs that are always for women and certain jobs that are always for men.'

Inequality at work: are men favoured?

All the organizations, then, displayed patterns of gender segregation, although, as we shall see in Chapter 5, changes had been occurring which had begun to weaken those patterns. How did this register with the employees?

It is indicative of the changes taking place in these organizations that the employees were more likely to perceive gender inequality in the employment sphere generally than in their own workplaces. Eighty-four per cent of women and 68 per cent of men felt there was still sex inequality at work. Women are more strongly aware of gender inequality and this was reflected in their attitudes to their own workplaces. Fifty-five per cent of the women felt men were favoured, as opposed to 36 per cent of the men. A minority of both sexes felt that women were now favoured (11 per cent of men and 2 per cent of women). There were variations in responses between the organizations which were clearly linked to the differing patterns of segregation described above. Nearly three-quarters of the women at Pillco and Northtown Hospitals spoke of men being favoured, reflecting the established strength of horizontal segregation; whereas at the other three organizations half the women considered that women and men were equal: where women and men work in similar jobs and segregation is mainly vertical it is less likely that inequality will be perceived.

It must be stressed that nearly half these employees saw relations between women and men in their organizations as equal. This was expressed in statements which linked opportunities for 'getting on' with merit and hard work:

'Everybody's equal. If you're a lazy git you won't get on, if you work you do.'

'Women have as many chances as men, definitely... If you show you're keen it doesn't matter who you are.'

Similarly some people suggested that if men were more successful it was because they were more career-oriented, had put more effort into gaining qualifications, or had natural advantages; such justified differences were not seen to compromise equality:

'The reason why we have men at the top is they've pushed more, they've done the courses. The opportunities are there.'

'If the women have taken the exams they will have equal opportunities with the fellas who have taken the exams.'

'Blokes lift coins on Friday, the heavy jobs, that's the only difference.'

There was also a sense that things had recently improved and men were quick to point to the increasing number of women who were getting promoted:

'They have the same opportunity. No bias either way. There hasn't been for many years.'

'Opportunities for women are as good if not better than for men, but, overall, it's still the best opportunities come up for men... Women have done well recently in promotion.'

This last quotation, from a male bank clerk, points to the complex and sometimes contradictory nature of comments about equality: the speaker was struggling to reconcile a view that women were now getting some kind of (unfair) advantage with the fact that there still were evidently more men in top posts in the bank. There was a sense in which some of my interviewees appeared to be trying to 'explain away' segregation, by seeing it as justified (because of men's greater career orientation), inevitable (because of women's domestic commitments), or as currently under attack (through equal opportunities programmes). Behind such comments lingers a traditional view of gender differences as natural and inescapable. What perhaps was more remarkable was the degree to which many of the women I interviewed had come to a very different view, seeing gender inequalities as unwarrantable. Rather than taking the fact of men's greater career commitment and women's domestic responsibilities as givens, they were beginning to challenge the bases of such assumptions and the social processes that lie behind them; it is important to stress that these women were not the highly educated middle-class women commonly associated with this type of gender politics.

Women challenging inequality

Where women did perceive inequalities, they often expressed their views very strongly:

> 'They favour the men, in every way. Especially if you're a married woman. If you want to go on, like the girls, there are one or two of them who are trying to be managers, they have to be in at all times, but if you're a married woman you couldn't do it.'

> 'The men have a better prospect. The men get more pay than women. The men get away with a lot more, at least I think so. The supervisor would ask a woman to do a job that they wouldn't ask a man to do, where he would refuse to do it. Women are soft like that.'

> 'I think the men are given the easier jobs to do... I've always found that the men tended to be faster movers than the women. A token woman is promoted... They tend to pick a pretty face and the right accent.'

Some commented on the way women were denied training opportunities, sometimes linking this to the bias of male managers:

> 'I've noted a lot more men getting the training opportunities.. There's only two women on a management training course. I do think it's more for men.'

'I'm not a feminist...but I don't think women are held in the same light. I think you can break through it but I think a lot of men don't realise how chauvinist they are.'

Women were having to challenge a longstanding ethos that somehow it was 'natural' for men to work for promotion while women were still ultimately destined for motherhood:

'Once you get promoted to Grade 4 and above, there it's not so equal. If you're a man, management assumes you are out for promotion. But a woman has to put herself forward to be considered.'

'Men get more opportunities than women, definitely. The bank feel that women are going to leave and have children so they promote the men.'

'Well, I think I've got a biased opinion but I think that men get on more quickly...Mebbes it's the time we have off for maternity...Men get away with more, they do less work.'

The latter speaker introduces a common theme, that women were in fact harder and better workers, but because of their gender they had to prove themselves more than men to get their efforts rewarded, to be 'twice as good' as male colleagues:

'The young lads sometimes, they don't know what work is, and if they can walk around with an empty basket and look busy...And the hard jobs, the women get them. You've got to stand up, you can be put on.'

'They get away with a lot of work...making beds, putting people on the toilets, cleaning up vomit...They see that as woman's work.'

'It's the women who do the hard work. Women do a lot more variety of jobs before they can go up a grade.'

All these factors come together to confirm to women that they are subsidiary to men within the workplace:

'I would say speaking from experience men do get on more easily...Men are favoured...It's an historical thing that men should be bosses and women should be servers.'

While this speaker, like many others, seemed to accept philo-
sophically that these attitudes would endure, a minority of women
had explicitly taken on the feminist task of fighting discrimination
and inequality in their workplaces. Among these were two women
at the Bureau who had reached the coveted top executive grade.

June, who is in her late thirties, has no children and has followed a career path in the Bureau since she left school; she is a
Grade 4, and has been managing a floor of her office since it
opened. Claire, who is 50, has had a more 'typical' female career.
She has three children, now grown up, and took seven years out
of the labour market. She experienced a more fragmented
employment history than June, holding several different jobs and
starting as a part-timer at the Bureau. She had recently been promoted to Grade 4 and was running a sector in her office. Both
women are proud of their management skills which they see in
terms of 'people-orientation', and smooth organization of the
work process.

Both June and Claire spoke of the past climate of discrimination in the Bureau: June described the unspoken assumption that
careers were more important for men:

> 'A few years ago they weren't equal. It was unspoken...well, there's a
> chap who's been here ten years, why isn't he getting on? Well, a woman,
> they didn't expect her to want to get on. As recently as ten years ago the
> emphasis was on men getting on. If a man got stuck at Grade 2 it would
> be seen as a problem.'

In these circumstances, women had to work doubly hard to
prove themselves:

> 'Generally the women would be the better workers. You worry some-
> times that you're a token woman. You do feel that you have to do over
> and above what the men do.'

These forceful women, who have made it to the top on the basis
of their achievements and talents, acknowledge improvements in
the last few years, but highlight women's own efforts in achieving
this against male opposition. In Claire's words:

> 'Men are still given preferential treatment...It was my generation who
> took them on. We're breaking through.'

Both women have had to tackle male sexism. June describes the social discomforts she still faces being a lone woman at her level. At a Christmas dinner in a restaurant with a large group of her male colleagues she was aware of 'cramping their style'. She has had to cope with sexist comments and jokes being made by the men about the female staff:

> 'There are still areas where I've got to say I do feel different... I am still aware of being a woman. There are situations in which I am uncomfortable. There are an awful lot of people who would like to think they are new men, the new age man, but the male chauvinists are still lurking amongst them.'

June's account typifies the subtle undermining and social uneasiness which women so often have to suffer as pioneers when they enter a male domain. Spencer and Podmore (1987), Cockburn (1991) and Marshall (1995), among others, have described the struggles women face in such environments as they try to retain their femininity while establishing their competence as workers. Marked out inevitably by body, by dress, by voice, women in top positions have to contend with being viewed as the 'other', an intrusive and alien presence in a world run on male lines. Often they are seen to disturb well-established and prized patterns of masculine social interaction, the easy climate of 'homosociality' described by Kanter (1977). It is no wonder that high-flying women may sometimes be forced into actions which seem to their sisters lower down the hierarchy as selling out, compromising with men.

Yet June and Claire have clung firmly to feminist ideals. Claire tells me how she has countered male objections to equal opportunities as undermining the principles of meritocracy, that the 'best people should get the best jobs', by pointing out that in the past women were forced to accept men getting the best jobs simply because they were men! Claire, who comes from an activist Labour background, describes herself as passionately committed to equal opportunities for all, regardless of sex, race or class. For her, the way ahead is for unions to help women to view themselves more positively so that they can cope with male teasing and sniping when they make mistakes at work:

'If we could teach women to live without guilt and show them that when men make a muddle they don't worry about it for three weeks!'

For both Claire and June, the focus of change is seen to be from the bottom up: it is attitudes, especially those of men, that must change.

Men and equality

As we have seen, men are much less likely than women to acknowledge gender inequalities at work. It is harder for those in receipt of privileges to accept that they have attained these because of their gender, class or ethnic attributes, rather than because of their own individual efforts. Accordingly, many men seek to legitimate manifest sexual differences in terms of their own superior qualifications, experience or strength. For many men the implementation of EO programmes threatens privileges they had taken for granted or viewed as rights, by opening access to skilled jobs and career paths to women. If women are indeed to be equal competitors, then men see their own chances of promotion and economic advantages weakened. In a minority of cases this had led to the development of a 'backlash', and an assertion of bias to women, as we shall see in Chapter 6.

But men are no more an homogeneous group than women. While 60 per cent of men (compared to 42 per cent of the women) considered that women and men were equal in their own workplace, it must be remembered that over a third of the sample acknowledged men's advantage. 'Men are still classed as number one,' said one; while another commented, 'There are still too many men in top posts.' They accepted that promotion procedures were still stacked in their favour:

'It's an advantage to be male in this place. Once you get beyond the two clerical grades men outnumber women two or three to one.'

'Today if there's a chap of thirty odd he'll be in a higher post.'

Some men who expressed sympathy for women attributed the situation to different characteristics of men and women, although not citing these as sufficient justification for inequalities:

'Women can't do heavy jobs so men have always done a little better.'

'I know the Bureau maintains it's an equal opportunities employer. But I think it still favours men. There's not that many women get up to Grade 4 and above…Having said that, a lot of them are quite happy where they are.'

But a few men stated that women were harder working and indeed superior to male colleagues who fared better:

'You see men who get promoted and you see women who aren't who are much better.'

'They tend to work better than men. But the bank still doesn't expect them to go into management. They still expect women to leave after a few years and bring up children.'

Men who held such views were in a minority, albeit a sizeable one. But where the number of such men builds up to a critical mass, it will be easier for women to assert their rights to be treated as equal competitors, while managers will find it more possible to pursue EO policies with vigour. The gender-aware men whom I interviewed were often in their thirties with wives in employment and with children. I shall argue in the next chapter that it is in families of this type that new gender relations are being worked out. Such men are accepting the necessity for change.

Gender, power and inequality

In Chapter 3, I outlined an account of gendered power based on the notion of differential access to and control of resources, which I shall now apply to the preceding account of gender segregation. Five dimensions of power are implicated in gender segregation in these workplaces: economic; positional; technical; symbolic; and collective.

Historically men commanded the greater share of economic resources. Disparities of income between the sexes remain

widespread and are seen as inextricably linked to gender segregation. Men's access to career lines leading to higher posts helps to
ensure their economic dominance over women. The concentration
of women in part-time employment is also a crucial factor. Such
trends ensure that men are still *seen* as the main earners. Arber
and Ginn's (1995) analysis of data from the General Household
Survey revealed that in the majority of dual-earner families men
earned more than their wives, even in some cases where women
had achieved occupational status equivalent to their husbands.

It should also be remembered that the most crucial form of
economic power relates to ownership of wealth, not income,
and here class considerations intertwine with those of gender.
There are few women directors, chief executives or board members within capitalist organizations. It is here, as Hartmann argued
(1976), that the interests of men as capitalists and as the dominant
sex may run together in influencing the distribution of social
resources.

Accordingly, patterns of vertical segregation in the case study
organizations meant that men were more likely to earn high salar-
ies. For example, we have noted the concentration of male nurses
in F and G grades (43 per cent). At the time of my research (autumn
1992) basic nursing pay was £13,750 to £16,830 a year for Grade F
and £16,200 to £18,750 for Grade G. Most men, then, have a good
chance of receiving a moderate salary. By contrast large numbers
of women are found at Grade A which paid only £7,000 to £8,570
or are stuck as enrolled nurses on Grade C earning from £9,450 to
£11,180. Nursing is 'woman's work' and correspondingly low-
paid: men, however, enter the occupation on the understanding
that they will rise to the higher echelons and get reasonable economic rewards. The same is true of the civil service and banking.
Those at the lowest grade in the Bureau, in which, as we saw,
women predominated, were currently earning only about £3.30
per hour, less, one man told me, than he had formerly earned in a
supermarket warehouse. But retail, too, is a low paying area.
Rates at TradeFare in 1993 were £5.90 an hour for supervisors,
£4.07 for cashiers and £3.85 for assistants; the average employee
earned £227 a week or £11,927 a year. This is high pay for retail
and TradeFare prides itself on this. But it was notable that few of
the male employees I spoke to had family commitments. The job
provides pay levels that single men and youngsters starting on a

working life may find acceptable: but, unless male recruits progress into management, as many hoped to do, economic prospects are poor in terms of any idea of a 'family wage'.

The association of women and what Siltanen calls a 'component wage', that is a wage insufficient to support a household unit at a minimum standard of living (1994, p. 6) is still strong. By definition the majority of part-time women earn only component wages. I was told by numerous men (and several women) that married women were only working for pin money since they had husbands earning good wages. While evidence presented in the next chapter on earning responsibilities challenges such a view, it is clear that the skew in earnings power between women and men persists and is propped up by structures of horizontal and, especially, vertical segregation.

Vertical segregation also reflects men's near monopoly of positional power. In all these organizations management positions were held by men, with the exception of some personnel posts. I did not meet one female general manager. Men also predominated in intermediate tiers, as supervisors, although to a lesser extent. None the less, the majority of positions which entail decision-making and the management of control structures were held by men. This has many consequences. First, women are accustomed to having men in authority over them, which confirms views that men are 'naturally' suited for authority and women are unfit for top posts. Secondly, decisions are mainly made by men and are likely to reflect male definitions and interests. Thirdly, men are likely to be in positions in which they are able to 'hire and fire' and make recommendations for promotion: the tendency for men to appoint 'in their own image' has been noticed in many studies (e.g., Cockburn, 1991; Savage and Witz, 1992; Marshall, 1995). Fourthly, it is mainly male plant and line managers who are responsible for implementation of EO policies. Though we should beware of seeing all men as sexist or holding traditional views on gender, it was clear that some male managers were hostile to some aspects of official gender policies and in some cases were undermining them.

In seeking to maintain gender differentiation, male power-holders often resort to naturalist stereotypes of male and female attributes. This is linked to male deployment of technical and physical power. At Pillco the male process operators had managed, though as we shall see with increasing difficulty, to assert their right to monopolise the more highly skilled work. The issue of strength was central here, since the job involved handling heavy sacks and cans of chemicals, but there was also a general sense that women could not perform 'the whole of the job'. Likewise fork-lift driving and computerized stock control had till recently been male specialisms at Pillco. Similarly at NDH, renal technology, involving the handling of complex kidney machines, had male associations and there was a higher concentration of male nurses in the renal unit, reflecting the greater technical requirements of this form of nursing. It is interesting, however, that the operation of electrocardiographic machinery was a female specialism: but, as Cockburn as shown in the similar case of radiography (1985), where forms of expertise have become associated with women, they are often devalued and lesser paid. This had been the case, too, with speech therapy. An NHS concerned to cut its costs may find it politic to feminize professions, as it was implied was happening with laboratory work.

In the white-collar jobs there was no link to machinery other than computers, but there was a tendency at both Albion and the Bureau for men to be channelled into the more 'technical' tasks. This was exemplified by the position of Grade 4 at the Bureau. This job was horizontally divided into two functions: there were 'technical' Grade 4s and 'management' Grade 4s. The women Grade 4s I interviewed were all of the managerial type, whose task was to run sections of the office and co-ordinate staff efforts. Men dominated as technical Grade 4s whose job was to manage expert teams working on case work of a particularly complex nature. The examples of both the Bureau and TradeFare suggest that the much charted entry of women into managerial positions masks a continued monopoly of technical power by high-level males which may limit the impact women have on management systems.

Underlying all these arrangements are relations of symbolic power. Men are still able to control the deployment of symbolic resources in relation to gender. It is men who set the rules of the workplace, and who define the meanings of such key terms as 'worker', 'skill', 'merit' and 'competence'. Gherardi (1996) describes women who enter male-dominated occupations as outsiders entering an alien culture or, in Marshall's phrase, 'travellers in a male world' (Marshall, 1984). Even in feminized cultures men remain the scriptwriters. In Gherardi's terms: 'the presence of women is tolerated because it is one of the rules of the game, although writing the rules of the game is a male activity' (1996, p. 193). In the imagery of the workplace, certain functions still are represented as fitted either for men or for women: women are portrayed as good at handling people, at training, at routine administration; men are good with figures, with machinery, at decision-making. In the words of one male bank clerk:

> 'Women are certainly more organised than men. Jobs like secretary, administration, et cetera, I think women are better at, but at decision-making I think men take things with more thought, rather than just looking at a colourful picture and dithering.'

Such assumptions, as we have seen, leave some gendered occupations quite untouched, as in the case of typists and car-park attendants, so strongly is their imagery that of one gender, even in organizations with conscious strategies to de-gender other jobs.

At work, men remain primary definers. In the past they have controlled the means of communication and the discourses which deal with production, employment and jobs and used them to maintain gender divisions. Often, as Still (1997) has argued, such gendering is concealed by a purportedly neutral economic discourse which portrays employees, producers and consumers as equal and free agents. But behind this also lurks the broader social division in which women are assigned the role of domestic specialist. This freight of femininity and domesticity, which women carry into employment, enables men as primary definers to present them as deviants in terms of the ideal 'neutral' (read 'male') employee. Thus non-standard forms of employment in which women are disproportionately represented (part-time employment, temporary employment, casual work, homeworking) are still portrayed as not 'real work' (Tilly, 1996). Some of the women I spoke to described such work as 'little jobs'. The concentration of women in such jobs, exemplified in most of these organizations, confirms the symbolic view of women as 'secondary' employees. Such a view was expressed by many men I interviewed and internalized by many women in the absence of an alternative female-centred discourse on women's work.

The importance of this source of male power cannot be under-estimated. The argument I am putting forward in this book is that resources of power are multiple and that this accounts for the complexities of power in given locations. None the less, it is pos-sible to see the control of meaning as the keystone of men's social domination. As Edley and Wetherell argue:

> Men have dominated over women, by and large, because they have managed to gain a stranglehold on *meaning*. What it means to be a man, what it means to be a woman; what jobs constitute men's work and what jobs constitute women's work. (Edley and Wetherell, 1996, p. 107)

Finally, male control in the workplace of the major share of all these resources of power has been backed (at least until re-cently) by male collective power, the ability of men to dominate in the collective organization of employees, using this to press demands reflecting male interests. Male dominance within trade unions facilitated this; and, as I argued in *Men's Work, Women's Work*, a collusion has historically developed between male union-ists and employers which has helped maintain gender segrega-tion, the sex-typing of jobs and pay differentials between men and women. Thus, for example, the trade union at Pillco had in the past supported the male monopoly over the process operators' jobs, negotiating an agreement in which women who filled the jobs had only 'temporary status' and were paid less. Unions have also supported the ideology of non-standard forms of work as 'secondary labour', putting their efforts into organizing full-timers and protecting their interests. This, too, was exemplified at Pillco where the temporary employees (mainly women) had until recently been accorded secondary status in the union, denied vot-ing rights and access to overtime (which was handled by the union).

Yet a key change of the last decades has been in the role of unions, as will be discussed in subsequent chapters. By their delib-erate espousal of EO policies designed to appeal to their female membership, unions have been involved in a major shift in the balance of collective power. Thus male employees experience diminished protection of their interests on two fronts as EO pro-grammes threaten their longstanding hold on the best jobs.

Conclusion

These important recent developments are the topic of Chapter 6 which deals with equal opportunities and challenges to gender segregation. Nevertheless, this chapter has demonstrated that gender segregation remains widespread, even in sites most favourable to its breakdown. It has been maintained in the past by the collusion between male employers and unions; by employers' wish to pay female workers less which sustains a gendered division of labour; by male views about their own superior abilities and commitment which give them rights to the best opportunities; by a symbolic apparatus which maintains a powerful set of gendered images about masculine and feminine attributes and their association with particular jobs and forms of employment; by gendered work cultures based on homosociality which cause difficulties for those who cross the boundaries of gendered jobs and deter many from leaving the shelter of sex-typed work; and by the constraints placed on women by domestic responsibilities.

All these factors were at play in the five organizations and have contributed to the persistence of gender segregation. But the response to this situation among the women and men who work there was varied. A minority of women and a majority of men saw the situation of the sexes as equal, despite the clear evidence of segregation. They comprehended this not in terms of discrimination (which would be seen as unacceptable) but as due to genuine differences between women and men, relating to acquired assets (exams, experience) or to attributes viewed as 'natural' (female domesticity, male strength and authority). Thus gender differences are seen as 'fair' and the notion of 'equality' is not compromised. Indeed, as we shall see in Chapter 6, a minority of men and women are opposed to recent initiatives which they see as favouring women and therefore 'unfair'.

On the other hand a vocal majority of women and a sizeable minority of male sympathizers read the situation as one of gender inequality and wish to redress the balance towards women. Some women in this group have developed a radical critique of prevailing gender relations and see themselves as working towards reforming them, even if only at the level of individual career endeavours. Such women, and male sympathizers, are beginning to question the whole basis of the sexual division of labour inside and outside the workplace. While structures of gendered power in these workplaces still support male dominance, these structures are currently under attack.

Note

1   All names are pseudonyms and some details have been changed to protect identity.

Chapter 6

'Breaking Through': Equalizing Opportunities and Change

'In twenty years I have seen a vast improvement but there's still a long way to go. It was my generation who took the men on. We're breaking through.' (Claire)

Established patterns of gender segregation are persistent, supported as they are by gendered meanings endorsing male dominance. But the picture is not all gloom. This chapter explores processes of change in the workplaces, linking them to feminization. The development of a 'climate of equality', along with women's own growing belief that their contributions should be better rewarded, are two key factors in promoting change: but aspects of the class dynamic (changing employer attitudes to women's labour; the changing position and policies of trade unions; technological development) are also at play.

There are also factors which work against the breakdown of segregation: men are able to use their command of power resources in the organization to block change or slow it down, thereby maintaining their positions of privilege; while individualistic attitudes also work against the effective operation of equal opportunities programmes. But prevailing domestic arrangements are cited by women themselves as the most significant barrier to gender equality. Yet even here change is afoot as couples adjust to a changing economic climate in which dual-earning is becoming the norm.

Equal opportunities in the organizations: a climate of change

Equal Opportunities (EO) policies have proliferated in Britain during the past twenty years, following the passing of the Equal Pay Act and the Sex Discrimination Act in the 1970s and the establishment of the Equal Opportunities Commission as a monitoring body. In addition, EO has been fostered by the influential example of the United States, with its stronger and longer-established equality programmes, and very specifically by the European Community which has kept a sharp eye on discriminatory practices in its member countries and which forced the British government to improve its legislation on the issue of equal pay for equal value in 1984 (the Equal Value Amendment Act). Recently, an additional impetus has come from the government's own Opportunity 2000 scheme, initiated in 1991: companies affiliating to this were obliged to submit an action plan, which specified targets and objectives and dates for achieving these, and to develop monitoring procedures.

Feminists have been critical of these management-led schemes (see Webb and Liff, 1988; Cockburn, 1989; Liff and Wacjman, 1993), which are often viewed as rhetorical window-dressing, part of a public relations exercise on the part of firms wishing to appear progressive. Indeed, the motivation of firms for joining Opportunity 2000 remains obscure. Union officers suggested that some companies see EO policies as an insurance policy against legal action from their employees. However, Freely (1996) has suggested that EO has become perceived more broadly as part of 'good business', a finding confirmed by Carter (1996) in his interviews with personnel managers. Cockburn's research (1991) revealed that commitment to EO was likely to come from top managers concerned about their organization's image and from graduates employed in personnel management whose education and personal beliefs incline them to EO: some of these explicitly espouse feminist ideals. Opposition, however, comes from line managers and supervisors who dislike the way EO disrupts established employment practices and norms.

Jewson and Mason's well-known typology of 'liberal' and 'radical' approaches to EO on race (1986) highlights some of the ambiguities in the formulation of programmes. The liberal approach hinges on removing blocks to 'fair' competition in order to ensure that meritocratic principles of selection and promotion are not being compromised by bias and prejudice. But the radical approach, which is based on the premise that competition is unfair because some of the competitors are disadvantaged and cannot enter on equal terms, advocates more radical intervention to change the conditions of competition, such as setting quotas or providing special training for women or non-white employees. Many programmes, such as Opportunity 2000, sit rather uneasily between the two and may encounter considerable resistance to the more radical aspects. This was reflected in my study.

The five organizations had been chosen partly because of their liberal stance on gender. Four of the organizations were members of Opportunity 2000 and had developed or were developing EO programmes. Pillco was the sole exception, but here there was a personal commitment to EO on the part of the very influential personnel officer which operated on a more informal level. As we have seen, the sexes were highly polarized at Pillco, but paradoxically changes there appeared more radical than elsewhere, as will be discussed later.

Albion, like other banks, had very well developed EO policies. It was the only organization to provide creche facilities (sponsored places in local nurseries): it operated a holiday play system and offered maternity leave and a five-year career-break scheme designed to allow women access to career tracks where in the past motherhood had disqualified them. The longstanding mobility requirements, which had disadvantaged women in the past, now appeared to be waived. Job-share schemes were also available (one manager cited two cases as 'working like a dream') and the bank, with some pressure from BIFU, was improving conditions for part-time employees. Nationwide, Albion's push to get women into management had quadrupled the percentage of women managers over the past decade to 21 per cent, though the regional position was less positive.

The Bureau and Northtown District Hospitals were bound into national policies on EO: both provided me with details of programmes which on paper looked extremely impressive. The Bureau action plan dealt with recruitment, career development, childcare, awareness of EO issues and sexual harassment. All selection boards were mixed in gender and all recruiters had EO training. The relaxation of mobility requirements for promotion had clearly helped women move up the career ladder. While there were still no creche facilities provided, the adoption of flexi-time arrangements had been crucial in allowing women with children to cope with their domestic responsibilities. Pro-rata rights had been obtained for the part-timers. There were plans for women-only self-development courses and a creche was under consideration at one office.

Northern District Hospitals also had a very ambitious action plan with eight specified goals. These included targets for increasing the number of women employed as general managers (from 18 per cent in 1991, to 30 per cent in 1994) and as consultants (from 15 to 20 per cent over the same period). Encouragement for women to enter management was reflected in staff development policies and in training courses: the latter were praised very highly by one of my female respondents. Between 1990 and 1992, 68 women as opposed to 28 men had undertaken programmes organised by NDH's development centre. Women were entitled to maternity leave and career breaks (a three-year scheme) and to return to work at a level commensurate with their leaving grade. Part-time arrangements or job share were available to facilitate such a return. NDH had a very strong policy on sexual harassment, which also took into consideration the needs of gay and lesbian nurses: this involved the appointment of contact officers and fairly severe disciplinary sanctions against harassers. There could be no doubt of the strong commitment of the personnel officer to these policies and the vigour with which she sought to promote them

TradeFare had more recently taken up the EO option and its programme was less developed, but included targets for getting women into management, provision of non-managerial career opportunities for women, monitoring and training for all recruiters. It was emphasized in the company literature that TradeFare was committed to offering equal opportunities to all employees. The company had produced glossy materials for training staff in EO awareness, which also covered sexual harassment. All jobs in the stores were said by the managers to be open to both men and women (the limits to this were discussed in Chapter 5). Job share was possible, but apparently little used, perhaps because part-time work was so freely available and women had leeway in choosing hours to fit domestic commitments. Part-timers had some entitlement to benefits, such as the profit sharing scheme. A term-time working scheme was under consideration (student labour could be used in school holiday periods). TradeFare had won an award for its policies on employing disabled people.

The next section explores the extent to which changes in the structure of job segregation were occurring. It would be wrong to impute these directly to the EO provisions, as these were in their early stages and effects were still working themselves out. Other factors were also at play, as will be shown in the detailed discussion of changes at Pillco. But I judge that *at the least* the EO programmes helped to induce a 'climate of equality'. Such a climate enables women to pursue claims for equality more easily and allows progressive managers to open up opportunities for female employees; while men who resist such changes do so with some uneasiness and feel the need to justify their resistance, as shown in Chapter 5. The spread of such a 'climate of equality' was also promoted by the activities of trade unions which will be discussed in Chapter 9.

Equality and change: challenges to segregation

'The men had the higher positions and the women the lower positions. Now it seems to be equalling out a bit. Just really the last two years.'

This comment from a female factory worker exemplifies the attitude to EO in the case-study workplaces. There was a definite sense that long-established patterns of gender segregation were fraying at the edges: such change, however, was perceived as slow, gradual, and something that women must fight for. Perhaps the most significant development was the challenge to vertical structures of segregation caused by opening up career ladders to women. The removal or weakening of mobility requirements was crucial to this process in the two white-collar organizations: but more subtle was the shift of climate which ensured that top posts were no longer *seen* as reserved for men. Two male bank employees commented on the changes they had seen during their stay at Albion. The first had started work in the 1950s and had seen opportunities opening for women in the bank:

'When I started ladies did all the routine jobs. It's more equal now...When I first started all the senior jobs went to men.

There's more grade 5 women managers now, more women in senior positions.'

In the view of his colleague the old structure which had reserved career posts for men had been completely overturned, with the advantage swinging to women:

'In the 1970s it was virtually a closed door for women with ambitions to further their career. However, in the 1980s women now have the edge over men in terms of job development and promotion.'

Crompton and Le Feuvre (1992) and Savage (1992) have charted the shifts in gender segregation in banking. The old practice, whereby men took exams and climbed steadily up the hierarchy, while women stayed at the bottom stuck in routine clerical jobs, forming a kind of 'white-collar proletariat' (Crompton and Jones, 1984), has been replaced by a two-tier entry system whereby potential managers are taken on for 'fast-track' training. This change may indeed favour women, though Crompton and Le Feuvre suggest that high-flying women are channelled into gendered 'niches', for example controlling the largely female clerical staffs within regional centres which process basic data on accounts and transactions. Certainly, the two fast-track candidates I encountered at Albion were male. Change is occurring, but slowly. Similarly at the Bureau many employees spoke of the slow movement of women into higher posts over the past ten years:

'It's fairly equal. A few years ago it wasn't, men were considered more of the career go-getters.'

'I think now it's a lot better. There's a lot more women in management now. When I started [1984]...there were no women at all in management.'

These changes enhanced the position of married women. The career break arrangements, combined with the advantages flexitime offers in enabling mothers to cope with domestic demands and crises, had made it easier for women to continue their careers. While in the past career success for women had been reserved primarily for a few 'exceptional' single high-fliers, married women with children like Claire have made their way into the hierarchy.

At TradeFare, too, women believed that promotion chances were improving for them. Here the key change was the organizational restructuring which had resulted in the new three-tier hierarchy. The new supervisory grade was more open to women:

'Since they've created the new position I would say it's quite equal. Women used to be only on checkouts and in grocery. There are now more women in posts of responsibility.'

This removal of hidden (and not so hidden) barriers to women's climb up the hierarchy is particularly significant since, as we shall see, it locks into greater aspirations for promotion among women themselves. Some of the young women had long-term ambitions towards management and rightly or wrongly perceived such opportunities as being open to them: two young women spoke (accurately) of their own quick movement up the ladder in comparison to some of their young male colleagues:

'Equal. I don't think there's any discrimination or anything. I started at the bottom and I've come on quite quickly.' (civil servant, aged 24)

'When I first started, I would have thought that men would get on quicker and faster, but since I've spoken to managers they say that it's going the other way.' (bank employee, aged 25)

But structures of horizontal segregation were more resistant to change. There was less sign of movement across gendered boundaries and this often took the form of men moving (though in small numbers) into female specialisms. For example, at TradeFare there were young men to be seen on the checkouts, and I was told that there was an increase in the employment of men in part-time posts, though no statistical proof of this was offered. In fact, the majority of part-time males turned out to be students: there was little sign of permanent male employment on checkouts. Although this job is apparently becoming less gendered, in actuality women and men enter it on different conditions and in different circumstances. For young men, it is a job they pass through on their way to higher things (a university degree and professional employment, a management post); for women, especially older married 'returners', it is a permanent job in which they become expert and which may lead to a supervisory post: but no further – the ladder ends there.

At NDH I was told by several nurses (again I have no statistical evidence for this) that more men were being recruited and that it was easier for them to find jobs after training. This was ascribed by one male nurse to the effects of the 'patients' charter' and the demand by some male patients to be looked after by their own sex. However, another man suggested that the image of nursing remained feminine, resulting in bias against men: 'There still is a bit of "nurses should be women" going about the hierarchy.'

While the movement of men into nursing might be welcomed as a challenge to gender stereotyping, the result has been that men have disproportionately gained top posts (see Chapter 5). The female nurses were well aware of this situation, yet many blamed themselves for it, accepting the view that men were more 'career-minded' or ascribing women's lower success rates to their domestic priorities. But one or two respondents suggested that here, too, things might be changing:

> 'It used to be there was less men in nursing so they always seemed to get higher up and to get the jobs after training, because there are so few of them. There was more competition for the women. It's changing a little bit now. Women are pushing more. More women are coming back from maternity leave.'

As one example of this, a number of enrolled nurses expressed frustration at the limitations their lack of qualifications imposed on their chances of career advancement. The position of enrolled nurse has historically been a gendered and racialized ghetto. As Carter's research shows (1997), many young women from Britain's former colonies were brought into the NHS and virtually trapped into these 'dead-end' posts, with little awareness that they were being effectively excluded from registered status.

Katie and Jayne, two enrolled nurses I spoke to, were actively involved in the local branch of the National Enrolled Nurse Forum, working to improve the situation of the 700 enrolled nurses in their district. They told me that the area offered only six to eight places annually for the conversion course to registered status. They are also debarred from the Open Learning courses available to staff nurses and from Project 2000 schemes which were designed to improve the educational qualifications of nurses and thus enhance their professional standing.

As a result women such as Katie and Jayne are frequently stuck at Grade C, earning £9–10,000 a year. They cannot rise above D as they are not permitted to teach student nurses, a requirement of E and F grading. The Forum is campaigning to open up opportunities for SENs and to get the English Nursing Board to change its rules on issues like training. Katie and Jayne told me of colleagues who were struggling to improve their chances by taking other forms of qualification, such as part-time university degrees or City and Guilds. Katie, for example, has a City and Guilds certificate in teaching and had taken several specialist courses on theatre nursing; but such courses are not considered equivalent to conversion. With a small daughter to care for, Katie was forced to work part-time (30 hours per week) and this in itself disqualified her from the conversion course. Katie, Jayne and their colleagues, like the women at Pillco, are full of frustrated ambitions and energies, with nowhere to take them. Surprisingly, the personnel staff did not seem to register the plight of these trapped and low-paid women in EO terms. Yet, as Katie and Jayne explicitly argued, this is a kind of discrimination with effects similar to sexism and racism: in fact most enrolled nurses are women and at least in the past many were of minority ethnic origin; this *is* an issue of gender and race.

Indeed, one criticism directed by feminists at EO policies is that they only benefit a minority of already privileged, highly-qualified and relatively well-paid women, by opening up top professional and managerial posts to them. Meanwhile, the lot of the majority of women stuck in low-paid, low-status jobs remains unchanged. In addition, the movement of women beyond the 'glass ceiling' is taking place in the context of organizational restructuring of management, in which special 'niche' jobs are created for women. Rather than a strategy of exclusion, a new strategy of inclusion is being adopted which brings women in, but places them in inferior positions to men.

On the face of it, my data confirms this analysis. The major effect of EO in these workplaces was to encourage women into management: at Albion, TradeFare and the Bureau this was concurrent with management restructuring, which accommodated women in lower management and supervisory tiers. Women were considered good at 'managing people' and 'communicating' and jobs were created which employed these 'female' talents, while men retained for themselves posts which required technical and financial expertise. A reframing of gender meanings at work is occurring, rather than the abolition of gendering.

None the less, I would argue that the picture is more complex. For one thing, the women who were grasping these new opportunities were not privileged middle-class women with university degrees, but 'ordinary' women from lower-middle and working-class backgrounds (see Chapter 8) who had worked their way up from the bottom. Moreover, while it is true that patterns of horizontal segregation (including the concentration of women in part-time jobs) had not changed greatly, the 'climate of equality' produced by EO was leading to a more general contestation around gender roles and meanings. This is best exemplified by events at Pillco.

Gender wars: change and resistance in the factory

On the face of it Pillco was the most traditional of the workplaces in terms of its pattern of gender segregation. But processes of change of a quite radical nature were discernible beneath the surface. These involved the movement both of women into men's jobs and men into women's. One operative neatly summed up the changes: 'At one time there was a definite dividing line but now the management have been putting men in categories which used to be done by women and women in what were men's jobs.'

In the course of this women and men were openly brought into conflict. Women asserted their rights to equal treatment, while men resisted the erosion of their traditional advantage:

> 'Ah well, there is a little competition, men here have sort of got themselves into jobs that they think are theirs ... and they don't like women encroaching on them.'

The two main male specialisms on the shopfloor were process operation and warehousing. Women were now found in both. The reasons for their move into process work were a little obscure. At some stage there had been shortages of male labour on certain shifts, resulting in women being taken on as temporaries. They were initially paid less, but their threat to take an equal pay action against the company had led to equalization, which was resented by the men. Some had left the trade union over this issue and feelings remained bitter. Men claimed that women were not doing identical jobs:

> 'Some of them are getting paid the same weekly rates as the men but they're not doing the whole range of jobs.'

> 'It's totally unfair... Because they were going to be taken to court for equal opportunities, they upgraded the pay. Women don't do lifting or dirty work. They're paying the same for doing one little bit of the job as I do for doing the whole lot... The company brought women in on false pretences saying it was temporary. But they've now been doing it for eight years.'

Strength was a key issue here: the job involved lifting 50 kilo cans and packages of chemicals and tipping them into the mixers. Men claimed women could not do this and should be excluded from the job. In fact, even men can find 50 kilo weights a burden. Several reported back problems: and one man complained that his suggestion that chemicals should be packed in 25 kilo cans had been ignored. The job could thus easily be reconstructed in such a way that men's possession of physical power would no longer be justification for keeping women out. This had already happened in the warehouse. New techniques utilizing pallets and fork-lift trucks remove the heavy graft out of warehouse work and allow women to enter it. This was the case at Pillco as at TradeFare. As one man acknowledged, 'the warehouseman's job used to be a man's job, but a girl can do it now'.

I interviewed four women who worked in the warehouse. These were tough, self-confident young women who had pioneered women's entry to the area and had established their right to work as fork-lift drivers. It had been hard, however, as Jacqui's story made clear.

Jacqui is 30, married with a small child. She had worked in the warehouse for eight months when I talked to her. She describes herself as very independent, noting 'I couldn't live off my husband', and is evidently fit and strong: she keeps herself in trim with gymnastics, but says wryly, 'I don't know where I get my energy from.' Although she prefers her new job to working on the line Jacqui confesses that it is a demanding one – it is heavy and the cold can be very bad.

On moving into the job she had faced opposition from the men:
'It's hard trying to be accepted in a man's job...Things are changing but I think in the main men do get more chances. I'm very
surprised I got the job. In a way I'm trying to prove a point. They
slip the odd woman in but they prefer men I think.' In particular
she had faced harassment from one particular individual, who
made a point of assigning her all the most difficult jobs, such as
shifting crates that were hemmed in by other boxes. Jacqui was
doing more than her share of work, but in her determination to
show that women can cope without special treatment she had
rejected the option of reporting this bullying to either management or union: 'I don't know if it's because I'm a woman but he
keeps passing work on to me. I could go to see the manager, but
I'm afraid he'll think I'm moaning because I'm a woman. A lot of
people think this is a man's job. Rather than moaning I've got to
try to stick it out.'

It is not only men, however, who resent encroachment into
'their jobs'. Women expressed concern that men were now being
taken on as line workers in packaging:

> 'When we came in as temps, it was just women, but now they're trying
> to get more lads and men in. I've heard it being said it's going to be a
> male factory, this, eventually.'

Entry into jobs of this kind can prove problematic for men who
have to adjust to routine monotonous working, traditionally seen
as only tolerable for women:

> 'There are jobs women can do that men aren't very good at.' (male
> process operator)

> 'They find the job very tiring although it seems easy.' (female packer)

While these changes might seem to be favourable to women
and had brought operatives of both sexes to confront gender stereotypes about jobs and attributes, Pillco women still saw themselves as disadvantaged. This reflected the continued dominance
of men in top posts. These women faced what we might term not a
'glass' but a 'brass' ceiling: there was no sense of tempting opportunities visible but beyond their grasp, but rather of a complete
blockage to possibilities of advancement. While formerly there

was a route up from the shopfloor, first to team leader and then to supervisor, the creation of a new tier of 'group leaders' consisting of graduate entrants (almost entirely men) to replace supervisors had cut off this option. Women, then, were denied access to authority which many believed they merited. A number of women commented bitterly on this development:

'I tell you, they [the old female supervisors] did a lot more work than what the men do. Now you've got all these young people with degrees and that, they don't know a thing about the factory floor.'

Joy, who was 42 and had been at Pillco for nearly twenty years, described how she had managed her section, until a young graduate aged 20 was brought in – she had to train him. Since he left, she had effectively again been running the section, but was only rewarded with the title – and pay – of team leader. Her claim to higher pay had been lost because, she claimed, the Hay evaluation scheme which was used to rate her work was stacked against her. Joy was running a section which involved some technical complexities and required continual monitoring; her expertise, based on long experience, was, she claimed, vital to its successful running. Her interview with me was cut short when she was called away to sort out a problem: the line had stopped. 'See what I mean!' was her parting shot.

Challenging gender segregation: forces for change

The above accounts indicate processes which have promoted reshaping of the gender order in these workplaces. Four major influences can be distinguished: processes of technological and organizational change, allowing the redesign and redesignation of jobs and hierarchies; employers' attitudes and policies; the changed role of trade unions; and women's own actions and aspirations.

1 Processes of technological advancement open the door for changes in the sex-typing of jobs. At Pillco and TradeFare technological change in warehousing made jobs 'lighter' and allowed the entry of women. The increased use of computerized

systems in white-collar organizations, like Albion and the Bureau, means more keyboarding work which may contribute to the feminization of these occupations. Similarly, restructuring of organizational hierarchies allows for re-inscribing of gender meanings on particular jobs, which may provide new opportunities for women (as at TradeFare and NDH), or block them (as at Pillco).

2   These developments link to changes in management practices in the deployment of labour. There is currently a tendency to feminize jobs or to employ higher proportions of women. In part this may result from EO programmes: as I have suggested, sometimes this arises from genuine belief in EO ideals; at other times it stems from fear of legal action or concern about public image. But there are more pragmatic reasons involved: women are cheaper; they are considered to be less resistant to control; their employment may undermine established union organization; and it is easier to introduce flexible working practices, such as increased use of part-time and temporary contracts, when employing women. All these 'advantages' of female labour have long been cited by employers. Jane Humphries argued that women constituted an ideal proletariat for an industrializing society (1983). Now there seems to be a new push towards 'female proletarianization' in the current phase of capitalist accumulation as women are seen to possess qualities apt for consumerized service employment: skills in customer care and 'emotion work' (Hochschild, 1983), communication skills, the ability to manage other women.

3   In the past employers' desire to feminize the labour force received a check from the resistant actions of male workers, especially through unions. The 'truce' or collusion between employers and male unionists resulted in the characteristic allocation to men of the top jobs and the clustering of women at the bottom of employment hierarchies. A crucial feature of current employment relations is that this truce has broken down. There are two reasons. First, trade unions have been so weakened in the past decades that they can no longer exert much influence of any kind on employers' policies (see Chapter 10). Secondly, unions in their desire to rebuild themselves are forced to acknowledge their need to recruit women and other formerly disregarded groups. Consequently they have

espoused EO and can no longer nakedly act to preserve the interests of white, male skilled workers. This constitutes a major jolt to male deployment of collective power in the workplace.

4   Finally, women themselves are increasingly unprepared to tolerate old structures of male privilege. Women are forcefully asserting their own right to well-paid jobs and are refusing to see themselves as inferior to men. My case-studies reveal the effects of this attitude shift. Some women, as yet in small numbers, but increasingly, are pushing their way into male specialisms, such as fork-lift driving at Pillco. In the same way individual women are pressing upwards towards high posts, as at Albion and the Bureau. Individuals (like Joy) and groups of women (such as the SENs or the speech therapists who were pursuing a claim for equal pay with male pharmacists) are challenging the traditional low evaluation of 'women's jobs' and pressing for their skills and achievements to be acknowledged and upgraded. This is perhaps the most important effect of what I have called the 'climate of equality'. Only a minority of women are actively involved in these challenge But my reading is that what as yet is a trickle could wel become a tidal wave. The gender wars commencing at Pillco are set to continue.

Barriers to change

There are forces which act in a counter direction, retarding the processes of change. Here I discuss three such tendencies: the resistance to gender change of some men, often referred to as 'backlash'; the individualistic ideology of merit which makes both sexes wary of radical forms of EO policy; and, without doubt the most important factor, women's domestic responsibilities.

While many men, as we have seen, are sympathetic to women's claims for equality, a vociferous minority oppose them, claiming that things have 'gone too far'. In their view, men are now the disadvantaged sex. They complain that women are being promoted on the grounds of sex not merit, that women are being allowed into jobs for which they are under-qualified while deserving men are passed over. Such a backlash against EO was in evidence at Pillco, Albion and among some groups at NDH:

'Women get promoted faster than men. Just for this so-called equality, they're going the other way now... The bank has to been seen to be promoting women, so it's the men who are suffering. I mean they're the ones with families to run.' (bank clerk, aged 19)

Men complained that 'positive action' programmes existed which not only favoured women but resulted in them taking jobs for which they were unsuitable:

'Positive discrimination, I think that's over-emphasised. I think that positive discrimination means they deliberately go about to put a wo-man into a job... In the bank it's gone too far. There are some jobs which men are in which you could call a woman's job.' (bank clerk, aged 37)

Such men struggled against changes in the gender order. They tended to see feminization as a problem because it was taking jobs away from men and clung to the old order of male breadwinner and child-minding mother. In the words of one of them, inequality between the sexes was 'necessary and inevitable':

'Mothers should stay at home and look after their children. There's too much encouragement for women to go back to work.' (laboratory scientist, aged 39)

'I don't think people's lives have been improved by two people going out to work. If unions fought to give the breadwinners a better wage then you could afford to keep the spouse at home.' (factory operative, aged 50)

'I don't want to come over as a sexist. But I tend to think that if children are born the mother should look after them when there's a shortage of jobs anyway.' (shop assistant, aged 18)

There is a generational element in the development of back-lash. Most of the men who expressed opposition to EO were older married men. These men might have experienced blockages to their own careers, or simply were unable to accommodate changes to customary arrangements. The significance is that men of this age group are often in positions to make decisions over recruit-ment and promotion. It was clear that some middle managers and section heads fell into this category and were using their power to retard change, a phenomenon also noted by Hochschild (1997).

At the other end of the age-scale a few young men also expressed what might be called traditional views on gender roles. This may arise from the feeling that they are losing out on career chances to young women: the public concern over boys' poor examination performance in schools fuels such anxieties. However, there is some ambiguity here. The same student working at Trade-Fare who expressed reservations about working mothers suggested that gender differences would be 'less and less with my generation growing up, my generation have grown up ... not in a sexist climate'. These young men have witnessed the gender order shifting and may simply be forced to adapt.

It is not only men whose views are ambivalent. Another obstacle to the successful application of EO policies is the contradictory sets of attitudes commonly displayed to them. My respondents were asked several questions about unions and EO. For women, this emerged as a high priority with 69 per cent thinking it a very important objective for unions. In view of men's attitudes discussed earlier it is no surprise that only 36 per cent of men rated it very important. Yet despite this commitment to EO on women's part, women, too, espouse individualistic ideals. They were asked if they supported the idea of reserved seats for women on union committees and this question received sharply polarized reponses from both sexes. Overall more people opposed the idea than supported it, though once again there was a significant gender gap: 49 per cent of women favoured reserved seats, with 42 per cent against, while a male majority of 51 per cent was anti, with 37 per cent in favour.

Behind the opposition was strong attachment to meritocratic ideals and 'fairness'. The policy was denounced by its opponents as 'sexist', 'discriminatory', 'segregating men and women', 'taking EO too far'. Typical responses were:

'The places should be open to people who are interested in them. It should be the best candidate for the job.' (male)

'You should be there because of policies and the hard work you're prepared to put into it.' (female)

Previous studies have revealed the resistance shown by some activist union women to the idea that women might need a helping hand. This attitude was held by some of my interviewees:

'Women can do it on their own merit.'

'I think if women want the seats they'll get there through their own work.'

For example, Claire, who as we saw in Chapter 4 was strongly committed to feminist ideals and described herself as 'a passionate believer' in EO for all, rejected reserved seats as discriminatory and used the 'best person for the job' argument. Yet Claire had overturned precisely those same arguments when used by men about women getting 'unfairly' promoted at the Bureau; and she suggested that her union might run assertiveness training courses for women to 'show [them] how to be positive', a policy which might be seen as a form of the generally suspect 'positive discrimination'. Claire, like many women, demonstrated a mix of attitudes, reflecting her (and our) exposure both to feminist arguments and to the individualistic discourse of merit and achievement so strongly promoted in the 1980s.

Younger people, who gained their political understanding during the Thatcher epoch, were especially prone to be caught between feminist and individualistic discourses. Thus some of Claire's younger female colleagues at the Bureau affirmed at the same time their belief in gender equality and their rejection of 'discriminatory' policies designed to correct gender imbalance: 'There should be equal rights for men and women – that's positive discrimination' (aged 22); 'If you want to have equal rights, you have to be equal' (aged 24). There is some possibility that such a mix of attitudes can lead to young women adopting a 'post-feminist' stance, as was the case with Mandy.

Aged 19, living with her boyfriend (who works as a driver) and bringing up a child aged 13 months, Mandy puts herself across as ambitious and independent. In the lowest grade, she is targeting herself for a Grade 3 and says she is 'determined to do something' with her life. The Bureau's flexitime enabled her to return to work after only four months' maternity leave: 'I don't think I could come to work under normal working conditions.' While she feels she would like to spend more time with her baby, she states explicitly that she wants a career, as well as needing the money. Despite flexitime and using her friend as a childminder, she finds co-ordinating her childcare arrangements difficult and repeatedly emphasizes that the union should work for the provision of better childcare, especially a creche. In many of her actions, and in her aspirations, the needs she articulates, Mandy behaves as one would expect a young feminist to do: but, in fact, she declares herself expressly anti-feminist. Men and women, are equal, she tells me; feminists have got what they wanted. She is 'fed up' with feminist activities and opposes reserved seats: 'If you're on about EO sort of thing between men and women, so why be prejudiced against half of them?' Mandy's attitudes about women are starkly opposed to those of the older women at Pillco, and suggest future problems for feminist-inspired campaigns among at least a section of the younger generation.

Mandy is struggling to cope with the demands of her domestic circumstances and appears, on balance, to be winning. But it was clear that in the eyes of most women, domestic responsibilities and childcare were the major remaining blocks to equality. The importance of childcare provision was stressed by women in all the organizations. Without it, women with children could not compete equally with men:

> 'To me that's the only thing that holds women back, it's looking after the children.'

> 'My personal view is that men don't have the hassles at home. They can just leave the home behind.'

Women in all the organizations believed that managers discriminated against women with children (and indeed, by extension, against *all* women, since *any* woman may give birth):

> 'I think if you're married and likely to have kids, I think you're pretty well frowned on. If you're single or you've been married a long time and there aren't children on the scene it stands you in good stead.'

Dinah's story illustrates the complex intertwining of work and family and how they affect women's careers. Dinah has two children in their teens. She trained and qualified as an MLSO in a particular specialism, but left her job for five years while the children were small. Then aged 35, she tried to return to her career, but wished to work part-time. Indeed, had it not been for the fact that 'I have got wonderful grandparents', she might not have been able to return at all, while her youngest was only two and a half. However, the only work she could obtain in her old specialism, as a part-timer, was that of an unqualified assistant. Dinah's story here typifies the experience of women returners, forced to take on jobs below their level of qualification and experience. However, a stroke of luck befell her. A vacancy occurred in the blood transfusion department while somebody was on maternity leave. Dinah took it, stayed on, eventually becoming full-time and regaining her former qualified status. She enjoys her work, with its contact with patients and nurses, although ironically she has not been trained for it.

For Dinah balancing the demands of job and home has been a continuous problem. She has not sought promotion in the past because of coping with housework and childcare: 'I used to find it enough just being at work in the circumstances.' Flexitime, she feels, would help greatly, as she could do her shopping in the morning before starting work. Her comments show how she is torn between work and family orientation: when asked her reasons for going out to work, she spoke first of extras for the family: 'Children cost you an arm and a leg. Having said that, I wouldn't mind being part-time but I wouldn't like being at home all the time. I think I need to work.' At 45, she is at last beginning to take interest in the possibility of promotion, but is in a difficult situation since her training was in one specialism while her past ten years' experience is in another. Unsurpringly she is jaundiced about gender relations in the laboratories:

> 'Our chief's quite sympathetic about working women with young children... But, I tried to get back into the other department, but there was no way they would take me on part-time. I know there was two other women, they left to have children at the same time, who wanted to do a job share and they wouldn't have anything to do with it.'

While job share and arrangements for returning part-time were now part of the official EO policy at NDH, it was apparent that some managers continue to evince the suspicion towards married women which has been reported in other hospital studies (Rosser and Davies, 1987; Homans, 1987). Women still have to deal with entrenched traditional attitudes among senior males:

'They're not really willing to give the women the responsibility. It's always the chaps that get it.'

A comment from a woman at TradeFare sums up perfectly the internal pressures women face in reconciling domestic and waged forms of labour:

'If you're a married woman... the opportunities are there, but carrying it out is a different thing. If you want to go on, like the girls, there are one or two of them who are trying to be managers, they have to be in at all times. But if you're a married woman you couldn't do it... It always ends up being the woman's responsibility, no matter how good your husband is and even if it doesn't you feel guilty. Especially as everyone thinks you should be looking after the children, they make you feel guilty.'

A new gender order: renegotiating the division of labour

Yet despite these familar problems, there are some signs of change in the arrangement of what Miriam Glucksmann has called the 'total social organization of labour' (1995), encompassing wage-earning, domestic work and other productive activities needed for individual and social reproduction. Women's disadvantaged position in the social division of labour has often been explained in terms of their lack of career-orientation. This traditional view is captured in a comment from one of the men at the Bureau:

'No disrespect, but a lot of women can't get out of the idea that their job is a second job. They're not looking to develop themselves. They're concerned to marry, have a family and keep money coming in but no more.'

But this view cannot be sustained by an examination of the responses of this particular sample of women. As a group, the women were almost as ambitious as men for promotion (Bradley, 1996); they did not see their earnings as 'pin-money' and they were as likely as men to make statements indicating strong commitment to employment as many of the women's stories recounted in these two chapters have shown. They valued their jobs for bringing them independence, freedom from domesticity and allowing them, exactly, 'to develop themselves':

'After a couple of weeks you want to go back to work. You get bored, you get lazy. I'm not that sort of person. As long as my health's fine I'll work, I like to be on the move. You need something to get up for in the morning.'

'I felt as if I were vegetating at home. I wanted to get back, I felt I had something to offer.'

'It helps us to be a person in our own right, not just mam, not just the wife.'

The women were asked whether they considered their earnings essential for their household: two-thirds said that they were, with another 28 per cent considering them important. Only 6 per cent thought their earnings unimportant, these mainly being young unmarried women living with their parents. A substantial number of the women were the sole or main earners in their household, because they were single, divorced, their husbands had died or were chronically sick or unemployed. Nearly as many women as men in the sample reported themselves sole earners: 26, of whom 12 were single, compared to 28 men, 10 of these being single. As one male sympathizer said of his female colleagues at Pillco, 'They're not just on second incomes, working for pin money, as so many men say.'

The majority of those I interviewed, both women and men, were in families with more than one earner. This, too, is an area of important change. Harrop and Moss (1995) have charted the trend to the dual-earner family which is now 'the most common form of family life' (p. 433). This is significant not so much as a quantitative phenomenon (economic need has characteristically driven working-class wives to supplement the family income) as a qualitative one. In the North East at least, dual-earning is becoming the *social norm*, replacing the expectation of breadwinner male and dependent wife. This in turn affects the way couples view their work situations as these comments from TradeFare workers show:

'To have a good standard of living, with your own car and holidays and that sort of thing, I think the woman has to work all her life.' (aged 24)

'I have my own car and for holidays which we couldn't have otherwise. I don't want to be a housewife. I'd go crazy staying at home. I like my own bit of independence.' (aged 45)

As they mutually construct dual-earner life-styles, women and men are rethinking the place that work of various types occupies in their lives. If my sample are anything to go by, women show greater aspirations concerning their careers than previous studies have suggested. Hakim (1991), for example, suggests that women are less ambitious than men. But, as Table 6.1 shows, there was very little difference between men and women in the younger age groups in terms of aspirations for promotion.

TABLE 6.1 **Percentages of women and men wishing for promotion at work, by age (full-time workers only)**

Age group	Women	Men	All
under 25	86	89	88
25–29	78	79	78
30–39	33	78	56
40 plus	39	17	28
All ages	56	64	60

Moreover the older women were actually *more* ambitious than their male counterparts. It was only in the age group at which domestic responsibilities tend to be at their height that women lagged behind men, and some of these women expressly put it down to the burden of domestic work, as we saw with Dinah.

While women sometimes were more modest in their promotion plans than men (aspiring only to rise one grade up the hierarchy) this difference disappeared among the young people. Many young women expressed managerial ambitions. While it may be argued that their hopes will be dashed when they face the realities of looking after children, there are tendencies which run counter to that. First, as Table 6.2 indicates, the time taken off to rear children has steadily decreased. Mandy and the TradeFare worker quoted above were typical of young workers who had taken minimal maternity leave.

TABLE 6.2   **Time taken out of the labour market to bring up children**

Age	No. of women	Time out of employment
Under 30	7	l year
31–40	12	2 years 9 months
41–50	21	5 years 3 months
50+	5	10 years 7 months

Such young women showed a disposition to 'have it all'. One woman said 'I'd like to get on in the bank, but I also want children as well'; while a nurse told me she was planning to have children and would like to work part-time, but was clear that she wished to become a sister.

In coping with women's desire to 'make something of my life' couples are readjusting the way they share out family and domestic work. Childcare remains a major problem. As these are not high-earning couples, professional childminding is a drain on budgets, but was the only option for some. Grandparents, parents and other relatives were the major source of help. Fourteen out of the 31 women who reported having help with childcare had used parents. But husbands and partners also played their part.

A number of men spoke of their involvement in domestic work and family commitments. A twenty-year-old Bureau worker felt he couldn't move area to get the promotion he wanted because of his responsibility to his invalid father. A nurse (aged 30) described how he shared childcare with his partner (who was in private nursing), by dovetailing shifts. This couple also cared for his disabled mother-in-law. A machine operative praised Pillco for allowing him time off with pay to care for his sick mother; and John at Trade-Fare told me that he could not seek promotion to a managerial job at the moment because he was 'a little tied up by family'. John's wife was just starting a nursing course as part of Project 2000 which would take eighteen months; John felt he needed to be free to help with their two-year-old child and promotion would mean moving around the region, disrupting his wife's career plans.

Where women become main earners they may call more on their partners for domestic help. Such was the case with Hazel, an SEN at Northtown. Hazel wished to do the conversion course to SRN but was concerned that with her fifteen-month-old daughter it would be too difficult to manage. However, her husband, who was currently on shift work, was doing most of the childcare and offering her excellent support. Hazel described her baby as 'Daddy's girl' since she spent so much time with her father.

Louise, for very different reasons, was also currently a main earner. Her husband was 'on the sick' with a bad hip and was about to take early retirement because of stress and problems in his job. Her story exemplifies the shifts and turns in the lives and motivations of women. Louise was 44 and typical of the older generation in having spent thirteen years out of the labour force to bring up a family. She had held a number of jobs in factories and shops before starting as a temp at Pillco in 1988. While valuing the companionship and independence she found in her job, she made it clear that she was strongly family-centred. She spoke of the hard work that she and her husband had put in to rear their three children; he had worked nights driving a taxi on top of his NHS job. Louise's money was now vital for the family, with her husband off work and two children still at home. However, she hoped that when recovered her husband might set up a consultancy, which would enable her to retire once the children were 'settled and married'. After a hardworking life, she said, she wanted a time of leisure and enjoyment alone with her husband: 'There's more to life . . .'

Divisions and differences: family-centred women?

Louise's orientations appeared more 'traditional' than those of young women like Mandy and Hazel or many of the older women at Pillco. While in these chapters I have been concerned to stress the common experiences of gender inequality shared by the women I talked to, it is important to acknowledge divisions and differences among women, which have figured so prominently within recent feminist work.

This discussion has highlighted some aspects of difference. Age is an important factor here: younger women are more likely to express long-term ambitions and to espouse the dual-earning family model, returning to their careers with only a short break after the birth of their children. At the same time, they are often more individualistic in their thinking than older women, and this leads them to deny the existence of structured inequalities of gender. Differences in achievement are ascribed to individual merit and efforts. Older women, by contrast, are more likely to read gender meanings into work relations.

There are occupational differences too. Since gender segregation manifests itself differently in these different locations, it is not surprising that the women at Pillco and NDH, where horizontal segregation was most marked, were most critical of prevailing gender arrangements. But the Pillco women also expressed most vigorously their commitment to employment and rejection of the housewife role. Perhaps the hard graft of housework where money is short means that being a 'lady of leisure' is less enticing for manual women than their more affluent white-collar sisters.

I have stressed the strength of commitment to work among my sample; but a minority of women, such as Louise, had followed a more traditional female pattern in their work histories, moving between jobs before having a long break to bring up their families. Some of them conformed to Hakim's account of 'family-centred' women, who would prefer to work part-time or not at all; and these lukewarm attitudes to work were more likely to be found in the clerical groups. Rhoda was one such. A charming, elegant woman of 48, she had taken thirteen years out of employment to bring up her three children, the youngest of whom was now 12. She had then helped her husband running his business until they split up and she found her present job. Rhoda, who described herself as a 'real woman', told me she longed to find a 'real man' to support her. She needed to work full-time for the money, and did not dislike her job, but would have preferred part-time or job-share arrangements to allow her to spend more time at home. Unambitious for promotion Rhoda said, rather sadly, 'I just want to be happy.'

The stories I was told suggest that women do indeed have differing orientations, but there can be no simple division of women into 'career-oriented' (largely full-time) and 'family-oriented' (part-timers). Women's aspirations and orientations change as they move between jobs and between stages in the life-cycle. I found some full-timers, like Rhoda, who would have preferred part-time employment; while some of the part-timers at TradeFare were strongly committed to their careers. Many factors influence the meanings that women bring to their jobs and those meanings are altering as younger couples frame their lives in expectation of dual-earning. Waged labour and domestic labour *both* play a central part in the lives of these women – and of some of their male colleagues too.

Conclusions

While this chapter has discussed continuing barriers to gender equality, such as male resistance and women's domestic responsibilities, I have been concerned to highlight change and positive developments. Dynamics of class and gender come together to disrupt patterns of gender segregation as employers seek to deploy women's labour in new ways and women themselves demand greater opportunities for promotion and self-development.

This is gradually leading to shifts in the balance of power between the sexes, as women gain greater command of economic resources relative to men. At the moment men continue to dominate in positions of authority at work and are able to use these to block women's advance. Yet this may change as the effects of EO policies play themselves out. When this happens, women may be in a position to utilize power in the symbolic field, contesting prevailing meanings that surround gender and employment. In individual households, where dual-earning has become the social norm, change in gender meanings is occurring as couples renegotiate the division of labour and redefine the contributions of women and men to the total social organization of labour. However, while this bodes well for the position of women in the future, a major problem is that these changes are occurring at a time when the dynamic of class is adversely affecting the lives of many employees, both women and men. This is the subject of the following chapters.

Chapter 7

Competitiveness at Work: Restructuring and Its Impact

'There's not much good about it at the moment. The pressure of work, it really destroys you. There's no incentive. There's no promotion, no pay rise ... Before I used to enjoy coming to work. But now it's just a job and you get paid for it.' (civil servant, female)

'Things will get worse rather than better. They have done in the last few years.' (bank clerk, male)

The last two chapters have examined the position of women and men as employees in the five organizations, exploring the changing gender dynamic as women become more ambitious and more prepared to challenge male domination at work. But these changes coincide with others which result from the operation of the class dynamic. As women contest more openly with men they find themselves in competition for decreasing numbers of higher posts. While equal opportunities are vaunted, the reality is one of diminishing opportunities for all. Women are having their expectations raised in a climate when it is harder to realize them; and the situation is worse if you are young or from a minority ethnic group. It is in this context that the male backlash, discussed in the last chapter, must be viewed.

The next two chapters examine the changing class dynamic. A longstanding problem in the study of class has been the gap between the material experiences of class (poverty, wealth, deprivation, exploitation) and the expressed meanings of class, in terms of subjectivities and identities. This contrasts with the study of gender. Women are not likely to 'mis-identify' themselves as men in great numbers (though there are of course boundary cases which challenge binary sexual identifications). But sociological research into class shows that such 'mis-identifications' are relatively common; many who are subject to the material conditions seen by sociologists to typify working-class experience call themselves middle-class (and vice versa). In the case of gender the transition from what I have elsewhere called a 'passive' (potential) identity (Bradley, 1996), to active identification is relatively straightforward. As the last two chapters showed, many women in my study had an active awareness of gender and a minority had developed politicized identities of an expressly feminist kind. But the path from passive to active or politicized identification of class appears more complex, contingent and unpredictable. Consequently, in these chapters I have chosen to study these two aspects of class, material experience and class meanings, separately.

This chapter considers the relations of wage labour as a manifestation of the class dynamic. Although I argued in Chapter 3 that class cannot be reduced to production relations, they remain an important aspect of class difference and the one I had access to for my respondents. I offer an account of the experience of wage labour as they described it to me. I asked them several open-ended questions about their jobs: what were the good and bad points about them? What problems did they experience? What would most improve the quality of their working lives? The questions allowed them to describe events in their own terms and air their own concerns, not those of social scientists, though in analysing responses I have linked them to sociological accounts of change.

The chapter considers the changes that were occurring as described to me by the employees, managers and unions. I show how these changes, associated with globalizing capitalism, affect everyday work relations within a regional economy. I consider the attempts of organizations to alter working practices in response to heightened competition, and to a perceived need for 'leaner, fitter' production methods, increased productivity and a heightened emphasis on market and customer priorities. The chapter highlights increasing stress, insecurity and collective powerlessness as characteristic of this particular phase of capitalist development, especially among public-sector employees. This reflects the attempt to reconstruct the public sector by importing the techniques and principles of private enterprise, what Du Gay terms the 'progressive enlargement of the territory of the market' (1996, p. 56). While in the past service-sector employment was seen to pose problems for class analysis as its prevailing relationships were different from those within private enterprise (Crompton and Gubbay, 1977; Parkin, 1979), it can now be argued that public-sector employees, too, are firmly located within the evolving capitalist dynamic. The changing configuration of class positions, linked to these changing relations of employment, is then explored in Chapter 8, where the focus is on the meaning of class and processes of class identification.

The experience of wage labour

'It's all right. It gets pretty boring. You get left in a job for quite a while. It's all right, it's a job.' (bank clerk, female)

'It's close to where I live. For the type of work I suppose it's not too badly paid. We're lucky to have a job. They're not too strict. They let you have a bit of rope, a bit of leeway... There are unpleasant things but I'm used to that. Your brain stultifies. They assume you're stupid because you're a production worker.' (process worker, male)

'It's tedious. Mind-numbingly tedious at times. You go home feeling completely blank.' (clerical officer, male)

'I don't like it at all really. It's boring.' (checkout cashier, female)

Wage labour has had a bad press in sociology. Marx's account of alienated labour has set the tone for subsequent discussion. In its classic manual form, wage labour is characterized by lack of control, powerlessness, monotony and repetition as a result of task division (what Marx called the 'detail division of labour'). Harry Braverman (1974) argued that the development of the capitalist labour process was marked by a long-term tendency to degradation, involving the removal of skill, discretion and autonomy from the worker. Empirical studies of factory work (such as those of Beynon, 1975; Haraszti, 1977; Nichols and Beynon, 1977; Linhart,

1981) confirmed the negative view, emphasizing the monotony, the stress and damage to mental and physical health, the lack of control, the frustration. Studies of female factory workers (for example, Herzog, 1980; Pollert, 1981; Cavendish, 1982) replicated these findings, also indicating that the most pressurized and repetitive tasks were assigned to women, who were subjected to tighter control than men. As two of my own Pillco respondents put it:

'We can go off the line and after ten minutes they're looking for us and men go off for ages and they don't bother.'

'I think women tend to get put on in the factory. And women do jobs that men will not do, they refuse to do them and they get away with it.'

The negative experience of wage labour for some of my sample of employees is reflected in the quotations at the head of this section. Monotony was experienced especially by those at the bottom of each particular job hierarchy: women on the line at Pillco, cashiers and trolleyboys at TradeFare, junior clerks at the Bureau and Albion Bank. Many of these lower-level employees complained of boredom and lack of stimulation as the worst features of the job. It might then appear surprising that the overall picture was of considerable attachment to jobs. A quarter of those interviewed expressly said that they liked their jobs: the features they liked are summarized in Table 7.1

A number of factors may account for this apparently high degree of satisfaction. As we saw in the last chapters, a general sense of work commitment was common, especially among women: these workers were in no hurry to abandon the work ethic. Moreover, in the context of high regional unemployment, any job, especially if it was relatively well rewarded and secure, received a high valuation: 'any work is good'; 'it's a job, for one'; 'I'm very glad to have a job in this day and age'. Another common response was that the organization in question was 'a good firm to work for'. Pillco and TradeFare workers, in particular, viewed their jobs relatively and saw them as preferable in a variety of ways to employment they had experienced elsewhere:

'It's a canny job. It's not a very hard job. It's easier and better paid than other jobs I've had.' (factory worker, male)

'I prefer it to the shop. Here you just get on with your job and you do what you have to do and you get your money, there's no hassle...You've got nobody on your back...Mind, you have to work hard, but that's what you're here for.' (factory worker, female)

It is common to make a distinction in sociology between the conditions of manual and of 'white-collar' work: although both are forms of wage labour, the conditions, rewards and character-istics are very different (Lockwood, 1958; Wedderburn and Craig, 1974). White-collar workers are habitually accorded a greater degree of autonomy and discretion, what Fox (1974) characterized as relations of 'high trust'. Also the content of higher-level white-collar jobs tends to be more varied and interesting and to present greater chances of upward mobility or progression, appearing as a 'career' rather than a mere job. On the other hand, there has been a longstanding debate over the possible 'proletarianization' of white-collar employees as capitalism develops. Braverman, for example, argued that the lower echelons of service employees, such as clerks and sales assistants, had seen their jobs degraded so that they differed little from factory work.

TABLE 7.1   Reported good features of jobs (number of mentions)

Contact with public	32
Responsibility/challenge	25
Good colleagues	25
Variety	18
Good pay	15
Flexitime	13
Just having a job/secure job	12
Good conditions	11
Autonomy	9
Fits domestic needs/helpful hours	9
Good managers	7
Teamwork	6
Providing a service	4
Pleasant atmosphere	4
Pensions/benefits	3
Working with computers	2
Generally I like my job	52

My survey reveals a complex picture. Low-level bank and civil service clerks viewed their jobs as negatively as their equivalents at Pillco and TradeFare. Simply being a white-collar worker gives no guarantee of greater fulfilment and control in one's job. But within each workplace, those higher up the hierarchy tended to experience more interest, more variety, more autonomy in their work. Across the sample the same things were valued by my interviewees as good aspects of their jobs: contact with the public (which headed the list of positive features); responsibility, challenge and variety; good workmates; good managers; and of course good pay and conditions. For women, hours that fitted with domestic needs and flexitime were also a particular asset. Generally, the more of these characteristics a job displayed the more valued it was likely to be.

The jobs which came closest to the career model, however, were found at Northtown District Hospitals. Even the lowest-level jobs here seemed to offer a level of involvement, interest and, especially, service to patients, which made up for low pay and sometimes rough conditions:

'There's a lot involved in it, looking at the whole patient. I like the fact that you form relationships with patients over a long time...At times it gets a bit samey, but...you can talk to patients, and find out their psychological problems and their social problems.' (nurse, male)

'It's brilliant...Job satisfaction, to see people get better. The team work between all the staff, there's never a dull moment on the ward. I look forward to every shift.' (nursing auxiliary, male)

'I enjoy the work, find it interesting. You get satisfaction from it, feeling you're doing something...I enjoy using my mind.' (MLSO, female)

However, this positive response to the content of their jobs and to providing a service was only one side of the picture at NDH. Against this must be set the tide of discontent over what was happening to the NHS. As we shall see, the net response to these changes was negative and hostile: in the eyes of many of my respondents change meant decline:

'The government is currently eroding what they see as the fat of the Civil Service...They're now down to the bare bone.' (male civil servant)

'I find the job interesting or I wouldn't have been in it for twenty years. But it's appalling what's going on, it's all money, everything's money, they're not remotely interested in the quality of the service you provide... I'm very very cynical.' (MLSO, male)

Restructuring and work organization in the public-sector

Public-sector workers in my study offered the most negative accounts of current changes. As other research has suggested, public-sector organizations are at the forefront of attempts to restructure employment relations (Fairbrother, 1991; O'Connell Davidson, 1993; Filby and Shelton, 1996). The British Conservative government led by Margaret Thatcher deliberately used the public sector to promote its own view of how work organizations should be run, as a stimulus to private-sector efforts to increase efficiency, productivity and thus competitiveness. In the postwar period the state has constantly acted as a model employer, originally promoting corporatist industrial relations as embodied in the Whitley arrangements (Beaumont, 1992; Seifert, 1992). Subsequently, as Fairbrother (1991) points out, the Conservative government in the 1980s–1990s used the public sector to promote New Right ideals of flexibility and the 'enterprise culture'. In this way, Du Gay argues, public-sector organizations have been 'reimagined as enterprises' (1996, p. 181). The principles of the market and of entrepreneurialism have been promoted, through, for example, the introduction of the 'internal market' as a device for regulating expenditure within the NHS along with the creation of self-governing and competitive trusts and the deployment of professional managers to introduce the techniques of 'New Public Management' (Osborne and Gaebler, 1992; Webb, 1996).

Such techniques include performance appraisal, performance-related pay and quality monitoring; the re-identification of clients as 'customers'; the introduction of new flexible forms of contract into employment relations, such as compulsory competitive tendering (CCT) in the NHS or market testing in the Civil Service. Du Gay suggests that these policies are an attempt to remake public-sector employees as entrepreneurial selves, while both Beaumont and Seifert argue CCT and the establishment of trusts in the NHS are designed in part to fragment a stongly unionized workforce and to weaken or marginalize the unions.

The effects of these policies were clearly felt in the two organizations under study. The Bureau was feeling the brunt of the government's attempts to slim down the service and cut costs, with a package of policies for change, many of which were actively being resisted by the BWU. These included: plans to merge offices to create larger units thus shedding high-paid top jobs; an attempt to replace a previous merit pay scheme with a fully-fledged performance-related pay scheme and performance appraisal (which was currently being boycotted by the union); market testing, that is the contracting-out of some of the more routine tasks (one pilot scheme tried locally was said to have ended in disaster because of numerous mistakes by the subcontractors); a delayering scheme, the Management Practices Initiative, whereby the complex hierarchy of 14 grades would be reduced to five pay bands, and which involved redistributing duties between management grades, reducing the autonomy of district management and losing a number of posts (the target was that 25 per cent of offices would be delayered by 1995). While these changes were being introduced, a freeze on jobs had been instituted and under the Clerical Resources Allocation Guidelines (CRAG) the Northern region was told to lose 120 jobs; the service was also currently subject to the 1.5 per cent public sector pay freeze. No wonder that the 40 Bureau employees were almost unanimously negative and embittered about their jobs:

> 'The way things are they're going downhill rapidly. You can work like the clappers but you don't seem to get anywhere. You don't get appreciated for it... If you were doing 101 they wanted 102.'

> 'We're working under a lot of pressure. There's a lot of change being brought in and the pace of change seems to be quickening. They're trying to revolutionize in five minutes and for the staff it's a nightmare.'

At NDH changes appeared equally momentous. Northtown was putting together its second bid for trust status, the previous one having been turned down for financial reasons. The hospitals had been told to get their budgets in order and were achieving this by cuts in staffing and some ward closure. Nurses complained of lack of staff and equipment. A typical comment as to how jobs might be improved was this from a female SEN: 'Having more staff on the ward and better equipment. *Some* equipment!'

Other aspects of restructuring were also viewed negatively: the clinical regrading of nurses (some 100 appeals were still outstanding); the initiation of performance review; the recording and monitoring of performance indicators; the implementation of GRASP, a manpower audit system, which was said to be extremely time-consuming to carry out and the findings of which, it was claimed, were ignored; the institution of flexible 12 hour shifts; and most especially the attempt to alter 'skill mix' through the employment of a greater proportion of less-trained and cheaper nursing staff. But the greatest preoccupation was the issue of trust status and its likely effects in terms of possible redundancies. This was explicitly linked in the minds of the employees to the penetration of market principles into the health service, a development resented by professionals who were strongly committed to a service ethic. Any attempt to reconstruct their values along entrepreneurial lines appeared so far to have failed:

> 'The workload's too much, staffing loads are deplorable. I personally feel as though that money is the name of the game ... being just out to cut costs at all costs. I know I could be doing a better job if I had the resources ... It's beyond a joke, you're just pushed and pushed and pushed.' (charge nurse, male)

> 'The privatization. I can't see any good coming of it. I don't think you can run a health service for money.' (laboratory scientist, female)

Restructuring and work organization in the private sector

Things were less dramatic in the three private-sector firms, though all had undergone some recent reorganization. TradeFare had developed new policies to improve competitiveness in the mid-1980s. There was a push to improve standards of management and to foster a corporate culture of commitment. A delayering scheme resulted in a severely flattened hierarchy (three tiers only), and a team system. To promote a more upmarket image, there was a stress on quality and on staff training. Commitment among employees was courted with a package of benefits and inducements (discounts on goods, profit sharing scheme) designed to limit staff turnover and enable the company to retain good-calibre employees: turnover nationwide had sunk from 75 per cent in the early 1980s to 37 per cent in 1992 (29 per cent in the stores under study). The company described itself as 'people-centred' with a policy of promoting employees' skills, and claimed that a philosophy of counselling had replaced a former disciplinary approach. These policies had been successful and the firm's profits had increased, while the TradeFare employees registered as the most contented group I interviewed.[1]

A similar attempt to develop a 'new corporate culture' had been instituted at about the same time by Pillco. This involved promoting 'corporate citizenship' with greater stress on 'people-oriented' skills, weekly briefing meetings, redesignating production units as teams, and replacing the old supervisory tiers with 'group' and 'team leaders'. As we saw in Chapter 6, one effect of this was to institute a sharp break between production workers and management. The employment of graduates as group leaders had cut off the ladder from the shopfloor, depriving production workers of promotion chances. There was talk of introducing a flexibility arrangement in the warehouse, integrating the two sides (stock control and transportation of goods). Another major change was the increased employment of temporary workers: all new recruits now started on temporary status.

Albion had been the beneficiary of the financial boom of the 1980s but had recently suffered setbacks and been forced to retrench. This chiefly involved branch closures (98 in the first half of 1992), merging of smaller branches and the concentration of some routine tasks in regional centres, a process that drew on the labour of female part-timers. Like the public-sector groups, the bank employees were concerned about job security and possible redundancies. A major cause of discontent was the introduction of performance-related pay for managers (there was also a yearly appraisal scheme for staff); and this was linked to another major policy change, the push towards a more market-oriented approach, involving the selling of the bank's increasing range of financial services. Managers and their staffs were under pressure to achieve targets in promoting these new services:

'I don't like the hard sell attitude that we're told to do. It's got worse here. I think people feel if they don't tend to do it they'll be out on their earhole.'

'The bank has lost its professional image to an ethos of selling.'

Gall (1997) notes the development of a greater degree of 'union-ateness' in the banking sector, as a result of the breakdown of the old framework of expectations whereby loyalty was rewarded by security and good promotion chances. His arguments are con-firmed by my research which revealed bitterness among some older male employees. In Gall's words 'banking was the quintes-sential career for a (relatively) well-paid, high-status job for life, especially for young working class people' (1997, p. 230). In this it resembled the civil service and, as we shall see, the effect on both Bureau and Albion workers was a heightened sense of job insecur-ity and a firmer commitment to unionism.

While all five organizations were preoccupied with the need to achieve greater competitiveness and efficiency, they were seeking to achieve these goals in differing ways, and change was proceed-ing at very different levels of pace and intensity. How did these changes affect the employees?

Job intensification and pressure

In a review of employment change in the Northern region, Richard Brown (1995) has suggested that three interrelated factors are currently shaping the experience of work: 'insecurity; the intensification of work; and employers' demand for flexibility' (p. 179). As Table 7.2 shows, many bad features about their jobs were linked by the interviewees to changes, with stress, pressure, and lack of staff being mentioned by a quarter of the sample.

There were many indications of pressure felt at work among all the groups. Work overload and pressure were also mentioned by nine people as a response to the question about problems with their jobs or careers. Seventeen people stated that the thing that would most improve their jobs was an increase in staff (the second most popular choice) and another seven called for less pressure. Public-sector workers in particular focused on increased workload, reflecting reorganization and cuts in funding in the NHS and Civil Service:

> 'You just get fed up with pressure from management all the time. They only seem to care about numbers for all they say they're concerned with quality. You seem to be more like a machine these days. They still stress that quality should be there but they still push you to do a great deal.' (civil servant, female)

> 'Just really all the stress you're under because of the staffing levels.' (nurse, female)

Private-sector workers also reported increased workloads and adding of extra tasks to their specified jobs:

> 'Workloads have increased. Statements used to be a two-person job but they took some things off and made it a one-person job. Jobs contain more work and you can get overloaded.' (bank clerk, female)

TABLE 7.2   Reported bad features of jobs (number of mentions)

Problems arising from changes	
Stress/pressure/work overload	43
Understaffing	11
Deteriorating conditions	11
Uncontrolled change	9
Low morale	9
Profit/money orientation	8
Uncertainty about future	7
Unnecessary paperwork	4
More traditional problems	
Monotony/lack of mental stimulation	32
Bad pay	11
Bad management	10
Problems with colleagues	10
Tiring/heavy	8
Lack of recognition	8
Problems with public	4
Cold	3
Underload	3
Isolation	2
Shifts	1
Nothing good about the job at all	11

'Since they've changed the job titles, you know, it's just been getting used to... we have extra responsibilities.' (store supervisor, male, who claimed seven more duties had been added to his workload)

'I do a lot more work than I've ever done before, because there's a lot more involved. Computer work, paper work – so it is harder... He's ruling us with an iron rod. This man will not budge an inch. He watches every move you make. All he talks about is money, cutting costs. We've just got to shut up and put up with it.' (machine operator, female)

Job insecurity

There is good reason why people feel they have to 'shut up and put up'. Job insecurity and fear of redundancies were widespread. As Table 7.3 shows 35 people identified this issue when asked about problems with their jobs, while another 11 spoke of a generalized fear of the future. Linked to possible job loss was the strong preoccupation with lack of opportunities for promotion. Several people declared that the only way up was through 'dead men's shoes'.

TABLE 7.3   Problems experienced with job or career (number of mentions)

Job insecurity and redundancies	35
Worries about future	11
Lack of opportunities/promotion chances	26
Worry about privatization	11
Work overload/pressure	9
Responsibilities/performance anxieties	9
Problems with managers	8
Pace of change	5
Cutbacks	4
Money	3
Deskilling	2
Prospects of relocation	2
Having to go on shifts	2
Other	7
Nothing/no answer	91

Fear of redundancy was least marked among the shop workers (although TradeFare announced national job losses in 1994 soon after my research), and the factory workers. It was strongest among the public sector workers (with more than half the Bureau workers mentioning it) and preoccupied many bank employees:

> 'Like everybody else, in the back of your mind, worries about the future, redundancies. At one time the Civil Service was considered the most secure job, once you were in you were in for life, but like everything else that's changing.' (civil servant, female, 42)

> 'I was at my wit's end last year. It's not so bad now, but I would be worse if I were in the bottom or the top grade. I think perhaps I have learned to live with the insecurity.' (bank cashier, female, 22)

This suggests that it is white-collar workers who formerly felt secure and who, indeed, often chose their careers especially because they appeared to offer 'a job for life' who articulate the clearest subjective experience of insecurity. One woman who had joined the bank in 1971 said: 'I feel a threat to job security for the first time since I worked at the bank.'

The threat of unemployment, which is another important aspect of the class dynamic, hangs over the Northern region workforce. It was mentioned by many people, including Pillco and Trade-Fare workers. But perhaps these occupational groups have 'learned to live with insecurity' over a longer period and took up their jobs with lesser expectations. That, of course, does not mean that objectively they were any less insecure. As one female factory worker told me, managers can bring workers in line with this threat: '"If you don't like it there's the dole." Most women in this plant are frightened.'

The comments of Betty are exemplary here. Betty is in her forties and works in packaging at Pillco. She held various factory and clerical jobs before starting at Pillco in 1978. She speaks of declining conditions and tightened control: 'I loved me job when I first started ... I don't know, things have changed over the years. It's become stricter.' She reports increased pressure and work intensification, although she says the company denies it. While not entirely negative about her job, she clearly suffers from the monotony of line work: 'Sometimes you get bored out of your mind, the jobs in here are so repetitive, that's the trouble...but you've got to hang on to the job.'

Betty is under considerable economic pressure because she and her second husband bought a house and her wages are needed to pay the mortagage: 'Sometimes I worry whether we did the right thing, starting a house so late on.' The threat of unemployment surrounds the family. Her husband was made redundant from the army after 17 years: he got a part-time job in local government which subsequently was made full-time, but the latest round of cuts again faced him with redundancy. Her son, in his late twenties, is himself now in the army; after leaving school he was on the dole, tried various YT schemes, couldn't find a job. Betty must retain her job because, as she told me, it is difficult for people her age to find work if they become unemployed. Betty, who returned to work in the evenings as a waitress when her son was three, is typical of the North East women who have adopted a major breadwinner role. No wonder if she, and women like her, are frightened to protest about changes. They know they are lucky to have full-time, reasonably well-paid jobs when so many face life on the dole or the option of insecure, part-time or temporary jobs.

Numerical flexibility

The growing provision of such insecure jobs has been understood in terms of employers' policies of deploying labour in a more 'flexible' fashion, to cut costs and increase competitiveness. Numerical flexibility involves using variable amounts of labour to meet fluctuations in demand, both of a cyclical and a weekly nature. All five organizations were using labour in some way to promote numerical flexibility.

Part-timers, or 'key-timers' as one organization revealingly called them, were heavily used by Albion, the Bureau and TradeFare. Contracting out, an increasingly common feature in the public sector, had occurred at NDH in the form of CCT and was being resisted at the Bureau. The use of temporary staff was an important new feature of work organization at Pillco. All new production staff were first employed as temps. Andy Danford (1996), noting the same phenomenon in his study of a car components factory in South Wales, argues that this policy serves an important control function. Workers undergo a trial period to demonstrate that they are hard-working, disciplined and reliable before being taken on as permanent staff. Beynon *et al.* (1994) also show this to be increasingly common in Teesside factories. Part-timers were used in exactly this way at the store. It is clear that a major trend in work organization in Britain has been the development of stronger internal labour markets, which heighten managers' control over recruitment, selection and promotion.

The trend to numerical flexibility has important connotations for gender relations. The majority of part-time workers are women, as we saw in Chapter 5, although TradeFare also employed male students as part-timers. Contracting out in the public sector has meant that low-paid but secure domestic jobs for women have been turned into even lower-paid insecure jobs. Women are the preferred choice for these non-standard forms of work. Men, here, might seem to be the losers. However, the jobs which women gain are in Siltanen's terms 'component-wage jobs', insufficient to support a household at a minimum standard of living. So while there may be more jobs around for women as the result of a drift to a part-time economy, such jobs do not make women independent of men or the state.

There is some debate as to whether such jobs designed to enhance firms' 'flexibility' are really on the increase (Pollert, 1991), while Gallie and White (1993) suggest that it is full-time rather than part-time or temporary workers who are concerned about increasing insecurity. But the concerns of the full-timers, like those in my study, must be placed in the context of their awareness of the spread of insecure employment. Beynon *et al.*'s Teesside study (1994) demonstrates the regional increase of temporary contracts and contracting out. My research endorses their claim that 'formerly-held notions of "jobs for life" were rudely ruptured' (p. 119). In Teesside, as in Tyne and Wear, it is the context of widespread unemployment that allows employers to pursue such policies and trade upon a climate of fear to mute worker and union opposition. It may be that nationally such developments are balanced by securer jobs in areas where greater labour market opportunities make it harder to recruit casual labour. Yet doubt as to whether *objectively* the chance of redundancy has actually increased does not invalidate my finding that *subjectively* employees' sense of insecurity has increased, a finding in accord with the analysis of SCELI data by Burchell (1994). It is this sense of insecurity which compels workers to accept work intensification and heightened levels of stress.

Functional flexibility and empowerment

While numerical flexibility increases insecurity, employers are also said to be seeking 'functional flexibility' by increasing the range of skills and job tasks carried out by individual employees. In the postmodern or Post-Fordist vision this is viewed positively and claimed to result in the enskilling and empowering of workers. But my research confirmed other studies' findings (Elger, 1991; Pollert, 1991) which suggest that functional flexibility is more common in theory than practice. It was notable that when asked what job they currently occupied the majority of respondents gave very exact job and task specifications. This was so even in the two organizations which most emphasized how their policies were designed to achieve flexibility. TradeFare had recently undergone a complete restructuring of its job hierarchy, reducing it to three simple grades: general assistant; supervisor; management. All general assistants, I was told, were trained to do all the jobs in the store: 'We believe in multi-skilling.' However, the majority of respondents described themselves as carrying out a specialist task: grocery, stock control, wines and spirits, cafe assistant or household goods, for example. Indeed one or two complained about the lack of variety:

> 'If you weren't stuck on a till for eight hours a day. If you were varied, a few hours in one department, mebbes another.' (cashier, female)

> 'You know, if you got to, to learn other parts of the job, sharing, and things like that.' (stock controller, female)

A similar picture emerged at the bank. A few employees described their jobs as comprising a batch of tasks; one woman worked on enquiries, as cashier and also ran a sub-office two days a week, while a man dealt with DSS business, and also helped with the share shop and assisted on the counter at the weekend. However, there were just as many complaints about inflexibility:

'In a large branch you get more specialized. It's better in a small branch where you avoid the monotony of doing the same task over and over again.' (male, 19)

'I'd like to get moved again. It's more interesting than sitting on the counter all the time.' (male, 20).

Where lower-level employees *are* used flexibly, it seems to be mainly a way to cover for absences or gaps. The interviews suggest that functional flexibility is more common among the higher levels in the job hierarchy. It was supervisory and lower managerial staff who reported taking on new responsibilities and functions. Here, it is not always welcomed since work overload and intensification can outweigh the pleasures of a more varied job. There were complaints either that insufficient training for the new functions had been provided or that task extension had made the job intolerably burdensome. This combined with frustration where expectations of 'empowerment' had been raised but not actually realized:

'A tremendous amount of change in my role. I've been brought up in a culture of change so it doesn't worry me … But I still feel I'm not given the reins of the ward as much as I need. I'm not really able to employ the staff who I want, dismiss, I'm not a budget-holder … One of my concerns is that I can't give my hundred percent at all. The things I've learned in courses at the Poly. I feel as though a lot of my potential is wasted.' (charge nurse, male)

'I'd like a greater ability to actually be responsible for meself, to plan what I was actually doing. Rather than obviously at the moment we've got to work to an office plan dictated by regional office.' (civil servant, male)

Moreover, where job content had been altered and enlarged, the move away from accustomed expert functions could be experienced as deskilling, as in the case of these two higher-grade civil servants:

'I'm totally dissatisfied. I'm not doing the job I was trained to do. The work I'm doing could be done by an officer in the grade below me. My expertise is not being used. They've taken away the interest.' (male)

'I think it's a dilution of skills if you like. Your skills often go in one direction or the other. Management I think is a full-time job.' (female)

Gallie and White's analysis of the 'Employment in Britain' survey (1993) revealed that a majority of employees reported increased skills in their jobs (though this was less so among the lower skilled and was often linked to increased workload). Postmodernists and post-industrialists have suggested that this kind of upskilling will lead to the enrichment of wage labour and empowerment of employees. But no sense of extensive enskilling emerged from my respondents' accounts. A few people spoke of challenge and of learning new skills, but this was linked with moving into new specialist jobs (student adviser at the bank, trainer at the store), rather than change to existing ones. My research also reflects Gallie's suggestion of a polarization in skill development between higher and lower tiers in the employment hierarchy. As mentioned before, a common complaint among less skilled workers was monotony. The only new skills that drew mention from any at these levels were those associated with computer systems; and process operators complained that no official recognition was given to this skill extension in the job evaluation scheme.

Power and relations with managers

Powerlessness and lack of control are central to classic accounts of wage labour. Contrary to postmodernist speculations, my employees did not feel empowered. If anything the power differential between managers and employees was seen to be expanding. Common complaints were lack of consideration and respect from managers, failure to consult with employees or to listen to their opinions:

'You get torn across the field when you're doing something wrong. You're never sort of appreciated, you know? So you feel you're worth something. Even just saying thank you, so you know you're appreciated. Because you never get any return for the job.'

'Sometimes when you are talking to management, you feel like you are talking to a brick wall. They say they want you to talk to them but they don't really. They listen to what you say, but nothing is ever done.'

Such feelings of being treated with disrespect, of not being valued, of one's comments not being taken into consideration, represent the subjective experience of alienation and lack of real democracy at work. This feeling of increased powerlessness expressed by many was linked explicitly to the decline in union power, which will be discussed in Chapter 10:

'Management is in charge. They [the union] go through the motions and that's it.'

'Unions had too much power in the past, but they've had it all taken away from them, and it's definitely to the detriment of the workers.'

Conflict at work?

Is conflict between workers and managers still endemic then, as in the classic models of wage labour, within these restructuring workplaces? Considerable discontent was expressed about relations with managers. When asked what would most improve the quality of working life, better relations with managers or better management was by far the most popular choice, with 33 people mentioning it, one-fifth of all those who responded to this question.[2]

On the other hand, as Table 7.1 shows, some interviewees cited their managers as a good feature of the job. A few respondents, mainly male workers at NDH and Pillco and women at Trade-Fare, expressed views supportive of managerial objectives and endorsed policies designed to tighten up efficiency and clamp down on 'lazy' individuals. There was praise for individual managers, often on the personnel side, who were singled out for their friendly and approachable style and their progressive policies. If managers can adopt a less authoritarian style the attempt to win support for their policies is likely to be more successful. As one woman at Albion commented:

'When I left school and started at the bank it was very silly. The manager sat at one end of his padded office. Now management are approachable and nice.'

Line managers and supervisors were more likely to be the target of critical and hostile comment:

'There are too many managers hanging about and getting in each others' way... They are all supposed to have different jobs, but in fact they stand around and boss you about.'

'If the managers could be more civil to you. You get the ones that say "move that" instead of "will you move that please".'

The attitudes of workers towards managers, then, are complex and varied, especially at the level of individual relationships. It was also apparent that there were variations between the workplaces in who was blamed for the adverse changes and who was therefore potentially identifiable as 'the enemy'. At Albion it was 'the bank' (that is, its central executive functions) which was blamed for loss of security, not the local managers (who have risen from the ranks of clerks and are all members of BIFU). The Bureau staff were unanimous in identifying 'the government' as 'the employer' and condemning its approach. Some individual workers at Pillco and TradeFare, too, held 'the government' responsible for the general bad state of things at work, rather than blaming their own managers. At these two workplaces the local managers seemed to have had greatest success in the new managerial endeavour of 'winning hearts and minds'. By contrast, at NDH, area managers came in for the criticism:

'If the health authority managers would get off their backsides and listen to what we want to say.' (nurse, male)

'I think a lot of people who are managing especially the NHS have no understanding of what the NHS is about.' (MLSO, female)

Yet behind these often quite sophisticated accounts of the complexity of change, responsibility and power, there can be glimpsed a more fundamental reading of workplace relations which surfaced particularly when my respondents talked about trade unions and their role. This is a continuing discourse of opposing interests, of two sides, which suggests that the Marxian analysis of the capital/labour relationship retains its relevance, as highlighted by the italicized phrases in these comments, taken from workers of a range of ages:

> 'I tend to think a lot of the changes in management approaches are just cosmetic. There remains a potential *clash of interests* betwen the employers and employees.' (civil servant, male, aged 50)

> 'I think the union are *on our side* and I think the management are against us.' (civil servant, female, aged 22)

> 'I'm not satisfied with the people who's in charge of the union. They listen too much to management instead of being *on the side of the people*.' (factory worker, female, aged 38)

Conclusions

It can be seen, then, that the impact of the dynamic of capitalist economic restructuring at the workplace level is strong, if manifested in complex ways. Overall, there is little in my research to support the postmodern, post-industrial view of empowerment and enrichment of jobs. The major effects of restructuring as experienced by the employees were increasing insecurity, diminished chances for promotion, work intensification, stress and a growing feeling of powerlessness.

However, these effects were most sharply felt in the two public-sector organizations. Change was apparently accompanied by less distress and conflict at Pillco and TradeFare. I have suggested that workers in private industry are already inured to the experience of insecurity, work intensification and limited autonomy as shown in many previous studies of factory workers (for example, Beynon, 1975; Cavendish, 1982; Westwood, 1984). This does not mean that their experience of wage labour relations is more pleasant, but it does explain the lower level of resistance to change. While the workers in the three service organizations were vocal in their opposition to restructuring, Pillco workers demonstrated a fatalistic resignation about the negative aspects of their work, seeing themselves as lucky to have relatively well-paid and secure jobs, while TradeFare workers also appeared to accept long hours, hard work and monotony.

If we relate these accounts of the experiences of employment change to the three sociological perspectives discussed in Chapter 2, we can say that for the TradeFare and Pillco workers it was a case of 'business as usual', the continued tolerance of the burden of wage labour and the struggle to avoid unemployment; whereas the non-manual groups' experience came closer to the radical model. These workers' subjective experience of declining conditions, increased exploitation and insecurity brought them more firmly into the wage labour camp.

The novel feature of this current phase of restructuring, as it is played out in this specific locality, is its impact on white-collar workers, and especially the lower-level public-sector professionals. It is in institutions formally marked by relations of 'high trust' and associated privileges (job security, promotion chances, greater autonomy in the job) that conditions of work are being most adversely affected. These changes stem partly from the Thatcher government's conscious attempts to reconstruct the public sector, in order to cut costs while also constructing a template for 'best practice' in the context of an increasingly competitive economic environment. But they also reflect the increased importance of services as a vehicle of profit and capital accumulation in the post-industrial capitalist economies. In the already tightly controlled and Taylorized conditions of private industry (and large-scale retail displays similar characteristics) it is more a case of continuity than change.

In gender terms these developments are felt similarly by women and men, except in the case of strategies designed to maximize numerical flexibility, which, as discussed earlier, create more employment chances for women, but chances of an inferior kind. Where the full-timers are concerned, men are particularly disturbed by declining career opportunities and increased job insecurity, since they have held higher expectations in these areas than women. Yet as the chapter has shown, both sexes complain of all facets of change.

There is a real significance for gender relations in the household, however. Where no job appears secure, both partners are impelled to cling to jobs; women's contributions will become increasingly important to household budgets. Both women and men are involved in complex 'juggling' exercises as they try to combine two insecure but highly pressurized jobs with household responsibilities. Thus the family developments discussed in Chapter 6 are given further impetus by the dynamic of capitalist development.

I will end this chapter with a set of comments from Lisa about her job, which illustrate some of the points made here. Lisa, who is 25, is a staff nurse, working in care of the elderly. She is a sharp, lively woman who trained as a teacher, but gave up because she disliked the work and drifted into nursing. Her account of her job reflects the service ethos of the profession:

> 'The job satisfaction is fairly good from the point of view of the patients. Seeing elderly people come, and go out better, is satisfying. Sorting out social circumstances is very satisfying. Communication with the doctors, district nurses et cetera...Team work, part of, being part of a family, feeling that you belong on the ward.'

But like so many public-sector workers, Lisa feels herself at the sharp end of deteriorating employment conditions:

> 'The bad things are the lack of staff, the responsibility for the amount you get paid, the frustration in not being able to give the care you want to give to the patient, the lack of equipment, the equipment that doesn't work...Being told you have to do night shift is a downer.'

The hospital's policy of seeking flexibility through variable shifts weighs especially heavily on Lisa as she and her husband live across the Pennines, a forty-mile drive away. No wonder Lisa cannot be active in the trade union of which she is a member (COHSE). Yet she describes herself as 'very committed' to the union, although she has limited experience of it, and comes from a middle-class family with no history of union activism. But her explanation of the need for unions exemplifies the feelings of powerlessness which were commonly expressed by my respondents as they faced up to the economic situation of the early 1990s.

> 'Well at the moment we're seeing that the unions haven't got much power and things are just getting silly. They'll have you working for blood.'

Notes

1 It should be remembered that the TradeFare respondents were selected by management not random sample, which may have led to
   bias.
2 Bank employees were not asked this question.

Chapter 8

A Post-Industrial Proletariat? Class, Change and Identity

'I would identify myself as being what I would call the working class. You're talking about two classes. All those who have to work. Britain's run by the class who do the employing. They're the people who have the power.' (civil servant, male, 34)

'If I had been asked that question ten or twelve years ago I would have said working class. But when I look around at what's going on around the country I'd have to class myself as middle-class.' (factory worker, male, 47)

'Classwise it's getting less because people are getting more and more affluent.' (shop assistant, male, 47)

Class, always a matter of fierce debate among sociologists, is becoming even more of a conundrum. In the 1980s, Andre Gorz (1982) argued that post-industrial change would bring an end to the working-class as classically conceived by Marx, Weber and their contemporary followers, replacing it with a 'neo-proletariat', a group something akin to the popularly-conceived 'underclass'. In the 1990s, as we saw in Chapter 2, some postmodernists have gone further and suggest that classes are disappearing altogether, as old collectivities are destroyed by processes of economic and cultural change. The popular form of this argument is the notion of the 'classless society'. Mainstream British class theory, on the contrary, continues to assert that class is a major influence in people's lives: however, class theory has long been riven by debates about how exactly to categorize classes, how to assign individuals to classes, how many classes there are in contemporary societies, where the boundaries are between different classes. John Goldthorpe's influential class schema is based on groupings of occupational categories. Erik Wright's alternative schema is also based on occupations, but organizes them in terms of relations of ownership and control, reflecting his continued espousal of Marxism. Ken Prandy and Bob Blackburn have developed an alternative 'Cambridge' scale based on patterns of friendship and association. Altogether, the analysis of class is so complex that many sociologists shy away from it altogether.

Avoidance of class has been quite marked in some forms of contemporary feminist analysis, as Barrett (1992) points out. Skeggs (1997a) also notes the retreat from class: 'Class as a concept and working-class women as a group have almost disappeared from the agendas of feminism and cultural studies' (p. 2). She ascribes it to a mix of factors: post-structuralist theory, espousal of 'the new individualism', the theoretical difficulties of defining class, publishers' wariness about the marketability of books about class. Walkerdine (1990), has developed arguments similar to Skeggs. She links the difficulties of speaking about class to previous errors of conception: 'the illusion of the proletariat as a steaming cauldron of revolutionary fervour' (p. 162). The subsequent failure of the working classes to function as a revolutionary force has led sociologists of working-class origin into disillusionment, denial of their own class experience, and a switch to other areas of sociological concern or a preoccupation with the middle classes; certainly a recent paper by Devine (1997) suggests that class analysis should focus on the issue of middle-class reproduction.

This chapter explores the complex issue of class identification. In Chapter 2, I argued that in some postmodernist writing there is a tendency to confuse class relations and class identification. Thus the 'death of class' (Pakulski and Waters, 1996) is pronounced because people no longer commonly identify themselves in class terms, despite persistence evidence that the material polarities caused by class relations are increasing rather than diminishing. To avoid such erroneous judgements we must carefully distinguish 'class relations', 'class position' and 'class identification'.

By *class relations* I mean the overall configurations produced by the workings of the class dynamic. Among these are the relationship between labour and capital as manifested in employment which was the subject of Chapter 6. Other aspects of current class relations include self-employment, unemployment, economic inactivity and consumption, but these fall outside the scope of my research. *Class position* refers to the way particular individuals or groups are located within the configuration of class relations (class location has much the same meaning). Finally, *class identification* refers to the processes by which individuals locate or align themselves in terms of class, that is how they develop (or not as the case may be) *class identities*. Class identity does not necessarily correspond to class position; class identification is a matter of meaning as opposed to materiality and, as argued in Chapter 2, these are closely connected but not identical. To cope with this conceptual problem, I proposed in *Fractured Identities* that class relations offer a *potential* source of social identification, but one that is frequently 'passive' and does not so readily take an 'active' or 'politicized' form as in the case of gender and ethnicity.

This chapter, then, discusses the class identifications of my sample, exploring the meaning of class in their lives. However, I start the chapter with a brief consideration of accounts of class and change and try to place my occupational samples within some of the class maps on offer, that is to consider their *class position*.

Classes and post-industrial change

The three quotations with which this chapter starts represent three views on class which correspond to current sociological debates. Mike, the first speaker, comes from a typical North East working-class background. His father was a miner, his mother worked in a shop before marriage. Mike is an 'old' Labour Party supporter, with strong 'them' and 'us' class attitudes and a clear view of employers as exploiters. His description of the British class structure corresponds to the classic Marxist view of classes as 'two polar camps'. Such an articulation of class was by no means rare among my sample and may reflect the seeping of sociological and Marxian theorizations of class into popular discourse.

Fred, the second speaker, comes from a very similar background to Mike: his father, too was a miner. Fred also displays the
political attitudes identified with working-class membership: he is
a strong Labour supporter and a union shop steward. But Fred is
picking up on something commonly noted by my respondents:
the superior position of those who have a job of any kind, compared to the unemployed. Many manual workers consequently
saw themselves as in a class tier above the very bottom class, 'the
poor', 'the lower class'. This position reflects the sociological
debates about the existence of an 'underclass' or 'labour reserve',
a group of people dependent largely on state benefits for survival
who have dropped out of the bottom of the class structure. The
existence of such a group is seen by some as a typical feature of
evolving class relations in contemporary post-industrial societies
(Esping-Andersen, 1993).

Finally, Walter represents a third group of people who suggested that class boundaries were shifting and changing. Walter
does not have the clear political commitments of Mike and Fred
and expressly states that he rejects the 'socialist ideals' associated
with trade unions. He describes his family background as working-
class (his father was a postman and his mother a school cleaner),
but is more tentative about assigning himself to a class: 'I suppose working class – but I don't know what people mean by working class. I'm not a pauper, not upper class.' He asks me how
other people respond to this question, do they all call themselves
working class? I reply, not necessarily, some say middle class.
Walter grapples to understand what class could signify. It is
something to do with money and lifestyle differences, which is
why he raises the issue of affluence and diminishing class inequalities. This third position links to the longstanding sociological
debate about embourgeoisement: does the boundary between
middle and working classes still exist. Walter himself is a shop
assistant. *Is* he working class? Or middle? Does it still make sense
to use these terms? Many postmodernists seem to operate with
an implicit version of the embourgeoisement thesis, while,
generally, many class theorists believe that the boundaries
between classes are increasingly less defined and classes are fragmented internally, themes associated with neo-Weberian class
analysis

The respondents on the class map

The above difficulties are writ large when we consider the class position of the occupational groups in my sample in terms of standard sociological theories. In Chapter 6, I treated the whole sample as part of the general category of 'wage labour' as analysed by Marx: that is, these are all people who do not own the means of production and must sell their labour to gain a living. In Weber's terminology, they are part of the propertyless. But within class theory these 'maximalist' terms (Parkin, 1979) have been considered too broad to be of much use in understanding contemporary class relations and the propertyless have been divided up into smaller groups on the basis of a variety of analytic strategies. Among my sample, one group, the factory workers, are clearly by any system of categorization part of the manual working class. But all the other occupational groups could be seen as part of what neo-Marxists have called the 'new middle classes', a heterogeneous grouping often described as 'contradictorily located' between the proletariat and the bourgeoisie.

The most influential class model in Britain has been that of John Goldthorpe, who distinguishes three main broad occupational class groupings: the manual working class, the service class (managers and professionals) and, between them, the intermediate class of lower-level service workers. In Goldthorpe's categorization, the majority of my respondents at Albion and the Bureau would fall into the intermediate class (Goldthorpe and Heath, 1992). Goldthorpe is ambiguous about shop assistants, who sit on the boundary between working and intermediate classes. Given the poor pay of shop work, and the fact that the TradeFare employees were drawn from similar communities and residential areas to the Pillco workers, I suggest that they should be categorized as working class. The TradeFare employees were less qualified than the other occupational groups: their average school-leaving age was 15.9, close to that of the Pillco workers at 15.5. For all other groups it was 17 plus. The nurses and P and T staff are part of Goldthorpe's service class, although in its lowest echelons. Each sample included a number of supervisory or lower management staff who would also fall into the service class.

The respondents were thus split between Goldthorpe's three classes. Fifty-four could be assigned to the working and 76 to the intermediate class. It should be emphasized that those who could be seen as service-class members (61) were certainly not part of a professional and managerial service elite. Across the whole sample only ten had any experience of higher education (apart from the seven male college or university students working part-time at TradeFare);[1] pay and salary levels were generally low; and many supervisors had risen from lower-level jobs in the organization. Over two-thirds of the sample, then, might be described as 'lower-middle class'.

There has been a long-standing debate concerning the 'prolet-arianization' of these groupings. Braverman argued that clerical and shop workers should be seen as part of the proletariat, be-cause their pay, working conditions and indeed the actual con-tent of their jobs (deskilled, routinized and Taylorized) were very similar to those of factory workers. Also, the fact that such occupa-tional groups are often highly feminized has a crucial effect. Shops and offices have long utilized the labour of women from manual family backgrounds. The low pay and poor conditions of such feminized jobs has made many see them as inherently prolet-arian (Braverman, 1974; Crompton and Jones, 1984; Clarke and Critcher, 1985).

The findings set out in the last chapter give some support to Braverman's arguments. Many white-collar employees believed that their working conditions were deteriorating. There has been an extension of methods long used to ensure persistent work intensification, heightened productivity and compliance among manual workers to white-collar workers, notably in the public sec-tor. These groups in my study were formerly the beneficiaries of high-trust relationships which were now under threat. In respect of power relations at work, if not in terms of economic rewards, such groups of employees are being downgraded towards the proletarian position. As Chapter 6 showed, many of them now experience the anxiety and insecurity at work which have long been the lot of manual workers.

However, some differences in the work and market situations (Lockwood, 1958) of the working class and the intermediate and lower service groupings persist. More complex mental skills are needed for some of the clerical jobs (though not the lower-level ones which were described as 'mindless'); while the lower profes-sional jobs in the NHS require a range of skills based on training and qualifications. There are still marginally better promotion chances in these jobs. In this sense I am hesitant to allocate the Albion or Bureau workers to the emergent 'service proletariat' linked by Esping-Andersen (1993) to the development of post-industrial economies, although this term might well be applied to the TradeFare employees.

None the less, it could be argued that the current phase of capitalist economic development is marked by a merging of the experiences of wage labourers in the lower tiers of the new middle classes and those in manual work. Contemporary class relations are subjecting the former to the vicissitudes and tight control typical of classic working-class jobs. If not quite proletarianized, these groups are at least losing some of the protection that was afforded them by their middle-class status.

But another important point emerged from the analysis of my respondents' class position. As a different strategy, I categorized the class of their parents. The rather crude indicators I had of this were, first, the occupation of both parents as stated by the interviewees and, second, the class to which they assigned their family.[2] What emerged from this exercise was the prevalence of family backgrounds which did not fit easily into a single category and the number of what have conventionally been called 'cross-class' marriages, a manual father and a clerical mother, for example, or conversely a father who was a manager and a mother who worked in a shop. Over a quarter of the employees' families (53) were of this type.

The difficulties surrounding the classification of women's employment in class terms, however, make this 'cross-class' terminology unsatisfactory. It is better to conceptualize these families as 'hybrid'. This tallies with an approach arising from recent work on class and gender (Mahony and Zmroczek, 1997), whereby class is viewed, like gender and ethnicity, as process and relation, not as a fixed entity. This entails rejecting the orthodox sociological approach of deriving class from occupational positions, exemplified by Goldthorpe's work; rather class is seen in terms of life narratives and relations with other people, especially parents. This opens up the space for seeing class, as theorists of post-colonialism have viewed ethnicity, in terms of hybridity. Class positions are not necessarily pure and unambiguous (though in some cases they are) and are themselves located in dynamics which shift and evolve, producing further 'structural ambiguity' (Crompton and Gubbay, 1977).

Both the class merging reported above and the experience of class hybridity will add to the confusions about class identifications which are explored in the remainder of this chapter.

The persistence and meaning of class

Despite confusions about class identification my respondents believed in the existence of classes. They were asked if they thought Britain was a classless society or whether classes still existed. Results are shown in Table 8.1.[3]

TABLE 8.1   Perceptions of inequalities in society (percentages)

	Women	Men	All
Class inequalities			
Yes	81	79	80
No	14	18	16
Don't know	5	3	4
Gender inequalities			
Yes	84	68	76
No	11	24	17
Don't know	5	8	7
Class more marked	36	59	47
Gender more marked	39	21	30
Neither predominates/ don't know	21	13	17
No inequalities	5	7	6

Eighty per cent thought class inequalities persisted while only 16 per cent believed that society was classless. Comments such as 'there'll never be a classless society', 'there'll always be classes', 'there'll always be the rich and the poor' were common. As the table shows, there was minimal difference between women and men and this contrasts with their views on whether gender inequalities still existed in society. As might be predicted, women were more likely to perceive gender inequalities. Following from this, when asked if they felt class or gender was a more important source of inequality men were more likely to cite class, 59 as opposed to 36 per cent of women. Thirty-nine per cent of women and 21 per cent of men put gender first. But, as we shall see, that did not mean that women's sense of class identity was weaker.

Class, then, retains meaningful significance as a way people understand inequalities in society. But what are people talking of when they talk of class? I did not ask my respondents to provide a 'map' of the class structure or specify what classes they thought existed. Scott Lash's research into class revealed the wide variety of models of class employed by American and French working people (Lash, 1984). Most of the North-East employees, in discussing class, used the commonly used terms 'working' 'middle' and 'upper', though some spoke of 'rich' and 'poor'. They also distinguished a number of refinements of these basic categories. It was, however, evident that the use of these terms may carry a variety of meanings as those who reflected on this issue indicated. My interviewees, like sociologists, found it difficult to specify a precise existential base for class

Mike was one of a number who made links between class and the division of labour at work. But a range of other bases for class were touched on as people reflected upon what the term might mean: it is something to do with money (a popular position), it may be to do with unemployment or with education, values and attitudes may be involved, it's about who you talk to and socialize with:

'It's more to do with having a job or not having a job.'

'It's got to be money. People who've got money think that they're better than you.'

'I classify myself as working class. I've got no high and mighty views.'

Tony, a young male nurse, recounted his political differences with his parents. He himself had 'discovered' socialism while doing a university degree, was a committed Labour party member and had joined NUPE not the RCN because he wished to belong to a 'proper union'. His father had been in the army and his mother he described as a 'salesperson' and they opposed unions. Tony saw himself as middle class but described a recent argument with his parents: 'They swore blind they were working

class and I swore blind they were middle class. They even read the
Daily Express for heaven's sake!' In this case, political values are
used as a yardstick of class.

This confusion about what class actually is (mirroring sociology's
conceptual contestations) adds to the problems of class identification discussed in the next sections. But it is important to note
that when talking about work relations respondents frequently
employed class imagery, talking of exploitation, of conflicting
interests:

> 'You're always going to get people – the entrepreneur, the exploiter –
> and that means people are going to be exploited.'

> 'There remains a potential clash of interests between the employers
> and the employees.'

They also stressed the role of unions as representative of class
interests:

> 'The unions have done an awful lot for the working class.'

> 'Especially with the current political climate they've got to protect their
> members' interests. Otherwise nobody else will.'

Class identities: Jim and Barry

Despite this persistence of class meanings, people experienced
considerable difficulties in placing themselves within the class
structure. The problematic nature of class identificationcan be
highlighted by discussing the views of Jim and Barry. Both men
are in their mid-forties, married with grown-up children. They
come from similar manual backgrounds. Jim's father was a lathe
operator and his mother worked as a nursing auxiliary. Both Barry's
parents were factory workers: his mother worked at Pillco and
procured him a job there when he was made redundant. Both
have been working for Pillco since the early 1970s. Yet their attitudes to class could hardly be more different.

Jim describes himself and his family background as working-
class and espouses a classic working-class political position. He is a
strong supporter of the Labour Party, has acted as a union rep in

the past and describes himself as holding 'socialist values'. He was despondent about the current political situation, seeing little hope of the policies he supports being realised 'while we've got this lot' (the Conservative government). He would like to see his union campaigning for a minimum wage and against privatization and deplores the abolition of the Wages Councils. He tells me how pleased he is that his daughter shares his ideals, describing how he watches television with her and explains to her what is really going on behind the stories in the news: political socialization of this kind has been mentioned by other people from similar backgrounds. When I ask for his reason for joining the union, he offers me one of the strongest statements I have come across of a collectivist perspective: 'I just believe in the *collective strength between the workers* trying to bring their hand to a better world.' In short, Jim views his world and his place within it, especially working relationships, through the filter of class. His understanding of politics is thoroughly informed by this class consciousness. There will always be a need for unions, he asserts: they would become redundant 'only when you have a Utopia. Because there's still a class society in Britain. The people with the money and power don't give the other ones a fair chance.'

Although his social background is so close to Jim's, Barry totally rejects any notion of class. He is one of the minority who believes that Britain is a classless society and he refuses to identify either himself or his family in class terms. He has nothing good to say about his own union and tells me that he only joined it because he when he came to the factory there was a closed shop. He criticizes the union because 'They fight for things that are trivial . . . They should concentrate on pay.' He is opposed to any kind of political role for unions and says he is a non-voter.

Barry's preoccupations are materialistic and his filter on the world could be described as pecuniary and instrumental, following Lockwood's typifications (1975). When I ask him about the position of women in the factory he tells me that women have got equality and that it's 'gone too far' but quickly moves on to complain about the unfairness of the job evaluation scheme as it affects *his own* pay rate. His negativity about unions is linked to his experience of a strike at Pillco, as a result of which, he tells me, the workforce lost many privileges, such as the right to choose shifts or the provision of taxi transports for those on early shift. Strikes are wrong, he believes, because you never get want you want and strike pay is too little to live on. While he is inclined to believe that unions have now become redundant, he equivocates in view of the fact that they might still be needed for pay deals. To some extent his extreme hostility to unions arises from his perception of their powerlessness, a theme he continually harks on:

> 'The union here isn't a union in fact. It's only a union in name. The company's got the upper hand all the time... Maggie T's killed the unions off. They have no legs to stand on.'

But while most of his colleagues would deplore this powerlessness, Barry considers it inevitable and natural because of his individualist view of life. He cannot see how unions can effectively work to help people, because individual needs are so diverse: 'Everybody is an individual, everybody wants different things.' Barry's espousal of a materialist individualism leads him to deny totally any sense of class or collectivist meanings, such as those displayed by Jim.

The complexities of class identification

The contrasting cases of Jim and Barry show that it is impossible to read off class identification from an individual's class situation. In occupational terms these two men share a common class position and are located commonly within the dynamic of class relations between labour and capital. But class, like other forms of social identity, is only a potential identity; there is no necessity for it to be realised. In this section I explore the class identifications of my respondents and consider the processes involved in the development of active or politicized forms of class identification.

TABLE 8.2   **Respondents' class identification (percentages)**

	Women	Men	All
No class	42	53	47
Working class	36	32	34
Middle class	12	10	11
Other class	10	5	8

As Table 8.2 shows, nearly half the respondents did not identify themselves as belonging to any particular class. Of those that did, the majority described themselves as working class. Given that, as we have seen, the majority of the employees would fall into Goldthorpe's intermediate or service classes (137 out of the total) it is remarkable that so few placed themselves as middle class. This contrasts sharply with the answers to this question offered by the teachers of Beechgrove School: 8 of the 13 I interviewed described themselves as middle class. This suggests that there is considerable ambiguity about the class identification of some of the groups allocated to the intermediate class by Goldthorpe: while membership of a long-established profession is more clearly identified with middle-class status.

Gender interacts interestingly with class. Women were more likely to identify themselves in class terms than men, despite rating gender inequalities above class. This is a highly significant point, suggesting that forms of identification are not, as is sometimes assumed in feminist analysis, in competition with one another. Those who develop personal gender awareness may also be more prone to demonstrate class awareness.

The difficulty that people had in answering the question and the confusion about class categories is reflected in the fairly high proportion of those I have classified as 'other'. Many people hesitated or fumbled to find a clear answer to the question: 'I can't really place myself'; 'I don't fit a certain peg'; 'Other people would say working-class' were some of these responses. Others struggled towards a definition:

'Well, I wouldn't say I'm lower class, but I'm not upper class, middling really, working class.'

'My parents see themselves as middle class, but I'm not sure, where's the barrier?'

Some, like Walter, linked this ambiguity to change:

'It depends what you mean. I think the bands have gone.'

'I would have [identified in class terms] a while ago, but with unemployment being so strong I feel things aren't the same any more.'

'I'm better off now than when I was a child. Mind, you're having to work to get to that class, to the better things of life.'

Thus some curious categories were offered to me: 'middle of the road', 'working middle', 'lower to middle', 'between working class and middle class', 'comfortable', 'normal', 'poor', 'improving working class' and even 'across the board'. The use of such terms is indicative both of confusion about personal identity and of sensitivity to the complexity of class positioning, especially in the context of change and increasing class hybridity: as one Bureau worker said, 'I belong to the class of people who has to work for a living so in that sense I'm working class. But there are many gradations within it.'

These comments mirror understandable confusions about the nature of changing class positions and also reflect personal experience of class hybridity. But there are other reasons for the difficulties experienced in answering this question. A number of people presented class identity as something that was imposed upon you by others:

'Stereotypically I'm working class. But that's not how I would see it.'

'It's probably what everybody would call working class.'

Class is presented here not as a freely-chosen identity, but, in Goffmanite terms as a spoiled identity (Goffman, 1964), even a source of stigma reflecting the condescension of 'higher' social groups. A hospital technician, describing himself as 'definitely not middle class', went on to say, 'manual workers are treated as though they are frowned on'. Other comments repeat this view:

'I would like to think that there wasn't any class, but there is still stigma attached. I feel people see me in class terms.' (female shop assistant)

'The Conservatives see it as upper class, middle class and lower class. To them we're all peasants.' (female shop assistant)

Thus some of those who rejected a class label stressed the desirability of bringing an end to class relations. Some endorsed the notion of classlessness, although as a desired goal rather than a present reality:

'I would like to think I'm not but I rather think I could be put in some
stratum. I'm not interested. I like to think we have friends from all strata.'
(female civil servant)

The ability to associate with people across classes was valued by
many. The views on class offered by Alec point to this. Alec had a
sad history. A former Bureau worker, he had lost his job through
illness and been unemployed for many years. Attempts to start his
own business had failed and he had ended up working part-time
at TradeFare. Alec told me that commitment to unions was something that had been passed down to him through the family and
the North-Eastern culture. Although describing his parents as
working class (they were a groundsman and a cook) he did not
offer a class identity for himself. While this might reflect the vicissitudes of his employment history, it was also linked to his view
that personal equality was desirable. Pointing to the portrait of the
TradeFare chairman which hung in the storeroom where I was
interviewing him, he said: 'I don't see myself any different from a
manager . . . If I met that chap there, I wouldn't knock on the door
and say, sir, I'd go up to him.' Alec believed that class distinctions
were fading. But he also rejected the view that there ever could be
a classless society, imputing this to other people's class prejudice.

The comments of Dick and Ivor, two laboratory scientists, show
the link between the ideal of classlessness and the view of class as
an imposed identity. Dick refuses any class identity ('I don't like
the term') for himself and his family (his father was a manager, his
mother worked in shops, a classic case of hybridity), but adds that
stigmatizing attitudes persist: 'People will look down on someone
who does a manual job.' Ivor also rejects the notion of class, saying
'I think it should be a classless society', but states that his background would be seen as 'stereotypically working class'.

Such accounts suggest that people view class in moral terms;
there is a tendency to confuse what society *is* with what society
should be. This was why some people endorsed the idea of classlessness and refused any class identity: 'I don't believe in class'; 'I
don't like the term'; 'I think it should be a classless society.' Pahl
and Wallace (1988) report this sense of stigmatization among
their Sheppey respondents in reference to being working class,
which is linked to poverty; and an even sharper sense of stigma or
even 'shame' emerges from Mahony and Zmroczek's collection of

pieces about the experience of working-class female academics (1997). While, argues Skeggs (1997a, 1997b), there is a possibility of celebrating male working-class identity in terms of the heroic rebellions of manual workers, female working-class occupations, such as domestic service, have historically offered little opportunity for this kind of pride in strength, toughness and skill; working-class women have characteristically taken on the task of procuring 'betterment' for themselves and their families, by achieving 'respectability', by encouraging their children into education. As Gail Fisher sees it,

> 'The working class is the only class that people do not aspire to! It is considered something to work yourself up from.' (Sayer and Fisher, 1997, p. 60)

What is interesting about my sample is that my respondents were no readier to accept a middle-class identity despite the fact that so many were in white-collar work. Possibly, in the North East with its history of homogenized working-class communities, moving up into the middle classes is a problem for individuals who find it hard to relocate themselves in terms of their roots. There is a sense that the idea of class is linked to a whole moral discourse of *how society ought to be*. The feeling that class is somehow 'wrong', undesirable, then leads people to see class as a pejorative label and this in turn problematizes the adoption of class as an identity for many. But not for all. As we have seen, other individuals, like Mike and Jim, display a strong sense of class belonging.

Influences on class identification

The cases of Jim and Barry show that processes of class identification cannot be read off automatically from an individual's class position. Is class identity, then, as postmodernists sometimes imply, simply a contingent matter, one of a batch of possible identities that may be picked at will from the supermarket rack? I would argue not. There *are* regularities in the patterns of class identification displayed by my interviewees. For example, the factory workers and civil servants were more likely than any other group to identify themselves as working class. Again, people who themselves came from working-class families were much more likely to offer a class identification than those whose background was one of class hybridity (59 per cent as opposed to 25 per cent).

Class identities are potentially generated by position within the class dynamic, but whether they become actualized, turning from passive to active or politicized identities depends on many factors, some of which will be unique to individual circumstances. My own data are not of the kind that would allow me to trace out such influences in any depth. However, they do suggest what some of the influences may be.

First, family background affects processes of class identification. In general people found it easier to identify their background in class terms than their own position. Seventy-eight per cent offered a family class identification. Although there was a high degree of upward intergenerational social mobility in the sample in terms of the Goldthorpe schema (32 per cent across the whole sample, 47 per cent among the white-collar workers), it was clear that people's perception of their family's class affected their view of their own class identity. Ninety per cent of those who were able to offer a class identification for both themselves and their family identified themselves as the same class as their family. Half of those who came from unambiguously working-class backgrounds (where fathers, for example, worked as miners or shipbuilders and mothers as factory workers or in domestic jobs such as cleaning or school catering) identified themselves as working class. Similarly, 31 per cent of those from unambiguously middle-class backgrounds, where parents were managers or professionals such as teachers or accountants, self-identified as middle class. This confirms my argument that class must be seen as a set of relationships arising from collective experience, not as a label for individuals based upon personal occupational status. Although class relationships derive from economic arrangements, families and neighbourhoods serve as transmitters of class cultures and meanings – and thus identities.

This can be seen in accounts of processes of class socialization within the family. Janie is 29 and a Grade 3 Bureau worker. Her parents both worked in the same factory and she identifies herself and them as working class. She describes how she came to join the trade union: 'I was young and never worked before. My first day at work, me mam packed me off with me bait and said, "Don't forget to join the union."' Both her parents were union members and she remembers them bringing home 'little magazines' and union information. Joining the union was seen as the normal thing to do, and, as Janie told me, loyalty tends to grow over the years: 'It's something that builds up and stays with you.' She had served as a union representative for a couple of years, though expressing herself somewhat disillusioned by the lack of support given by the national organization to local activists: 'They pull the rug out from under you.'

Janie's colleague Linda also has a background of trade union activism, having been a BWU rep for five years. Her uncle she describes as 'a hard-dyed union member'. She had worked for the Labour party, canvassing alongside him and with her husband's family: her father-in-law was a local Labour MP. Like Janie, Linda offered firm working-class identifications for herself and her family: her father was a factory worker and her mother worked in shops. Linda's view on class aligns her against the neo-Weberian sociological position on the mental/manual divide as she derides her colleagues who erroneously 'think they're middle-class because they're white-collared workers'.

Claire, whose feminism was discussed in earlier chapters, also recalled her political socialization in the family. Her father was a fitter, who was works convenor at his factory and became a branch secretary of the AEU: he was also a Labour councillor. She described his influence on herself and her siblings:

> 'I was brought up to trade unions from the age at which we could write. We used to make out all the new union cards... We were brought up to think for ourselves, very much so. My background, obviously, has got to influence me. I have a very strong social conscience and recognise that without the power of the unions I wouldn't be sitting where I am today. That collective looking out for each other is crucial for the work-place.'

All the children went to grammar school and gained professional jobs. Despite this family experience of upward mobility Claire rejects a middle-class identity: 'I would say I'm working-class.' Before working at the Bureau she had started to train as a teacher, which had till then been her lifelong ambition, but became disillu-sioned and dropped out because she felt that within the education system working-class children were 'given up as lost'. Claire makes it explicit that her family background has given her a 'passionate' commitment to social equality, in both class and gender terms.

Discussion of class socialization has often focused on men and the transmission of working-class values to boys through apprenticeships and union membership. It is significant that the stories quoted above are from women. These stories, and others like them, show that these processes operate for women too and that mothers as well as fathers play an important part in the transmission of class values and meanings.

The stories of Janie, Linda and Claire, also indicate the way in which class consciousness and gender consciousness are complexly related. There is certainly no simple opposition between the two: those aware of one type of inequality may well be more likely to be sensitive to other types. All three of these women have been union activists and display strong class values: but all three also stated that gender inequalities were greater than those of class. In the case of Linda and Claire, this view may have been linked to their experiences of sexism at work and within the union. For Janie, who offered no account of personal experience of discrimination, the reason seemed to be that class inequalities were inevitable and enduring (a common view among the class identifiers) while gender injustice was open to change:

> 'Class division has gone on for centuries. Whether someone lives in a mansion in the country, or whatever, let them get on with it. But men and women should be equal. That concerns me.'

While I have been stressing the family as an important source of class identification, Janie's comments also show that identification and the formation of class meanings are continuing processes. What happens at work will be crucial in confirming (or disconfirming) values learned in the home. The influence of work and occupation is suggested by the variations in levels of identification between the different occupational groups, as shown in Table 8.3.

The two groups demonstrating the highest levels of class identification were the factory workers and civil servants. The response from the Pillco employees was an expected one. Many of them lived in the local estate which could be seen as a typical working-class community and many came from unambiguously working-class families. But the response of the Bureau employees was more surprising. Apart from the fact that these workers displayed the highest level of class identification, they also provided the most articulate commentary on class relations.

TABLE 8.3   **Respondents' class identification by occupational group (numbers)**

Class identification	Bureau	Pillco	TradeFare	Albion	NDH
Working	21	18	13	9	5
Middle	4	4	5	5	3
Other	4	2	1	4	5
None	11	14	21	22	27
Total	40	38	40	40	40

The contrast with the bank staff whose class identification was low is sharp, considering that the job content, educational background and market situations of the two groups are very similar. A number of factors may account for the difference. It is possible that public-sector workers by virtue of their commitment to state provision develop different political values from those of their private-sector equivalents. But there are also significant differences in their background. Fifty-two per cent of the Bureau staff were upwardly mobile as opposed to 22 per cent of the bank clerks, with 65 per cent of them describing their family background as working-class compared to 25 per cent of the Albion employees. The civil service provided an opening for working-class children who did well at school, especially boys, to escape from the fate of mines, factories or shipyards. Yet the loyalty to working-class origins and values has not been shed.

As the table shows, the hospital staff were the least likely to offer a class identification, although their family backgrounds were not dissimilar to those of the civil servants. This may be due to a sense of professionalism, which was very strong among both occupational groups. Professionalism is clearly associated with being middle class. Yet what is interesting about both the bank clerks, with their more middle-class social origin, and the NDH staff, with their professional pride, is that the numbers who identified themselves as middle-class were no higher than in the other social groups.

Another factor which helps us make sense of these occupational differences is the role of unions. The Bureau and Pillco were the organizations with the most active unions; at the Bureau in particular a sense of political militancy was marked. There is a clear link between trade union activism and working-class identification, though it would be hard to say which is cause and which is effect. As Table 8.4 shows, 28 of my interviewees were or had been union stewards or representatives and of these 68 per cent described themselves as working class.

TABLE 8.4   Degree of union activism and class identification (percentages)

	Working	Middle	Other	None
Stewards (n=28)	68	11	4	18
Active members (n=14)	50	7	0	43
Passive members (n=126)	31	16	2	51
Non-members (n=23)	30	9	4	57

Those who were not union members or were passive members (those who did not participate in any union activities outside work time) were least likely to offer a class identification. This suggests that trade unions retain an important role in political socialization.

Pillco and the Bureau were politicized workplaces. They had strong workplace-based union structures (for example, there were regular on-site union meetings). Many of the employees held strong views on class and gender issues, were or had been active union members, were strongly committed to Labour politics and held radical views about what was currently happening in society. This degree of politicization was lacking among the more contented TradeFare workers, although they had a similar social background. Albion and NDH staff shared the critical attitudes to changing employment relations of the civil servants, but in both cases union organization was less developed at workplace level.

The hospital unions were fragmented and BIFU, although a successful union, is moderate in its policies. This suggests that class identities are more likely to take a more politicized form where individuals have direct experience of class-based organizations, such as trade unions and the old Labour party. If class identification is indeed generally diminishing in society, as postmodernists argue, it seems likely that the declining influence of these organizations, or their own attempts to distance themselves from any particular class allegiance, is at least in part responsible. Is this leading to the decay of working-class identification?

The decline of the working-class?

One clerk at Albion described himself as part of the working class, 'the real brains in the UK!' This burst of working-class pride is unexpected within such an occupation, the more so as there is a general sociological view that the rise of unemployment and the decline of unions have weakened longstanding processes of class socialization especially for young manual men (Hollands, 1990; Willis *et al.*, 1990). In Pahl's words:

> 'The collectivist solidarities of working-class unionism have failed to deliver and working-class pride has been undermined by deskilling, political attacks and employers' divisive strategies.' (Pahl, 1995, p. 120)

My data do not support this view, for despite the problems surrounding personal class identification, there was more assertion of 'working-classness' among those I interviewed than might have been expected from a sample which in most neo-Weberian class analysis would have been defined as largely middle class (Giddens, 1973; Abercrombie and Urry, 1983). My respondents were curiously reluctant to describe themselves as middle class: a few, indeed, offered their identification as precisely 'not middle'! This may relate to the broader context of the North East as a class milieu. Family background seems more important in processes of identification than personal occupational status; in the North East, people remain strongly embedded in family networks, and those families themselves are rooted in the working-class communities and residential areas, such as the estate on which Pillco and TradeFare were located.

While I have suggested that there is a discourse on class which presents it in terms of stigma, there also exists a counter-discourse rooted in these communities which is hard to destroy. Thus many of the employees located working-classness as somehow the 'norm' and preferred to attach themselves to that norm: phrases such as 'just normal' or 'just working class people', expressed this idea, if in an uneasy way. One Pillco worker said 'Poor class. Well I don't think of myself as being in any class to be quite honest. Just the ordinary working class.' Here being working class has become so much a part of normality as to become almost invisible.

Others more explicitly referred to a feeling of being rooted in the working-class communities. For example, a female worker at the Bureau told me that though her lifestyle was 'heading towards middle class' she still identified as working class because of her background. Her father was a bus driver and her mother had formerly worked with her at the Bureau. She believed that class inequalities were more significant than gender ones: 'There's still an awful lot of jobs that go on background or where you were educated.' Another Bureau worker, a young man of 21, similarly described himself as working class 'but on the way up', linking this to the common perception that 'the standard of living is much better for everybody'. Despite this perception, however, he stated that class distinctions were marked in the office. He identified his family as working class (his father worked as a painter and his mother was a domestic):

'I was asked about class the other day by someone who said, everybody says they're middle class now. But I feel I am still really working class.'

Conclusions

This chapter has illustrated both the persistence of class meanings and the complexity of processes of class identification. As Holloway argues (1997), class is pervasive and powerful in its influence on people's lives and yet puzzling because of its seeming invisibility. Moreover, the class dynamic is constantly evolving. In the North East, as elsewhere, the 'traditional' manual working class is numerically in decline. Most of those involved in the relations of wage labour now fall into what some neo-Marxists call the 'new middle classes' and Goldthorpe labels intermediate and service class groupings. There has been a longstanding debate about the class position of the lower echelons of these classes; should they be seen as a 'white-collar proletariat'? Are they part of a newly emergent 'service proletariat'? The occupational groups I have studied have been established too long to be part of the latter. Yet the claim that they are a white-collar proletariat is not without plausibility: the clerks and public-sector professionals pointed to it themselves in highlighting the decline in conditions, their sense of diminished autonomy and insecurity. The pay levels of these employees are in many cases lower than those of skilled manual workers and the fact that they are feminized contributes to a lower status for the occupations. While some differences in job content and promotion chances remain, a degree of merging with the conditions of manual wage labour is occurring. This adds weight to the suggestion that class identification in contemporary societies might be more fruitfully analysed through notions of hybridity.

The ambiguous class position of these groups indubitably affects processes of class identification, as does personal experience of a hybrid class background. The chapter has shown that, while belief in the existence of classes remains strong and class meanings are common in the discussion of employment relations, the sense of class as a form of personal identity is much weaker. Half of those interviewed were unwilling or unable to locate themselves in class terms. I have suggested that this reflects sociological confusions about what class is and where boundaries are drawn; in some cases it derives from an experience of class hybridity, both in people's background and in their own experience of upward mobility; it also springs from a widespread conviction that class relations are altering; and finally it links to a moral discourse of classlessness which presents class as socially undesirable. At one end of this is the perception of working-class membership as stigma, as described by Val Walsh:

> 'If, in a class-based society, working class means *lack*: of decorum and beauty, education and influence, knowledge and power, if it means *wrong* as in uncultured, unskilled, unintelligent; if it signifies poverty and dependence: how could it be admitted, let alone celebrated?' (Walsh, 1997, p. 155)

Nevertheless, around a third of my interviewees were prepared to acknowledge to me (a middle-class researcher) a working-class identification. This is indicative of the existence of an opposing moral discourse, which presents working-class membership as a source of pride and positive evaluation. Working-class values and identities are upheld within families, communities, learned in education or through involvement with the Labour party. At work, a link between class and trade unions still exists; a strong union presence promotes active or politicized class identification.

Middle-class identity is more problematic. The white-collar employees rejected a middle-class identification. I have argued that there is no necessary link between an individual's location within class relations and class identity. Class identification must be seen as in part a political process, in Devine's words 'a product of collective organization within an institutional framework...of political democracy' (1992, p. 27). Media or institutions for the transmission of middle-class identity appear undeveloped, at least in the North East. Membership of an established profession or possession of higher educational qualifications encourage middle-class identification. But in general it might be said that middle-class identity is a 'default identity' in Kitzinger and Wilkinson's phrase. That is, it is an identity which, since it is taken for granted, is not a source of personal reflexivity; default identities are 'less articulate...than are oppositional or oppressed identities' (1993, p. 32). The history of North East communities has constituted working-classness as an oppositional identity with its own values and discourses which are absent for the middle class in the region.

I have argued in this chapter that trade unions are an important locus for class meanings. In the next section of this book, it is time to consider the role of unions more explicitly, especially in relation to the challenge of gender.

Notes

1 The class position of the seven students is as yet hard to determine so they have been left out of some calculations.
2 Such allocations were inevitably crude and inaccurate as I had no time to probe into parents' work histories and had to rely on a simple occupational label (sometimes I was offered a little more); obviously both parents, but especially mothers, may have held many jobs in the

course of their working lives. It seems probable, however, that the occupations people offered me were the ones that had impinged most on their consciousnesses and were thus likely to have influenced their sense of their own class position.

3   At Albion and NDH a different version of this question was employed. Results, however, were consistent despite the variation.

Chapter 9

Sisters are Doing It...? Women in the Union

'Women have got to push themselves in the union. They cannot rely on men. They won't get the support from men.' (steward)

'Women should be more involved. It's easier for men. I still think there's a little...slight prejudice, in the case of the older men. They don't see it as women's business.' (female nurse)

'Now that the branch secretary is a woman and the reps are mainly female...I think it has made a difference because there isn't the selfishness there has been in the past. The men have a bias in the union to their own departments and their own sex.' (steward)

In the last chapter, it was suggested that trade unions continue to be linked with class meanings in the workplace and to play a part in processes of class identification. Such a link between unions and class is an historic one. In their role as the collective voice of working people, trade unions in Britain and elsewhere were among the few legitimate outlets through which members of the working classes could express their opinions, interests and needs before Parliamentary representation had been achieved. Marx and Engels, over-optimistically no doubt, believed that unions would be a vehicle through which the industrial proletariat would move from being a class in itself to a class for itself. Certainly E. P. Thompson, in his magisterial account of the formation of the English working class during the first half of the nineteenth century (1968), stressed the important role of unions in promoting class consciousness in industrial communities, as did John Foster (1974) in his study of Oldham. Accounts of union development in

161

the later part of the nineteenth century suggested that, though trade unions were still a crucial part of the labour movement, they were pursuing economistic and sectional interests rather than posing any radical or revolutionary challenge to the system of capitalist work organization (for example, Musson, 1972; Perkin, 1985). Nevertheless, if trade unions failed to develop socialist zeal, the interests they pursued were still taken to be those of the working class, or specific groups of working-class people. This was also reflected in their close link with the Labour party, in whose formation they played an important part.

In the twentieth century, however, the link of unions and the working class has become problematical. The rise of white-collar unions in the postwar period began this process, providing a challenge to the orthodox view of the unions' class role. Was this a sign of white-collar proletarianization? Or did it signify a new form of unionism, expressing individual needs and 'instrumental collectivism' (Hyman and Price, 1983) rather than any sort of class solidarism, however embryonic?

The fracturing of the union link with class, however, has been more marked and explicit during the past two decades. Four interrelated sets of factors have been involved here:

1   The general phenomenon of 'union decline', measured both by decreasing membership and by waning social influence. Union density has sunk from a peak of 55 per cent in 1979 to 31 per cent in 1995 (ONS, 1996; Williams, 1996). This has resulted both from structural changes (decline in manual jobs, rise of self-employment and of part-time and casual work, growth of service-sector employment especially of small private enterprises which are notoriously hard to organize) and from the attack of the Conservative government on union power, through restrictive legislation, through severing the corporatist alliance of unions with government and employers, and through ideological representation of unions as part of the 'enemy within'.

2   The triumph of 'managerial prerogative in the workplace', sanctioned by the Thatcher regime, and the attempt by management to achieve a 'decollectivization' of industrial relations (Smith and Morton, 1993). Decollectivization involves both an attempt to individualize employment relations, through a variety of strategies such an individual contracts, performance

appraisal and performance-related pay, and an attempt to marginalize trade unions and weaken their role as employee representatives. Where tolerated, unions may be forced to adapt to a framework of individualism (for example, by concentrating on individual grievance procedures).

3 The loosening of the connection between the Labour party and the unions. Both the Labour party and the unions have seen this as in their interests. 'New Labour' seeks to broaden its constituency by appealing to the 'nation' across the spectrum of class interests. The old structures of trade union power in the party, such as the block vote, are seen as inhibiting the modernization of the party and have been dismantled. Similarly, the unions increasingly see their political relationship with Labour as a hindrance to expanding their membership; white-collar unions in particular are apt to portray themselves as moderate and 'non-political'.

4 The realization by trade unions that union revival depends upon recruiting members whose interests were not sufficiently catered for in the past: women, part-time workers, minority ethnic groups, young people. Thus class becomes only one of a number of identifiable interests to be addressed by union policies.

Attention is given in Chapter 10 to the issues of union decline and renewal, decollectivization and the changing political affiliation of unions. This chapter deals with the fourth issue, focusing on women as a particular constituency within union membership. How are their needs being met by trade unions? Do distinct gender interests exist? And if so, are they in conflict with class interests? And can they be harmonized? The chapter starts by discussing the attempts made by the unions in the study to appeal to women members. It then explores the progress made by women within their unions as rank and file members and as representatives. Finally, consideration is given to the 'divided loyalties' (Phillips, 1987) of class and gender.

Trade unions and equal opportunities

While women have been involved in trade unions since their inception, unions in the past have been represented as 'the men's affair' (Beynon and Blackburn, 1984). Women have been relegated to marginal roles; they have been under-represented in positions of leadership; and, on the whole, their specific interests as working women have been subordinated to those of their male 'brothers' (Cockburn, 1983). They have taken a supporting role, as women often have done in the past in political movements, a role in fact crucial but seen as less valuable than that of their 'heroic' male comrades. I shall never forget my first experience of a union conference, when in the middle of an interesting debate a large number of women sitting in the hall suddenly got to their feet and disappeared into a side room: they were going to make the tea!

The portrayal of unions as male institutions arose historically because of men's dominance in the political sphere in the nineteenth century and because women's work was subordinated to men's during the process of industrialization (Bradley, 1989; Lewenhak, 1977). The prevailing tendency to symbolize both waged work and unions in male terms meant that the presence of women in unions was masked by the greater audibility and visibility of the 'brothers'. Thus women were constituted as 'second-class citizens' within the unions. Male officers often presented women as 'a problem': they were stereotyped as apathetic, less militant, more difficult to organize and generally less interested in union affairs (McCarthy, 1971; Boston, 1980; Bradley, 1987). Moreover, the way unions operate promotes values of 'masculine heroics' (Cockburn, 1991, p. 120). Male officers are expected to work in the evenings and weekends, rush around the country attending meetings and conferences, in a way that makes the job inaccessible for many women with domestic commitments. As Heery and Kelly found in their study of full-time officers (1988), a wife is a requisite of the job.

However, over the past decades feminism has posed a challenge to the marginalization of women in unions, while unions themselves have grasped the importance of appealing to women as members in the context of feminization and industrial decline. Nearly twenty years have passed since 1979 when the TUC drew up its ten-point 'Charter for Equality for Women within Trade Unions' (Hunt, 1982). Most unions now have strategies to promote gender equality and greater female participation: women's officers, women's committees, training courses targeted at women, policies on sexual harassment (Ellis, 1988; Cunnison and Stageman,

1993). Are unions now becoming as a much a 'woman's place' as a man's?

The unions in the case-study organizations had all made attempts to develop special provisions for women members and to address the issue of equality for women within the union. At national level, all either had women's or equality comittees or had appointed women's officers or equality officers. The larger unions, such as the TGWU and NUPE, also had local officers with responsibility for women. MSF had a local women's committee open to any woman and, like the TGWU and other unions, ran special courses for female reps. Local officers from COHSE and NUPE had jointly organized women's days with NALGO, in this period prior to the merger to form UNISON.

At both national and local level, all the unions were working on policies designed to improve conditions for women workers and to increase female participation. USDAW and BIFU were campaigning for better rights for part-timers, which had already been achieved by BWU. MSF had conducted a successful equal pay campaign on behalf of speech therapists (an undervalued female profession). NUPE and COHSE were campaigning vigorously for creche facilities at Northtown. BIFU had established a counselling service on sexual harassment. BWU's part in gaining flexi-time arrangements was praised by many female members. Many unions had carried out research on women's issues; for example USDAW had completed a survey of part-timers' experiences. Union publications carried features targeted at women, with stories about equal pay, harassment and desegregation of jobs, along with profiles of women activists. The unions, then, were aware of gender issues and were making serious attempts to address them. Had this resulted in the greater integration of their female members?

Women and men in the rank and file

National surveys show that women employees are less likely to be union members than men. In 1994, 31 per cent of employed women were union members as opposed to 37 per cent of men (CSO, 1995). In 1989 women constituted 40 per cent of union membership (Bird and Corcoran, 1994). The SCELI research, carried out in six localities in 1986, found that female membership was lower in all the areas: 38 per cent of women employees were members, compared to 52 per cent of men (Gallie, 1996).

However, research indicates that these disparities are not necessarily the result of gender *per se* but arise from the structural differences in women's and men's employment (Payne, 1989; Lawrence, 1994). Women are more likely than men to work in small, poorly unionized or non-unionized establishments; many are employed in private services, a poorly organized sector; and many work part-time or move between jobs, factors which discourage people from joining a union. Indeed the SCELI researchers found that if they looked only at full-time employees the gender difference nearly disappeared: 47 per cent of full-time women were union members.

This finding is born out by my study. Trade unionism is, in any case, more strongly established in the North East than in other regions. In 1995 union density in the Northern region was 41 per cent as opposed to a national figure of 31 per cent; only Wales had a higher rate (ONS, 1996). Membership levels were high in all five organizations. The survey suggests that full-time women in well-unionized organizations are little different from men in terms of their membership. Omitting the part-time employees at Trade-Fare, 92 per cent of my female respondents were members and 87 per cent of men. Similar numbers of women and men in the sample could be identified as activists (they were currently union reps or had been in the past): fourteen women and fourteen men. As reported in other studies (Rose, 1996), the majority of both men and women could be described as 'passive members' (Bradley, 1994). Such people described themselves as not being active in the union, expressed only moderate enthusiasm for unions and did not take part in activities which occurred outside working hours. Only slightly more women members than men categorized themselves as not active in the union, 77 per cent as opposed to 74 per cent.

Gallie (1996) reports that the SCELI women employees were less attached to their unions than the men, although noting that women's attachment seemed to be increasing during the 1980s. Perhaps Gallie was picking up on a developing trend or perhaps the North East women are different from those in other parts of the country: for, if anything, the women in my study appeared more attached to unions than their male colleagues. As Table 9.1

shows, they were slightly more likely to ~~be~~
committed to unions, while similar propor~~tions of~~
men (a very small minority) described themselv~~es~~

TABLE 9.1   Attitudes towards unions (percentages)

	Women	Men
Very committed	9	3
Quite committed	29	31
Neutral	52	55
Quite hostile	8	6
Very hostile	1	3

It is sometimes suggested that women join unions for more conventional or pragmatic reasons than men, for example because they feel the need for protection more strongly or because their friends are members. As one (male) union officer once told me, 'Women are like sheep: if one joins they all do.' Men, by contrast, are envisaged to have ideological reasons for their membership.

Little evidence to confirm this could be found in examining the reasons given for joining unions or for being committed to them. While more women than men did mention that they had joined because the organization operated a closed shop or because it was 'the done thing', similar numbers of men and women ascribed their membership to a belief in unions. The need for protection was a common reason given by both sexes. Both women and men spoke of the influence of their family background, as discussed in Chapter 8, and of experiences at work which had brought home the importance of unions, as shown in these quotations, all from women:

'I was and still am a great believer in the trade union movement.'

'Me dad said to me, "You must be in the union, no matter what happens, you must be in the union."'

'Listening to what goes on. My experience has convinced me of the need for a union.'

'We had a problem with a patient and it went to court. I'd been silly not to join before . . . I've seen a lot of people helped out of difficulties.'

... women *are* more likely to join for 'social' reasons than men, such 'sheeplike' behaviour need not be read in a derogatory way. Joining a union 'because everybody else was in it' can equally be read as evidence of a spirit of workgroup collectivism and solidarity with female colleagues. One man grumbled about women's voting behaviour at meetings because 'they look round to see what their friends is doing, rather than having an independent mind'. Women here appear more in tune with the traditions of the union solidarity than their menfolk, who by contrast seem imbued with the individualism of the Thatcher era.

Case-study research suggests that, where occupational differences are absent, women are not so different from men in their levels of membership and participation (Wertheimer and Nelson, 1975; Lawrence, 1994). My own study confirmed that, with only a small minority of members being actively involved in union affairs, the overall profile of women and men as participants is fairly similar. I asked the interviewees whether they had taken part in a range of activities; the findings are summarized in Table 9.2.

TABLE 9.2 **Percentages of women and men who had taken part in various union activities**

	Women	Men
Reading a union magazine or publication	90	96
Voting in a union election	86	86
Attending a union meeting	57	68
Attending a social event organized by the union	18	32
Attending an educational event organized by the union	12	11
Acting as a union representative	15	18
Taking part in industrial action	40	41

The table shows that men are slightly more likely to be active in most areas than women, but the only activities where this is strongly marked are those which take place outside the workplace. Women's capacity to attend meetings and social events outside work hours is limited by their family responsibilities. While lack of time was cited by both sexes as a major obstacle to greater participation, constraints of time press more heavily on women. Moreover, there is an acknowledged problem for women venturing out alone at night to inner-city venues such as pubs and clubs where branch meetings and socials are commonly held. As one male activist reflected:

> 'There's more men at our branch, to be honest. Perhaps the starting time is wrong...The only thing I can think of is the time we start. You know, they're working women, they're wanting to get home and get hubby the tea and do the house.'

It is significant that in the two organizations where meetings were held in the workplace during work time the difference between men's and women's attendance diminished: at Pillco and the Bureau 100 per cent of men, 95 per cent of women reported attending a meeting.

Despite the evidence that the women's behaviour and attitudes were quite similar to their male co-workers, the perception of unions as a male sphere remained entrenched. The imagery of unions seems to have altered little with the advance of women. Both women and men made this point to me repeatedly when asked if they thought women were as interested in the union as men:

> 'It's always been men-orientated really. In the past the workers were the men. It's more of a male-dominated sort of thing.' (male shopworker)

> 'If they're married and stuff they've got a lot of other things that are more important to them.' (female nurse)

Sometimes this was linked to the perception of women as secondary earners:

> 'If they've got husbands working, a lot of them are just working for money for holidays, so they're not that much interested in job evaluation, pay deals, et cetera. Some of the women never look at their pay slip from week to week.' (female operative)

'Women are only working for pin money so they don't want to stick their necks out...A woman is well paid and they don't want to rock the boat. A lot of them have husbands who are working. Their husbands could keep them on their pay.' (male operative)

Another factor was the link perceived between unions and aggression. As contributors to the study of women in unions have argued (Briskin and McDermott, 1993; Cunnison and Stageman, 1993; Lawrence, 1994), women appear to have a different style to approaching problems and to negotiation. They eschew the stereo-typically macho table-thumping style associated with collective bargaining, favouring a less confrontational, more consultative style of industrial relations. Certainly, nearly half the women I spoke to said they opposed strikes, as against only a quarter of the men. Because union officers were seen to operate by utilizing assertion and aggression, some felt that women were unsuitable as representatives:

'I haven't got the bottle to go and argue with anybody.' (woman)

'I think the men's always the fighters and shouters, more so than the women. You do get some women who are good arguers, but most of the women are only here for the wages.' (woman)

'Women are not prepared to stand up and fight.' (man)

A young woman made it clear that the imagery of traditional polit-ical conduct was a deterrent to her, and no doubt to many of her age group who are said to be disinterested in conventional party politics:

'I don't like the type of people, they seem a bit like dictators. The image puts me off...people standing on soapboxes and shouting a lot.'

Although the representatives of her own union (BIFU) were far removed from this stereotype, I had a graphic example of this when I witnessed a young male representative dealing with a grievance case on the phone. This man, who had been charm itself in his conversation with me, appearing gentle, caring and sensitive to gender issues, was suddenly transformed. He turned on a new personality, becoming furious and ferocious, bawling into the phone so that he could be heard through closed doors. A young woman in the room with me subtly conveyed that he was 'always like this'. If such muscular heroics are deemed necessary in dealing with employers, it is perhaps not surprising that women are daunted at the prospect or believe their own sex unsuited for union power:

> 'I'm not the kind to be in the front. I'd rather be in the background.'

> 'If a problem came up and a woman officer had to speak to a male manager she might not be taken seriously.'

This use of an aggressive form of masculinity as a weapon in union strategy serves to strengthen the accepted if artificial divide which locates women in the private, men in the public sphere:

> 'I suppose it's not a woman's thing. Men are more into politics and things like that.' (female)

> 'I think a lot of the women, they're more interested in the family side of life than the political side.' (male)

Women as representatives: coping with male norms

Despite this common perception, a minority of women launch themselves into the 'political side' of workplace life. The passionate devotion to unions that women can show was typified by Yvonne. She had been an office representative for three years. She joined her union after six months' part-time employment and became active when a problem arose at work; her husband, himself a union activist, had encouraged her to take it to a union meeting. Subsequently Yvonne herself had become an enthusiast. 'You can't get away from unions in our house,' she told me.

Yvonne was one of only two women at a local branch meeting I sat in on. She had served on the union's Equal Opportunities Committee, she was a Health and Safety rep and a sexual harassment counsellor. She was also on the union's National Committee (composed at that time of five women and 20 men). She is a formidable, lively woman, passionately committed to equality for women as well as employees' rights in general. She has ambitions to progress further in the union but they sit uneasily with her domestic responsibilities. Her children are now in their teens which makes things a little easier, but as she says, 'It's always in the back of my mind. You can't totally forget about it all.' With his own commitment to unions, her husband offers her help and support, but her possibilities remain restricted. What she would really like to do is work full-time for the union. It is clear she has the ability, energy and national standing to do so. But this would require her to move to Sheffield or London and this is impossible, she says, because of her husband's job.

Yvonne negotiates her role as a union activist within existing gender relations rather than openly challenging them, but is acutely aware of men's tendency to dominate. Like many women, the strategy she has adopted is to take them on at their own game. She described how she at first felt nervous and inhibited when joining the National Committee, especially because as one of the few women there she felt she was representing her sex. But soon she gained confidence as she observed that 'men seemed to waffle on'. Echoing other female representatives I spoke to, she commented, 'I've often found from my experience that men come out with a whole lot of rubbish. Women will only speak when they've got something to say. Men seem to like the sound of their own voices.'

Yvonne had apparently mastered the male art of talking copiously and confidently in order to operate effectively in the masculine union world, along with other necessary skills. She described to me how she had been on a 'teamwork and leadership' training course. Participants were briefed in advance that they must wear rough clothes, which had apparently deterred the only other woman enrolled from attending. Yvonne told me she had made it clear from the start, as the team embarked on an assault course, that she wanted to be treated as an equal, to become 'one of the lads'. It had worked and she'd been successful, but, as she ruefully told me, in the video made of the event, 'they kept photographing my backside'. Differentiated conventions about dress, appearance and deportment are a crucial way in which gender boundaries are marked out; women are visibly 'the other' in workplaces where maleness is seen as the norm (McDowell, 1997). Women like Yvonne have to tread a fine line to preserve both their femininity and the respect of male colleagues who do not have to worry about unsuitable clothing, untidy hair or bodily presentation.

Not all female representatives, however, shared Yvonne's feminism nor did they necessarily experience sexism. Some said they had found no problems arising from being a woman and reported strong support from male colleagues; while some are deterred by explicitly feminist campaigning, including Barbara, one of the Northtown reps. She was sceptical about what she saw as the overemphasis on equal opportunities, although she was very sensitive to the discrimination she believed occurred against part-timers, night staff and enrolled nurses; but she did not interpret these as gender issues. She had found herself uneasy at a woman-only meeting she had attended, saying that she felt it offered nothing for heterosexual women. A robust and outspoken woman, Barbara's motives for union activism were what Ledwith *et al.* (1990) describe as 'welfarist'. 'I enjoy my union work. I like helping people on a personal level. And I don't mind pitting my wits against the management.' Although vigorously involved in campaigns against the NHS 'reforms', Barbara explicitly denied being interested in the political side of unionism.

Sometimes the experience of sexism only occurs as women begin to move upward in the union hierarchy. Two reps who spoke enthusiastically about their work at grassroots level had found branch affairs more problematic. One, who described herself as a socialist feminist, reported that her branch was conservative, bureaucratic and dominated by men; when she tried to raise broader political issues rather than workplace matters she was stigmatized as a 'loonie leftie'.

The other had become active in the union when victimized by her manager: 'I said to myself,who can I turn to? So I thought let's get on the union and in no time I started to assert myself, having been a quiet little thing who wouldn't say boo to a goose.' Empowered by her experience, she had risen quite meteorically to branch level and commenced a union career, but her experience of union culture had slowly led to disillusion: 'I found there was a clique. Wherever you go you can spot who are the union guys. There's a lot of well-intentioned people on the exec, but they do like their beer. A lot of the business was done in the pub.'

While pub-based masculine camaraderie dies hard in some unions, it must be stressed that union cultures vary. Where unions

have tried to become more woman-friendly the experience of
women may be very different. Sheila's story illustrates this and
also the complexities of change and individual responses. Far
from being rebuffed by male activists, Sheila felt she was being
unduly pressured to climb within the union hierarchy. She had
been pushed into becoming a rep because she had 'the biggest
gob' and contrasted her initial experiences with the current climate:

> 'When I first joined, it was sister that, brother that, committee that,
> cloth cap stuff, Andy Capping. I thought I didn't like it, but you've got
> to stick with it...Things have changed and women's presence has
> helped to change it.'

Sheila is committed to her union work, 'I love my union,' but finds
it demanding. She has two children under ten, and as she says
ruefully, 'I need a wife,' although her husband looks after them
when she goes on weekend training courses. Getting a job share
has released her from a sense of chronic overload and gives more
space for union work; but while it had been suggested to her that
she might think of becoming an officer she feels that her male colleagues merit it more, expressing particular admiration for the
efforts of one young man, Doug.

Indeed, Doug was a live wire and could be seen to embody the
spirit of a new generation of male unionists who are sensitive to
gender issues. Doug had been central in a campaign for creche
facilities which was about to bear fruit. Aware of the offputting
nature of traditional bureaucratic procedures to many rank-and-
filers, he ran branch meetings informally, encouraging women to
bring their children along and bringing his own to set the tone.
He emphasized the importance of the social side of unionism to
attract new recruits, of making sure union business was not all
boring, that 'there's pleasure in it'. Full of energy and ideas, he
believed that the union was right to target greater female participation; he was trying to achieve it himself.

But there are ironies attached to Doug's commitment to 'feminizing the union'. The union in question was considering a positive
discrimination policy to increase its proportion of women officers;
but Doug himself had ambitions to be an officer and clearly was an

outstanding candidate. It is not surprising that he opposed a policy which might threaten his own prospects. Moreover, his very dynamism and effectiveness might prove daunting to less confident women. Doug acknowledged this problem himself when he told me that the union needed more strong women, women who were able to dominate and to shut men up – including himself!

It must be emphasized that male dominance is hardly the *main* deterrent for women to becoming union activists. I was repeatedly told that being a rep was 'a thankless task'. People had to be pushed into it, often because nobody else would stand, because a current rep was proving inadequate, or because they were perceived, like Yvonne, as a strong personality:

> 'The floor was not satisfied with the steward we had and I was more or less pushed into it. I'm not frightened to speak up.'

Unlike Yvonne, however, many women had been deterred by the negative sides of their experience: the pressure of combining union work with employment and family duties; the grumbles and complaints from members; the feeling of continually battling against hopeless odds:

> 'You felt as if you'd been through the wringer.'

> 'I found that no matter what you did...if you couldn't do something for them they always forgot about the things you had done for them.'

Men experience these pressures too, but for them family duties are less demanding; they were not mentioned by the male activists, while family considerations played a part in the stories of a number of the women. Beth, for example, came from a family with a union background and had been both a steward and a branch secretary for many years. She had, among other things, succeeded in getting cancer screening for her female members and her achievements were commended by others. She had enjoyed her activist spell but had given it up because she now wanted to spend more leisure time with her new husband:

'I loved it. It used to get the adrenalin going... It helped to keep my
brain going, break up the monotony of the job. But when you're happy
you don't have so much fight in you.'

Things had worked the other way round for Elaine. She had
been very much influenced by her husband who was branch secretary of his own union. Before her marriage she had been
management-oriented, coming from a business family:

'Before I married I would have voted Tory. But my husband changed
me. Because I used to be very quiet – coming out to work has changed
me. So I was kind of educated by him. He's more of a militant type of
person than I am.'

Like so many Elaine had been pushed into the steward's job: 'I
never ever thought that I would be a steward. Because it's a
thankless job.' She told me that she had enjoyed going to training
courses and got satisfaction out of working on individual cases,
describing herself as a person who would never give up halfway.
Backed by her local officers, she felt things were going well for the
union at the moment, yet she suffered the characteristic pressures
of the job: the lack of time, which prevented her from communicating with members as much as she felt she ought to, the unreal-
istic expectations of members: 'A lot of them want the union to go
and do their dirty work for them. They say 'I'm paying my union
to you' and I'm saying, "Well, you know, you are not paying it to
me!"'

Elaine believed that women behave differently as union members, reflecting research which presents women as more concerned, more democratic (Briskin and McDermott, 1993):

'They haven't as loud a voice or as selfish a reason. The women don't
want to see themselves earning more than the people they work with,
the men do like to see themselves earning more. Women want friends,
men don't care about having friends.'

For this reason she applauded the recent increase in female reps,
believing that it was improving the image of the union in the
organization. Ironically, however, the pressures of the job may
deter her from standing again. She said wryly, 'If I wasn't voted
in, I wouldn't be depressed.'

Women as officers: positional power

The pressures and dilemmas faced by women as representatives are magnified for those women who take the further step of moving into full-time union work. In preparing for my research, I spoke to fourteen full-time officers (FTOs) and one lay officer who looked after the affairs of a union that had no regional office. This included some officers from unions whose members were not subsequently covered in the study. Of these fifteen people, seven were women, four working for manual unions, three for white-collar unions.

For the four female FTOs who dealt with manual workers, sexism was a major issue. The other three women did not discuss this problem with me (which was not to say they had not experienced it). Two of these were organizing nurses in the NHS and each was the sole FTO for the region: in their current circumstances, they were less likely to confront sexism. Indeed one of them, when asked about the role of male nurses, viewed it positively in union terms; she saw women as too docile, enmeshed in an ideology of altruistic service:

> 'Men will not be trampled on... Nurses have never been ones to stand up for themselves... Managers want to do things and the men say you can't do that. Perhaps female nurses are getting more assertive, but we've got hanging over our head, you came into nursing because you're dedicated. However, now we have some very forthright women in nursing with very strong, free-thinking ideas. But there are still many nurses that have been fifteen, twenty years on the same ward. They're not going to rock the boat. But it's good that there are a growing number of free-thinking women.'

The seven women I spoke to could all have been described as 'strong, free-thinking women'. Ledwith *et al.* (1990) categorized female activists as traditional unionists, welfarists and feminists. Traditional union women shared the goals and attitudes of male colleagues, often seeing gender equality issues as a distraction from the real business of class struggle. Welfarists had become involved in unions because of their concern with the problems of their colleagues and often raised issues that affected women in the workplace, but did not have very strong political affiliations. Feminists, however, held political views on gender and were determined to raise them within the union context. All seven women FTOs I interviewed could have been characterized to some degree as feminists, even if their original entry into union activism had been for welfarist or traditional reasons. If they had not brought feminist ideals into the job (and most had) they had been politicized while doing it. All were vigorously pursuing equality policies, all were aware of women's specific problems, such as childcare, low pay or lack of opportunities; and the women in the manual unions had played out the dramas of gender in their own lives.

Mary had been a full-time officer for fifteen years. Her history is typical of the older breed of union officers, although she is atypical in having reached the topmost tiers in her union. She says she did not come from a background of left-wing politics, although she is from Scotland which has a notable tradition of female union activism. She worked her way up from the ranks having started out in a manual occupation similar to those of the workers her union represents. She recalled how when she first went to union meetings and heard people speaking she felt she 'couldn't do it in a hundred years'. Nevertheless she ended up as her shop representative in the familiar situation that 'nobody else would do it', and succeeded in raising the membership from 50 to 100 per cent. After such initial success, she gained considerable credibility in the union, and recalled a feeling of being compelled to voice her views, especially on equal opportunities issues. Mary seems to have developed feminist ideas quite early on in the 1970s. She described to me her first experience at the union's annual conference. She had picked a topic carefully that she felt confident to talk on, the shorter working week, and angled it as a woman's issue. Like many women, she reported the difficulty of overcoming her lack of confidence:

> 'Yes, I was very nervous. I can remember getting up, I could hear my heels all the way up to the rostrum...I'd never spoken into a microphone before, I heard the voice bounce back at me from the back of the hall. But I thought, I'm going to look more ridiculous if I come off, I've got to go through with it.'

Subsequently Mary progressed her way up through the union hierarchy to her current high position, but she has perpetually faced sexism and opposition from certain male occupational groups who, she says, would never consider voting for a woman. She knows that her record, her personality and honesty have gained her great respect from much of the membership, but doubts whether women are as effective in participating in the wheeling and dealing of internal union politics. Mary's refusal to join in these 'boys' games' may cost her the chance to make it to the very top of the power hierarchy.

Despite her feminism, Mary's story is typical of the older generation of female union officers. Younger women are likely to enter the job in rather different ways. Some base their careers on qualifications, using a university degree to acquire a specialist post (education or research officer, for example). A strong commitment to both left-wing politics and feminism is likely to have contributed to such a career choice. Others may start out from the ranks like Mary, but recognizing career possibilities earlier deliberately make moves like applying for a post in a different union. In both cases, women will be helped by the union movement's current concern to appoint women among their officiate.

Catherine was an example of the latter group. Like Mary, Catherine described herself as having no family background of union activism. Aged 38, when I met her, she had been an activist since she was 18; she has no children and did not marry until in her 30s. She had initially drifted into being a rep for NALGO: 'Basically I just got involved being difficult. It was an issue that nobody would take up and I said right and I took it to management.' Subsequently she climbed up the union lay hierarchy, although describing herself as having no clear career plan but simply being in the right place at the right time. Eventually, she found that opportunities to join the officiate were limited, so she applied for a post with her present union, which, unlike NALGO, advertises externally. Their keenness to recruit women and minority members was helpful to Catherine. She is now an area officer for her new union and is particularly committed to promoting equal opportunities and working on women's issues, such as sexual harassment and rights for part-timers.

Gaining access to union office is crucial for the success of women in challenging male power at work. Women like Mary and Catherine who acquire this kind of positional power can use it to promote women's issues, to bring forward other women in the union and to promote equality bargaining. However, there is a considerable price to pay for such power. Women taking union office enter a competitive and often hostile world in which they have to fight hard for acceptance:

> 'To succeed women need to be strong and to have proved themselves capable and efficient. You certainly have to prove yourself, more so than a man would do.'

> 'You've got to be hard, basically, to actively combat them trying to use the weapon of sex against you.'

The world of union officers is a tough and demanding one for men and women alike, as previous studies have shown (Heery and Kelly, 1988; Watson, 1988; Cockburn, 1991). One woman described it as a 'seven days' a week job'. Another told me she had worked 25 weekends in the year. It is difficult to combine this with a conventional married life, so many FTOs are single women or women whose families have grown up. If there are children, husbands must be prepared to help with childcare and also to accept patterns of behaviour that depart from marital norms:

> 'In some respects my husband was very good, but he wasn't very happy about the fact of me staying away over night. To be honest, it bothered me that he wasn't very happy. But I felt I had to stick to my guns, it was something I was doing for myself.'

> 'My husband had to put up with teasing. "You don't let your wife go away to London and stay overnight. You must be mad!" It's not seen as right for a woman to do this.'

If women officers are married with children they, like Yvonne, have a delicate balancing act to perform, exposing them to a double pressure which men may legitimately evade. As Mary told me, 'Men and women act differently...We are always having to think of other people than ourselves...I have always put my husband and children first in making decisions about my career.'

While struggling to reconcile domestic duties with their work, women taking up union office also have to contend with more or less overt sexism or stereotyping from the various groups involved: rank and file members, male representatives, fellow officers and employers. Older male officers and reps in particular present

problems, being unwilling to accept that women have the competence to do the job and sometimes openly refusing to accept their
authority. One woman told me of being reduced to tears during
her trainee period by her superior officer who couldn't accept
that she was tough enough for the job as her style of self-presentation
was not aggressive. Another reported that male representatives
referred to her with cases frequently asked to speak to 'someone
higher up', while a third spoke of persistent sexism from male
activists. She articulates a dilemma familiar to many women who
seek power: 'If you shout, then you're being aggressive. If a man
shouts, then he's being assertive.'

This problem is amplified in relationships with employers.
There is a common experience of not being taken seriously, of
being patronized. Women reported being told, 'You don't look
like a union officer,' or 'At least you're prettier than the last one.'
While one line is that women can use their sexuality to advantage
in these situations, this was not the prevailing view:

> 'To be honest, I'm not the type of woman who could use these so called
> women's charms... I think it weakens your case with management.'

The difficulty is compounded by women's different bargaining
style. Irina described her first pay negotiation with an employer
who 'thought he was Rupert Murdoch meeting Arthur Scargill'.
Despite feelings of inadequacy and depression, she had stuck to it,
worked out all the details and consequences of the offer and taken
it back to the members for discussion, earning their gratitude as
her predecessor had never bothered to do that, simply 'presenting them with the agreement on a plate'.

As they struggle to be accepted, such women may feel deeply
isolated because of their emotional distance from the prevailing
male culture. They encounter the established attitude that new-
comers should be thrown in at the deep end and demonstrate
their ability to survive. Irina, who works for a manual union,
described how the culture throws the burden of solving problems
on the individual. It is not acceptable, in such a climate, to show
weakness or even to seek help from more experienced officers.
'That's life, pet, you just have to get on with it' was the advice
offered to her by an established woman officer. Though this is
true for both sexes, the men are seen by these women to display

greater self-confidence, which is reinforced by the knowledge of being among their own kind. It is easier for them to integrate and be accepted. As studies of male managers have shown (Collinson and Hearn, 1996a), male bonding is a powerful force in promoting both the will and the ability to succeed in positions of power.

The women I interviewed, all of them in my eyes formidably competent, have had to find ways to maintain their self-esteem and survive in an androcentric environment. Their own record of achievements and display of capabilities is an important asset for all of them. They recognize the crucial importance of acquiring the right knowledge, of being well-briefed about issues and aware of regulations: 'The rule-book is my bible.' The women can also gain advantage from their gender in relationships with female members; they consider themselves better equipped to deal with certain types of grievances or cases where delicate personal issues are involved. Handling such cases is a way to build up a loyal following among the membership – as, indeed, is gaining a successful outcome in the more formal bargaining situations. Educational advantages can also be used as a weapon as long as they are linked to credentials of experience within the union movement. It is useful, too, as it is for men, to find a sponsor:

> 'I had an introduction to the office from an outstanding established organizer who was held in some esteem and she introduced me as a bright capable woman . . . It made life easier for me.'

The union world is a small one, and female officers are likely to have links with others in the region with whom problems may be shared. While such alliances are important, in a region where they are in a minority, opportunities for networking are limited. Inevitably, then, they must fall back on the force of their own personalities, digging their heels in, learning to 'hang on in'.

Catherine has taken a more assertive line in pushing issues of gender into the open. She has tackled the sexism she has faced in the same way:

> 'I've tried to deal with it head on. There's a lot of politics involved, not just about myself . . . I've had to deal with it by involving the members.'

The risk though, of tackling it head on, taking on the men at their own game, is that it can lead to co-option; surviving means joining with what you can't beat. Irina acknowledged this problem, confessing that she listened to herself telling juicy anecdotes about her confrontations with managers and the stratagems by which she had bested them and recognized her own adoption of the discourse of masculine heroics: 'It's the structure. It's a male-dominated structure. There's no collective spirit. You can't share your problems with anyone … The danger is that you end up just the same as them.' But Irina was hopeful for the future. She told me that the older men, even the 'nice ones', inhabited a different mental landscape in which they simply could not grasp the salience of gender. But younger male officers (like Doug) are different, having grown up in a new cultural climate in which race and gender issues have become part of the mindset. Echoing the Bureau women, Irina declares, 'We're getting there.'

Gender and class interests

If more women, and feminist women at that, are making headway, if slowly, in their unions, does that mean that greater prominence will be given to 'women's issues'? As we have seen these unions had addressed themselves to women's needs: childcare, pay equity, part-timers' rights, cancer screening were now on the agenda. But Ann Phillips' work (1987) has highlighted the potential clashes of class and gender interests. Did the women in this study experience themselves as torn between 'divided loyalties'? Were unions still privileging class over gender interests? Are there identifiable women's interests?

The answers to these questions are complex and indeed suggest that the questions may need to be rephrased. First, men's and women's interests converge to a considerable extent. The interviewees were asked to rate a number of union activities on a five-point scale. The rank order of the activities was little different for women and men except with regard to two items, childcare and equal opportunities. Both women and men rated health and safety, conditions and pay as top three priorities for unions. But women placed equal opportunities as fourth most important, while men rated it seventh. On childcare, 38 per cent of women and 15 per cent of men rated it very important.

Childcare may be considered a key 'women's issue'. The female members were asked if there was anything they felt unions should be doing to help women. The most popular issue identified was childcare and child sickness leave, with 22 per cent mentioning them. Childcare was particularly salient to the women at Pillco and Northtown (it should be remembered that Albion already had creche facilities, while TradeFare and the Bureau offered part-time arrangements and flexitime):

> 'If they could have more creches. Some of the young women in here are forking out a fortune in childcare.'

> 'Being a woman, I should like the union to fight for some kind of creche or some kind of allowance towards childcare.'

> 'Lack of childcare in the past has meant many women leaving the profession.'

Responses might suggest that the unions are catering pretty well for women members already; 82 per cent of women felt that the union represented them as effectively as men. Similar proportions of women (70 per cent) and men (73 per cent) expressed themselves satisfied with their current union. But the crucial factor here is that unions are still perceived as operating within the framework of class and class interests. The rank and filers see unions as serving the needs of *workers*, 'working people', 'the staff', 'the workforce as a whole'. The category of 'women workers' is here subsumed into the greater whole. It may be inappropriate, therefore, to conceive of class and gender in this context in terms of 'competing interests': certainly, it is not how the rank and filers see it. An indication that unions are seen as sites of class meanings, not gender ones, is that while the majority of women expressed themselves satisfied with their union, only a third knew about their union's EO policies.

It is representatives and officers who personally encounter sexism who are likely to develop an understanding of class and gender interests as in conflict. One representative faced this issue when she riposted to my questions, 'Are you asking if I am more of a socialist or of a feminist?' Her explanation of her involvement in unions balanced socialist and feminist motivations: 'In part it's to do with my general value system and wanting to see injustice and inequality removed; and an aspect of that more particularly it's to do with being in a female-dominated profession that's been badly treated.' For this women class and gender inequality were 'aspects' of one another: and this reflects a general tendency for people who were aware of one kind of inequality to be sensitive to others. In this sense gender and class consciousness may not be oppositional but additive.

This is a crucial point, for early writing on working women implied that women must choose between class and gender loyalties (Phillips, 1987). Gender 'consciousness' was conceived of as distinct from a general workers' class consciousness (Pollert, 1981; Cavendish, 1982; Porter, 1983). More recent work has also tended to portray class and gender politics as being of a qualitatively different kind, class politics being based on claims for redistribution, feminism deriving from a call for cultural recognition and inclusion (Fraser, 1995; Coole, 1996). By contrast my work suggests that gender and class interests and awareness are more intricately related.

But the notion of a clash of interests cannot be entirely shelved. Tensions around this issue surfaced most clearly in the answers to the question on reserved seats for women, discussed in Chapter 6 (p. 99). As we saw, both sexes were split down the middle on this issue, with 49 per cent of women supporting the idea but 42 per cent against. The contentious nature of the topic is indicated by the fact that this question almost always elicited comments rather than just a yes/no answer.

Those women who supported the policy displayed awareness that there might be a special women's angle which needed representing and that women might need some special help to progress within unions:

'Women have different interests. Women are in a different situation.'

'I think you need a woman so you can go and talk to her about personal things.'

'A female rep ... would encourage more female involvement.'

Opposition could be linked to two sets of perceptions. As discussed in Chapter 6, one reflected the discourse of individual merit. Even those who expressed awareness of gender inequalities and discrimination within their workplace might take the meritocratic line:

'The best person should be up there, whether it's male or female.'

'There shouldn't be any need... Whoever represents me, as long as they do the best they can, he or she, I'm not really bothered.'

The other perception subsumed the separate interest of women (which might be acknowledged) into the broader class interest, arguing that the needs of the workforce as a whole must come first:

'I do feel that women should be represented, but a man can do it. A union's representative should represent everybody whether they're men or women.'

On a practical level, while some people acknowledged that positive action might be necessary 'to get things started', others felt that it might be counter-productive and divisive: 'You have to get people to want to do things, rather than force them. You could alienate people by doing this.'

The attitudes of individual women often involved a complex mix of these various frameworks, mirroring the feminist debates over 'difference' as opposed to 'sameness' (Scott, 1988). Thus, for example, Elaine, despite her belief that the increase in female reps was producing a more democratic union spirit in her organization, expressed herself opposed to reserved seats and women's committees: 'I don't agree with woman this and man this. All right, it was nice to have a woman at regional office you could speak to, but I don't think they should have called her a woman's officer.'

An awareness that women experience special problems requiring different treatment vies with a deep-seated commitment to democratic political representation which is predicated on sameness, enshrining a view of the abstract, un-gendered individual. Many women (and men) expressed the view that there should be women at all levels of the union and on all committees. But they were uneasy about departing from established methods of election to get them there, seeing positive action as 'unfair' or 'discriminatory'.

Within unions, as elsewhere, the definition and pursuit of distinctive gender interests may be impeded by other political imperatives. Here, notions of the common interests of employees as an aspect of class relations still constitute the main political justification for the existence of unions. Moreover, there is a broader attachment to the principles of liberal democracy, which continues to foster the ideal of the 'universal citizen', transcending of gender and class.

Conclusion

This chapter confirms the finding of previous researchers, that within large, well-unionized organizations, the patterns of behaviour of women and men as rank-and-file union members are not very different. Women have a well-established presence as shopfloor representatives and are making progress in entering top union posts.

However, the study also suggests that the culture and ethos of unions is still framed in terms of masculine values and practices, making women uneasy entrants to the union world. Among the rank and filers unions are still considered as 'men's business'; and women who become union activists and officers are still having to contend with sexism. Union women need considerable personal skills to survive and succeed in this world.

Can unions, then, be feminized? In the sense that women officers are carrying feminist values into the union arena and raising 'women's issues' on the agenda, this is already happening. But the feminization of the symbolic universe of unions is a slower process. Just as in the organizations themselves, the setters of rules and the primary definers are still largely male. The preoccupations of unions and their style of interaction reflects the priorities of these men. Until more women become firmly established as holders of positional power this is unlikely to change.

Moreover, unions came into being as vehicles of class politics and, at least in the North East region, they still carry this historical freight. The majority of employees still comprehend unions within a framework of class meanings (though the extent to which this may be changing is examined in the next chapter) and this affects the position of women within them. My study suggests that the idea of women as a distinct 'interest group' within unions must be seen as problematic. Women relate to unions not only as gendered but as classed subjects. Although their location in the gender dynamic may incline them to particular concerns over, for example, the treatment of temporary and part-time workers or the provision of childcare, their location as wage labourers in the class dynamic leads them to share common anxieties with male colleagues, over pay or redundancies. If there are 'women's interests', then, they should not be conceptualized in universal or essentialist terms as pertaining to gender *per se*, but as the needs of a *specific group of women*, women employees.

The other side of the coin is that in the past *class* interests as represented by unions have been narrowly defined in terms of the dominance of men. There is now potential for a *redefining of class interests* to reflect the experience of women as class members. Thus the provision of childcare for employees may be seen as a class not just a gender issue: wage labourers in manual or lower-level service occupations do not earn enough to afford the private childcare options available to professional and managerial women. Workplace creches or state provision must be the best solution for working-class women. The workings of the gender dynamic, in terms of women's higher expectations and greater involvement in employment, are in such ways indelibly altering the nature of class experience and class-based union demands. In that sense class relations, as well as unions, are being feminized.

Chapter 10

Class, Gender and Power

Women in top posts in trade unions are contributing to the shift in the balance of power which I have identified in the workplaces I studied. Feminization and changes in the employment structure have increased women's access to economic resources in relation to their menfolk and allowed at least a minority of women to achieve positional power. Processes of change have also undermined some of the traditional bases of men's technical dominance, as new technologies replace old manual skills and a new stress is given to skills of 'people-management' and communication which are seen as 'natural' feminine attributes.

However, it is premature to say that this has brought an end to male dominance: as Burris argues, while 'men's and women's lives have changed dramatically in the past few decades' so that 'there are are many more options for women and men ... yet most paths lead towards the familiar reality of male dominance and patriarchal control' (Burris, 1996, p. 61). Men continue to control the symbolic apparatus of the workplace and predominate in positions of authority. They can use these resources to redefine notions of technique and expertise in such a way as to confine women to specialist ('feminine') niches as they move up the hierarchy (see Savage, 1992) and to reinforce traditional forms of sex-typing at the base. Men are able to define the meaning of key terms such as 'skill', 'merit', 'competence', 'value' (Ramsay and Parker, 1992; Collinson and Hearn, 1996a; Davies, 1996). They decide what is meant by 'quality' and 'excellence', setting the rules for their measurement and evaluation and, crucially, determine the level of economic rewards.

Nevertheless, I have suggested that, increasingly, feminist meanings are also at play in the workplace and are being inserted into the symbolization of work. As women become promoted and enter supervisory, advisory or managerial posts they may question the prevailing notions of what it is to be a 'good worker', taking advantage of EO procedures of equal opportunities. Although many have argued that this only serves the interests of well-qualified professional and managerial women and does little to help the majority of low-paid women in female ghettoes, the assault of feminism is two-pronged: within trade unions, women officers and stewards are also challenging established notions about work and worth. The victory in 1997 of the speech therapists in their claim for pay equality with pharmacists is one example. At all levels of the occupational hierarchy what I have termed a 'climate of equality' is being established.

These developments are slowly beginning to undermine the sex-typing which has for so long shored up gender and class hierarchies at work. This last observation brings us to the point of this chapter: the slow transformations of gendered power which I have been describing must be located within the dynamic of class relations with which gender divisions at work are intertwined. Feminization and the rise of feminist consciousness are occurring alongside processes of globalization and economic restructuring which affect the balance of class power. How is this manifest within the case-study workplaces? And how does the changing balance of class power alter gender relations? For we are not talking here merely of women and men as workers, but of men *and* women as employers, managers and wage labourers.

Class and power at work

Class power in the workplace is more skewed than gender power, as marxists have persistently pointed out. The institution of private property invests all the economic power within the workplace in the hands of capitalist employers and their agents. Positional power at work is entrusted to managers who must by and large accept capitalist economic imperatives to perform their jobs. Moreover, employers have managed historically to impose their meanings on work relations, although these were, as E. P. Thompson and other social historians have shown, bitterly contested in the early phases of industrialization in Britain (Thompson, 1968; Hearn, 1971; Hammond and Hammond, 1979). Since then capitalists have succeeded in gaining general social acceptance for notions of the primacy of profit, the managerial prerogative or 'right-to-manage' and, recently, the greater efficiency of privatized enterprise over public ownership. Thus, as Thompson (1967) and Williams (1968) have brilliantly argued, work under capitalism is made equivalent to 'wage labour' and wage labour becomes the shadow-version of capitalist enterprise. Enterprise is carried out for profit, not human need; wage labour is undertaken for money, not for the good of humanity or personal fulfilment:

> 'The meaning of work, in such a system, is reduced, against all other human interests, to a profitable return on the investment of capital. Labour is wage-labour, and to find the meaning of work in wages alone is a shadow – a real shadow – of this commanding fact, by which men's freedom to direct their own energies has been practically limited for so long that it can pass as a fact of nature.' (Williams, 1968, pp. 294–5)

Against the economic and symbolic might of capital, the resources of wage labour appear puny. Yet, as contributors to the labour process debate have argued, within the workplace capital's control is never absolute: the workplace remains a 'contested terrain' (Edwards, 1979). Wage labourers have been able to deploy countervailing resources, symbolic, technical and collective to varying degrees in opposition to the decisions and practices of employers and managers. As Chapter 7 showed, women and men resist the reduction of work to profit, seeking to assert their own meanings of service, competence, and self-development against management's economic imperatives.

Labour process theorists from Braverman (1974) onward have suggested that employees can use their skills and knowledge of the labour process to undermine managerial power. While managers have tried to counter this by various forms of control strategy (personal, bureaucratic, technical), attempts to take away technical resources from employees can never be complete; there are always forms of 'tacit' knowledge and skill gained in the actual performance of labour which can be used to subvert managerial control and gain space and autonomy (Jones, 1989). Professional employees, in particular, have long been able to deploy their monopoly of forms of expert knowledge to claim the right to autonomy and self-management (Johnson, 1972). Once such autonomy has been grasped, employees are more likely to develop the confidence to challenge the predominant meanings of work offered by capitalists.

From the onset of capitalist industry employees have developed their own ideas about work and its organization, culminating at times in broad-based campaigns for various forms of industrial democracy or 'workers' control'. As I have suggested above, such contestations appear to have diminished as capitalist economies have developed. One might instance the recent abandonment by the Labour party of the ideal of common ownership. Increasingly, opposition to capitalist definitions of work has become narrowed to claims around the effort-reward bargain, what constitutes 'a fair wage for a fair day's work'. Such claims are characteristically voiced by trade unions; through unions employees mobilize their most important resource, the collective power of the workforce. Collective power mediated by unions has been manifested in structures of collective bargaining and in various forms of industrial action.

However, the past decades have seen considerable increase in capitalist power both at societal level and consequently within the workplace. The rise to power in many western societies of New Right regimes has led governments to endorse capitalist objectives and employment practices to a greater extent than ever before. Thus in Britain we have seen the strengthening of the ideology of the 'market' and its introduction to public-sector organizations (such as Northtown and the Bureau) which had previously preserved some distance from capitalist principles and values (Fulcher, 1995). Moreover, globalization and the increased power of multinationals have been seen by many to erode the power of national governments to impose constraints on capitalist activities, even were they were to wish to do so. This may lead even social democratic governments to begin to modify their policies on employment. The election of a 'New Labour' government in 1997 does not appear likely to change things in this respect, since Tony Blair and his ministers have affirmed their belief that Britain must respond to the needs of the international market for a 'flexible workforce'.

At the level of the workplace, this has resulted in heightened managerial power. Where the government is the employer, there have been attacks on professional and semi-professional groups and on the values of altruism and public service which had characterized public-sector employment. We have seen the bitterness that these attempts to impose market values had provoked among the employees at Northtown and the Bureau. But while certain groups have struggled quite notably to resist the imposition of capitalist meanings in their own occupational contexts (teachers and hospital consultants, for example), it may be said that overall the symbolic power of capital has been reinforced by such developments. The collapse of the Soviet experiment has reinforced the sense that 'there is no alternative' to the marketplace; while the apparent success of capitalist consumer production, in its glitzy, hedonistic postmodern phase, has convinced many that we do not want an alternative anyway. As Terry Eagleton has written,

'The power of capital is now so drearily familiar, so sublimely omnipotent and omnipresent, that even large sectors of the left have succeeded in naturalizing it, taking it for granted as such an unbudgable structure that it is as though they hardly have the heart to speak of it.' (Eagleton, 1996, p. 23)

As consumers, we may be happy. As producers, we are characteristically less so, if my respondents have any claim to typicality. While consumption and leisure may offer increasing levels of choice, within the workplace the class dynamic imposes itself in the form of increasing constraints, as was argued in Chapter 7. Employees feel powerless to resist the imposition of greater workloads, fearful of job loss in a climate of employment insecurity. These feelings of powerlessness are increased by the sense that unions are no longer able to defend the interests of employees as they could in the past. Unions have been seen as in decline in Britain since the coming to power of Mrs Thatcher, both in terms of numerical strength and declining social influence (Beaumont, 1987; Hyman, 1991). This has been heightened by the increased legitimation of the managerial prerogative discussed above, leading to the development of more ebullient 'macho' management styles, and by the ailing fortunes of the Labour party prior to 1997 and the problematization of its link to the unions. How have these trends manifested themselves in these workplaces? Were unions indeed in decline? The rest of this chapter explores the fortune of unions as the agents of collective class power and how that power might be weakened or strengthened by the shifts in the balance of gender power.

Unions in decline?

Some commentators have suggested that the decline of unions has been overstated. Gallie *et al.* (1996) for example, argue that while the power of the unions has been eroded at the societal level they have retained considerable influence locally within workplaces and, in particular, have managed to maintain existing structures of voluntary collective bargaining. An earlier study by Batstone (1984) had also suggested that unions had succeeded in sitting out the attacks on them, largely by keeping their heads down, curbing industrial militancy, and concentrating on mundane issues so as to keep 'business as usual' virtually intact.

My research gives support to these propositions. In these five well-organized workplaces there was little sign of any major decline in union membership. All the unions had maintained their bargaining relations with the employers and their day-to-day arrangements with managers (for stewards' facilities or meetings in work-time, for example). There had been no attempts at de-recognition and all the managers I spoke to expressed their support for responsible trade unions. Whitley arrangements remained in place. TradeFare had retained its agreement with USDAW that all new recruits should be informed by the company about the union and encouraged to join. At Albion the branch managers were members of BIFU (indeed they were among its most active supporters) and membership had increased over the 1980s to be virtually 100 per cent. While the former closed shop at Pillco had legally ended, because of the restrictions imposed by the Trade Union Act of 1984 and the 1990 Employment Act, it appeared effectively to be still operating, a finding replicated in the SCELI research on trade unions (Penn and Scattergood, 1996). Any decline in TGWU membership in this well-organized plant was not due to managerial hostility but arose from sectional discontents within the membership.

Support for the unions remained strong (Bradley, 1994). Eighty-four per cent of those interviewed believed that there was a continued need for unions. Even though they offered critical comments, over two-thirds of them (71 per cent) described themselves as satisfied with their own unions. For most of these employees unions were viewed as a crucial source of support, both in cases of individual problems and grievances that might arise and to protect the conditions of the workforce as whole. There was clear recognition that unions served these two functions, operating, as one Northtown employee put it, on both 'a representational and a personal basis'. The following were typical responses as to why unions were necessary:

'Something to help and protect you... protect you from anything the employer's going to throw at you.'

'Someone to stand by you, to be not just you as an individual, you've got backing.'

'Negotiation of pay rise, oh, and to be there to represent you as a body of people and also as an interceder if you were facing some disciplinary charge brought against you.'

Despite this climate of support for unions, there was a prevailing belief that over the past two decades the workplace unions had suffered a decline in effectivity. This was in part linked to internal aspects of union organization. Many were critical of their unions for perceived weaknesses, such as badly managed meetings, poor communication, ineffective leadership at national level, and above all failure to consult with the rank and file:

'They don't start off with consultation.'

'Lack of information... and they, the committee, make the decisions without telling us before they make the decisions.'

'I've been here seven years and I've never seen anyone come in and actually want to talk to us. They need to come and listen to our views and let us see what they're actually doing. If they've got the strength of the staff behind them they could be effective. They need to wake up and get their act together.'

But more generally union ineffectiveness was ascribed by the employees to broader aspects of political development and in particular to the power of the government which had been turned against the unions, allowing employers greater freedom to impose their will on their workforces. The common view was that the unions had been 'smashed by legislation': 'Maggie Thatcher did for them.'

Perceptions of powerlessness

This perception of union powerless was extremely marked. Eighty-seven per cent of the interviewees rejected the proposition that unions have too much power. While many felt that unions had done so in the past and had used their power unwisely, the consensus was emerging that things had gone 'too far the other way':

> 'In the seventies unions I felt had a little bit too much power but now it's gone completely the other way.'

> 'Unions had too much power in the past, but they've had it all taken away from them and it's definitely to the detriment of the workers.'

> 'The trend of the last few years... It can be seen that the power of the unions has diminished to such an extent that companies and organizations can do what they want with employees' lives. If some employers could send children up chimneys for a shilling a week, I think they'd do it.'

This development was often viewed in terms of a return to the 'bad old days' in which workers lacked any kind of 'rights' or 'representation':

> 'I would want to know what other representation the working man has. It goes back to what my father told me about when he had to go to the mines at six o'clock, just to look for work. I wouldn't want to go back to that.'

> 'Well, I think you've only got to mention the name Mrs Thatcher, she tried to take us back to Victorian times... There's a lot of companies if they could would get unions done away with, that would mean taking away of wages and conditions and everything we've gained.'

This latter comment raises the spectre of the complete abolition of unions, which was certainly feared by some:

'I think they'll disappear. The management are too strong. People are frightened for their jobs.'

'The history of the working class.. everything the workers have got they've had to fight for, the unions are responsible... it's sad now to see it all eroded... It's going to mean the re-emergence of sweatshops.'

As some of these quotations show, the decline in the social power of the unions was explicitly linked to the actions of Conservative governments as embodied in Mrs Thatcher (a potent folk devil in the North East as a result of the 1984–5 miners' strike). The social influence of unions in the past has partly been an effect of their special relationship with the Labour party. The change in this relationship has left unions in a curiously disembedded political position and might be said to undermine their traditional role as a vehicle of class politics. Certainly, the old link was seen as problematic by many. The union's political role in campaigning for the Labour party was rated lowest on a list of priorities for union action; and around a third of the respondents (33 women and 32 men) believed that 'unions should not do this':

'I am not sure that unions should be involved in politics. They should represent all ranks in society... There is a need to detach unions from a working class image.'

'They're tied too much to the Labour party. Unions should be tied to no party. It makes it difficult for them to work with the Tory government.'

This kind of view, as we might expect, was held more strongly by the white-collar workers; and suspicion of party-political linkage was not incompatible with the widespread use of class imagery in discussing the role of unions. But it signifies acknowledgement of a more restricted, less politicized role for unions, even among groups of workers who believed strongly in their importance and many of whom were Labour party supporters or were critical of the Conservative government. Such contradictory indications may be read as a sign of the complexity of relationships between class location, class identifications and political attitudes (none of which, as I have already argued, can be deduced from one another). The complexity of attitudes is exemplified in the comments of a woman at Northtown who described herself as coming from a working-class background and was critical of current government policy on the NHS. Her comment on whether the unions should support the Labour party expressed a not untypical ambivalence: 'Personally I don't think they should, but if they don't do, where's the opposition going to come from?' But this ambivalence was combined with an appreciation of the broader political need for unions:

> 'If we didn't have unions, we wouldn't get anywhere. I'm not saying we're downtrodden, but with the best will in the world the people who hold the purse strings are not giving free gifts.'

However, some might interpret the rejection of the party-political function of unions as evidence of growing individualism and economism among workers. Recent work in industrial relations has highlighted the growth of a culture of individualism, arguing that the new techniques of human resource management have deliberately aimed at breaking down worker solidarity by treating each employee as an individual (Bassett, 1987; Marchington and Parker, 1990; Coates, 1996). This has been described as a 'decollectivization' of industrial relations (Smith and Morton, 1993). Steve Williams (1996), in a study of unions in the North East, suggests that decollectivization entails both attempts to oust or marginalize unions as the collective voice of employees and also the use of managerial strategies designed to individualize the employment relationship. But, if this has indeed been the objective of employers, in these workplaces at least it seems curiously to have backfired. As we have seen, unions have not really been marginalized; while, ironically, the very strategies designed to individualize workers and promote identification with the company (such as performance appraisal, performance-related pay, team organization, monitoring of individual output) have not only been resisted and resented by these groups of employees but have contributed to their feelings of frustration and powerlessness. And this in turn may drive them back to the union, rather than away from it.

Union renewal and collectivism

Such a prevailing sense of powerlessness is, Williamson argues (1997), a key feature of current social relations. She points to the paradox that, in a world increasingly obsessed by developing systems of monitoring and control, as individuals we have a growing subjective sense that the world is 'out of control': 'the flip side to a control culture is a general feeling of impotence, as if, because we can't control everything, we can affect nothing. People feel increasingly as if their actions and decisions have no impact on the world at all which isn't true' (p. 6). She points out that this expression of impotence can be often used by those in power, such as governments, to evade responsibility: all social problems, such as unemployment and homelessness can be blamed on a globalizing world economy beyond human control. Thus, within the case-study organizations those apparently invested with power (managers) often spoke of their own powerlessness in the face of national economic events; there was no choice but to cut services, increase workloads or limit intake of new staff. The frustration some experienced was sincere while responsibility for change was characteristically transferred to 'the company' or, most popularly 'the government'.

Thus, while those those with less power, the employees, strongly expressed a sense of impotence and linked it to the unions, this does not necessarily mean that the collective power of unions has eroded altogether or irreversibly. Fairbrother (1994a; 1994b) has initiated a debate as to whether certain aspects of current employment relations may not actually encourage greater involvement at grassroots level, leading to a form of 'union renewal': the trend to localized pay bargaining, for example, or the ending of check-off arrangements, which forces unions to give more attention to communications with members.

An alternative response to powerlessness is to take the route of individual 'self-help' and advancement, developing one's career and working up into the elite. Education and credentials are usually the major weapon used in such a strategy. P. Brown (1995) and Devine (1997) among others highlight the importance of education as a mechanism for middle-class reproduction. We saw earlier that some women lamented their own earlier rejection of higher education and dreamed of taking a degree to improve their labour market chances. At NDH, nurses and scientists saw training and gaining professional qualifications as a crucial way to better their positions. But overall this was not a well-qualified sample, with only around six per cent having higher education qualifications. Perhaps for this reason, faith in the promise of collective betterment offered by the union movement had not yet been entirely lost.

As we have seen, trade unions in these workplaces had managed to cling in through the lean years, aided by the strong tradition of union allegiance in the North East region, which has been illustrated earlier in my discussion of political socialization in the family. Despite the anxiety of officers and stewards and the cynicism of members, the unions had retained their bargaining rights and continued to operate existing practices of consultation, negotiation, representation and grievance handling. If officers, activists and members alike felt that the unions had been marginalized or ineffective during the past ten years, that was more to do with the broader economic and political climate than with the behaviour of employers and managers in the local sites. Moreover, there was some sense that where 'hard times' were being experienced, the unions were able to capitalize on this to strengthen their support among members. This was most evident in the two public-sector organizations, as the analysis in Chapter 7 would intimate; but at Albion, too, there was some sense of revived interest in the union, in line with Gall's (1997) account of the rise in 'unionateness' in banking.

It was at the Bureau that a sense of union renewal was most apparent. (Fairbrother also found a spirit of renewal marked in some civil service unions.) Some women explicitly stated that the union was more relevant to them than it had been in the past. BWU was actively opposing 'market-testing' at the Bureau and was currently operating a ban on a new performance appraisal scheme. One woman reflected on her growing advocacy of the union:

'I just lectured somebody today that they ought to be in the union. Just the way things are politically at present. The politics side of it is why we feel more committed. I feel we need to stand together.'

This linkage of increased awareness of the utility of unions to the current political situation was reflected in other comments by Bureau workers:

'I suppose the last year or so we have been taking a bit more interest in the union.'

'I think the unions are for you if you're in trouble, they certainly do help you. It's necessary in this day and age, you need somebody on your side.'

'Up until a few months ago they seemed not to be doing what we wanted them to do. Now they seem to be taking more note of what we're saying... The union seems to be doing what we want it to now.'

What is interesting about these comments is the use of the collective 'we'. It is 'we' who need the union, 'we' who are becoming more interested in it, although the 'we' is sometimes ranged against 'the union' (which of course is 'itself a 'we'). 'At the end of the day the union is us,' remarked a Pillco woman. Given that the Bureau women were hardly the stuff out of which industrial militancy has traditionally been forged, the assertion of a collective identity, interest or will is the more remarkable, but kept cropping up in discussion of the union:

'I think the union are on our side and I think the management are against us.'

'Without them [unions] there's nothing to look after the interests of the ordinary person. We'd just be walked over.'

'Unions are very important in that you present yourself as a body rather than being picked off as an individual.'

I argued in Chapter 7 that unions remain the site of class meanings; the explicit collectivism of such comments affirms this. Conflicts within the workplace continue to be generated by the capitalist imperative for greater competitiveness, whether taking the form of a quest for reduced costs (public sector) or for increased profits (private sector). What the Bureau example shows is that unions, if they act effectively, can take advantage of the resulting struggles around control and rewards; they can use them to strengthen or regenerate their members' loyalty and collective commitment. But such a commitment has a class base which may sit uneasily with gender issues in the union arena.

Gender, power and the union

In the last chapter I argued that it may be wrong to conceptualize
class and gender identifications as competing alternatives. Awareness of class injustice may make people more sensitive to gender
injustice, and vice versa. However, while not *necessarily* conflictual,
it is clear that in certain circumstances, class and gender interests
may collide. Women's increased involvement in the labour market and heightened aspirations for career advancement have
been encouraged at a time when there is increased competition
for jobs and promotion. While many people I talked to imputed
this to government policies or the economic climate, it is also possible that some men may blame women for the restriction they
experience on opportunities. This is the phenomenon of backlash, discussed in Chapter 6.

Backlash is likely but not inevitable; and this can be illustrated
by considering the contrasting state of affairs at the Bureau and at
Pillco. At the Bureau, the BWU had been involved in the negotiations around a package of policies designed to help women
employees with their careers: maternity leave arrangements,
encouragement for women to return to their jobs after childbirth,
either on a part-time and full-time basis; pro-rata benefits for
part-timers; the introduction of flexitime. These developments
helped women to compete more equally with men for promotion.
But no evident opposition to the organization's EO programme
had developed among the male employees I spoke to, even
though some of them held familiar stereotypes of women as secondary workers, less interested in their jobs and less militant as
union members. This seemed to be because the union, while
working for gender equality, had continued to display itself as
actively involved in campaigns to safeguard jobs and conditions
for *everybody*, for example by opposing market-testing and performance appraisal. Male employees felt the union was working
for them, indeed more so than did the women who were more
likely to criticize the union for its failure to consult.

The BWU has maintained a high profile by fighting for issues
involving the whole workforce. It appears to have succeeded in
balancing the specific needs of one section of the workforce with
the interests of employees as a whole. Put crudely, unions need to
reassure their members that if they are campaigning for one

group of workers (women) to get a greater share of the cake, then the size of the cake as a whole must increase. In this way they can redefine the agenda so that what were formerly seen as 'women's issues' become translated into general class interests.

Where this does not happen the union may become a site of gender contestation as was apparently the case at Pillco. As we have seen, women and men perceived themselves in conflict at Pillco. Women wanted to enter 'male jobs' and get equal pay and felt that they were discriminated against and their work undervalued. Men believed that women could not perform effectively in 'their' jobs and resented women's encroachment. This was reflected in the union politics of their plant. While the TGWU had traditionally been male-dominated, the current senior steward was a woman and women were increasingly active as representatives. But both women and men felt the union was biased against their sex. The women believed that the men continued to run the union to maintain their own privileges while the men felt the women, who were numerically dominant in the factory, had taken over the union to work for their own interests:

> 'Women are doing very well. They run the factory from a union point of view.'

> 'It represents the women better than the men because there's more of them in the factory.'

One man criticized the factory union committee for 'leaning towards the women'. Desire to win their vote had led, in his opinion, to a mistaken claim for across-the-board pay in the last round of negotiations; while another, asked if women were as interested in the union as men, replied laconically 'very interested in themselves!'

Here we see men struggling to come to terms with the threat to their position of dominance in the factory hierarchy. In the words of one of their number, 'In the past it was always men. The men were the kings. That's changing now.' Such change undermines at once the men's sense of gender and class identity, as man and as breadwinner. Hollway (1996) argues that, as industrialization developed in the nineteenth century, men as wage earners shored up their sense of masculinity through claims to different forms of 'mastery' (they were, of course, no longer 'masters' of their own work, but merely 'hands'). While managers gain mastery through the control of other men, manual men find it in bodily strength and the control of technology and machinery. Paul Willis' classic study of 'the lads' (1977) showed how respect for physicality and mechanical competence are developed in the adolescent anti-school culture of working-class boys; his fieldwork also highlighted how these processes of learning to (be) labour are effected partly through separation from girls and their construction as inferior. At Pillco the entry of women into process work took from the male operators their sense of mastery in these two fields (strength and technology). This disturbs their experience of a settled class and gender order, in a way reminiscent of Cockburn's (1983) description of the impact of new technology on male printers.

Some of the women, however, held a different view of the union:

> 'They will fight for the man's job and not the woman's job. They're not interested.'

> 'I don't feel they do enough for women – and I don't feel they do enough for temporary workers.'

These perceptions were linked to past arrangements, whereby union representatives had tended to be men drawn from all-male departments. They also reflected the events surrounding the entry of women into process operation. One woman reported being stuck on temporary status as a process operator for five years, despite repeated complaints to the union, which she believed would have responded differently to men. However, the fact that things were beginning to change was reflected in the way she spoke about male dominance in the union:

> 'We've got a woman chair at present, but I think they seem to...mebbe's not as much as in the past...as though they're fighting for the men more than the women.'

Other women suggested that things were improving with the presence of the woman senior steward and other female reps who were seen to communicate better with the rank and file. As we saw in Chapter 9, Elaine believed the women felt that the union now offered something for them as well as for the men. In the view of some of the men this was achieved at their expense; but Elaine contested that view in her assertion of women's greater democratic sense:

> 'They do [take as much interest in the union as men,] but they haven't as loud a voice or as selfish a reason for doing so. The women don't want to see themselves earning more than the people they work with, the men do like to see themselves earning more.'

These attitudes were beginning to influence some of the men. One male activist conceded that, 'Women are fully aware of some things that they experience at a job, where I can only look at it from a male point of view.' But where men feel their interests under threat from women's advance, and cannot come to terms with the impairment to their sense of masculine superiority, they may blame women for the ills they are experiencing, especially in a climate of restricted opportunities. At the extreme, women may be held responsible, because of their lack of militancy and family priorities, for the weakness of the unions and thence their failure to defend class interests. This point was alluded to by many men and articulated with particular clarity by one male Bureau employee. His analysis may well represent a common disillusion of men from working-class backgrounds with the current state of politics:

> 'The powers that the union now has are so restricted, they're under so many limitations anyway...At these particular times when jobs are the main issue, these things aren't implemented, the union has no influence. People you are looking towards aren't getting the message across. People aren't prepared to put themselves forward now, go on strike, take industrial action. They have family commitments, they just aren't prepared to step out of line. There's fear of losing jobs...There are quite a lot of young people in the Bureau now, married women. There just doesn't seem to be any commitment to a union...No disrespect, but there are a lot more women prepared to, just happy the way things are. A lot more women who are perhaps prepared to just accept.'

Conclusion

Clifford Geertz, reflecting on his career as anthropologist, declares that, 'all politics is quarrel, and power is the ordering such quarrel sorts out' (Geertz, 1995, p. 39). The task of the social scientist studying power, then, becomes that of discovering 'what sort of quarrel is going on' (p. 41). In my study of these five workplaces, the quarrels I have distinguished, and indeed those which seemed to emerge clearly from the accounts of my respondents, were those of gender and class: more precisely those between women and men and between labour and capital.

The social scientist, no doubt, finds what she goes in to seek; other forms of quarrel were, I am sure, also at play in the workplaces, for example, between different groups, levels and functions within management; between differing occupational groups anxious to assert their own claims (that between doctors and nurses was one which was revealed to me); between full-timers and part-timers (clearly articulated); and perhaps, if in a muted way, between the generations. Yet that issues of class and gender resonated in the workplaces can not be held in doubt (and some of the other contests listed above can be conceptualized in class terms if a Weberian as opposed to marxian framework is employed).[1] Class issues were volunteered to me spontaneously in response to fairly 'neutral' questions about work and jobs and unions. Gender quarrels required more teasing out by questioning, but once aired were discussed in passionate terms.

Such quarrels arise from the workings of the dynamics of gender and class as they play themselves out at the micro-level. The dynamic of gender, currently manifesting itself in the form of the feminization of work and feminist claims to equality, generates conflicts between women and men over prevailing definitions of masculine and feminine attributes, what tasks women and men are 'fit' to do, and about access to material rewards and coveted positions in the hierarchy. The dynamic of class, currently manifesting itself in the form of an increasingly globalized and therefore more internationally competitive capitalism, generates conflicts between employers and their agents (some managers, though not all, fall into this category) and employees, over control structures at work, over employment conditions and contracts, over how the labour process should be organized, and, classically, about the level of rewards employees should receive for their efforts. In these conflicts, the various resources of power discussed in this book (economic, symbolic, technical, positional, collective and personal) are deployed in a constantly changing ebb and flow to form and reform structures of domination and hierarchy.

Currently, the dynamic of class is itself contributing to the shift in the balance of power between men and women. Economic restructuring in Britain is clearly linked to feminization as new jobs are assigned to women rather than men. This can be seen as an unintended consequence (it just so happens that prevailing patterns of sex-typing favour women getting the new opportunities rather than men) or as a deliberate strategy (women are a preferred source of labour as they are 'prepared to just accept'). Yet, while this hands more power to women relative to men, this is occurring in the context of an increasingly insecure labour market and a shortage of desirable jobs. Gains in gender equality are made at a cost; while some women benefit from more equal competition with men, the majority lose from the weakened power of wage labour. Thus, the combined dynamics of class and gender are promoting a polarization among women, with those at the bottom of the employment hierarchy subject to greater economic insecurity, confined to low-paid jobs. The same women are likely to find their husbands and sons at risk of casualized employment or long-term unemployment. Increased competitiveness, then, means increased competition between worker and worker, between men and women. The role of trade unions in bringing together potentially divided workforces must be crucial.

Both Diana Coole (1996) and Nancy Fraser (1995) have discussed feminist politics in terms of the contradiction, or dilemma, between the demand for redistribution (linked to the old labour movement) and for recognition (associated with the various forms of 'identity politics': feminism, the gay and lesbian movement, anti-racist, ethnic or nationalist groupings, disabled people). Coole suggests that class interests are seen in terms of demands for economic redistribution, which serves to problematize class within a politics of difference (as discussed in Chapter 8, class may not be considered a thing to 'celebrate' but something to be done away with). By contrast she implies that gender politics are more to do with cultural recognition; such an analysis seems to imply that gender is mainly a cultural construction. However, Fraser makes it clear that gender is 'not only a political-economic, but a cultural-valuation differentiation as well' (1995, p. 79). Thus it should involve claims for both redistribution and recognition.

Certainly, *both* class and gender interests, as identified in the context of the workplaces by my interviewees, involved *both* redistribution and recognition. Women wished to achieve equal pay with men and gain equal access to top positions; but they also wanted their distinctive contributions in 'women's jobs' to be acknowledged and re-evaluated and not to be considered inferior workers. Similarly, the employees in their class role as wage labour wished for increased pay and more access to promotion chances; but they also wanted their talents and skills and their contribution to the organizations to be recognized and their dignity and intelligence as human beings to be respected.[2] The latter is crucial, since class relations have typically involved the denigration of working-class intelligence (Reay, 1997; Skeggs, 1997b) or even its negation (Morley, 1997).

Class and gender interests are distinct as they derive from different dynamics; but they need not necessarily be in conflict any more than they are necessarily in harmony. If trade unions are to thrive in the future, they must find ways to juggle both kinds of interest; where possible to reconcile them and work for both sets of objectives, bearing in mind the particular need for fair treatment of women (and of minority ethnic workers, disabled employees and other disadvantaged groups), while still foregrounding the need to represent the workforce as a whole. To do so, as I suggested in Chapter 9, may involve a recasting of definitions of class and gender: what it is to be a man, a woman, a worker.

Notes

1   The Weberian framework stresses conflicts and competition within the propertyless groupings as much as the conflicts between classes.
2   Wheelock (1994) in her study of households in Wearside makes the same point, while Willott and Griffin (1996), discussing unemployment, highlight the importance of 'respect' as well as material factors.

Chapter 11

Conclusion: Feminization and Globalization

Richard Rorty, debunking the pretensions of certain types of social theory, states that 'insofar as political situations become clear, they get clarified by detailed stories about who's doing what to whom' (Rorty, 1994). The aim of this book has been exactly that: to explore the politics of class and gender in workplaces in contemporary Britain by telling just such a set of stories about the specific and detailed experiences of certain groups of people. The stories, drawn from the accounts offered by my respondents and seen through the filter of my own interpretation, offer inevitably a partial view of contemporary social change. Those addicted to statistical testing and large data-sets might object that these accounts relate only to specific people in specific contexts; of course, they are correct. None the less, I would argue, with the ethnographer Geertz, that such specific accounts, 'particular events and unique occasions, an encounter here, a development there', can be woven together in the light of previous studies, factual material and interpretations to produce a sense of 'how things go, have been going, and are likely to go' (Geertz, 1995, p. 3).

But in this final chapter I want to return, *pace* Rorty, to some theoretical considerations in summarizing what the empirical detail presented in the book has revealed about changing relations of gender, class and power in employment. While the focus in this book has been on the minutiae of changes in one site, the workplace, in a specific region of Britain, the argument has been that these changes must be understood in the context of global changes: the feminization of work and the development of a more highly competitive internationalized capitalist economy.

Feminization, gender and change

Beverly Burris claims that recent changes in gender relations can only be fully understood by reference to changes in the organization of work and occupational structures. She argues,

> In advanced industrialized societies, paid employment is now central to the lives of the majority of both women and men, and workplaces are some of the most important arenas in which the drama of gender is staged. (Burris, 1996, p. 61)

I have suggested in this book that these changes should be explained in terms of the feminization of the labour market and the spread of feminist ideas among women. These developments have brought a shift in the balance of gendered power as women gain more access to economic resources. The effect of this is to render women's waged labour and their contributions to household subsistence more visible. Of course women have always 'worked', contributing to the household through their domestic labour as well as through various forms of earning: but the skew between these more fragmented economic activities and the traditional breadwinning activities of the male allowed women's contributions to be to a great extent concealed and devalued (Allen, 1997). The decline in male breadwinning (Land, 1994; Willott and Griffin, 1996) in combination with women's more confident assertion of their own value reconfigure women as major players in the economic sphere.

My research, like that of others (Spencer and Taylor, 1994; Sianne and Wilkinson, 1995), suggests that young women in particular are more committed to career development, in the expectation that much of their lives will be spent in the labour force. Walby (1997) considers this the basis of an important polarization between younger and older women. Younger women are making use of increased educational assets to grasp the opportunities provided by feminization; while older women suffer from lack of qualifications and from their experience of a previous 'gender regime' in which women were steered towards the domestic sphere. My research confirms Walby's thesis.

Such changes are in part a response to men's increasingly insecure hold on employment, particularly men without qualifications or from working-class backgrounds. In light of this change, couples are having to rethink their strategies for building a life together, adjusting and adapting to the climate of insecurity of which my respondents were markedly aware. This calls for reconsideration of the contribution of female and male partners in a relationship. As Pahl suggests:

> The so-called feminization of male jobs has far-reaching implications – it may be that the economic base for an increasing number of households shifts from one settled 'career' to two unsettled sequences of jobs – or no career or jobs whatever. (Pahl, 1995, p. 191)

Feminization arises from the interaction of class and gender dynamics. The changing nature of a consumerized global capitalism has led in the more developed western economies to a shift away from industrial employment to service work. The types of job created by this class dynamic have been stamped by the dynamic of gender as 'suitable for women': earlier processes of gender segregation had resulted in women being allocated to jobs involving caring, servicing, communicating and dealing with people. Because these jobs were done by women they were assigned lower social value, were less well-paid and were often offered part-time. As a result men are resistant to entering them, especially working-class men who have grown up in a culture valorizing male physicality and technical mastery.

Here we see again how class and gender dynamics interact to influence processes of motivation and action. Masculine identities are bound up with dominance at work, but take different forms for men of different classes (Collinson and Hearn, 1996b; Segal, 1990: Morgan, 1992). Both middle-class and working-class men have to contend with feminization at work but respond to it in different ways. Managerial and professional men, as I have argued, are able to use their positional power at work to buttress the culture of homosociability and keep women confined to 'niche positions'. Working-class men are the chief sufferers from feminization as they see their jobs vanishing to female competition, but they have not so far shown a disposition to compromise their masculinity by seeking to enter 'women's jobs' in great numbers. It may, of course, yet happen.

Women's motivations are also affected by the interaction of class and gender dynamics. Feminism, as a counter-tendency to the exclusionary practices of men, has contributed, I have argued, to the development of 'a climate of equality'. Women are no longer readily prepared to accept their subordination as something natural or to acquiesce with male views of their inferiority as workers. Even explicitly non-feminist women are affected by these views which have seeped out into 'common-sense' thinking. Andrea Stuart (1990) refers to this as 'popular feminism', noting its influence on young women. This may be the lasting effect of second-wave feminism despite its collapse as a formal movement. As Melissa Benn has it, now 'feminism is everywhere and nowhere' (Benn, 1987, p. 85).

But the 'climate of equality' is not the product of feminist ideology alone. Its message that women, too, can succeed is in line with the individualistic ethos carefully fostered by the New Right in the past decades; this is why the Thatcher era was so ambiguous in its effects on women. While contributing to the polarization of the fortunes of women of different classes by its policies on employment, welfare and social security, Thatcherism also encouraged a breed of ambitious managerial and professional women to tackle sexist barriers to promotion and success. In the (slightly hyperbolic) words of Henry Porter in a *Guardian* series on powerful women of this breed, 'for the first time in British history you can assemble a list of women who wield power – power of the actual hefty kind that does not rely on inheritance, sex appeal or manipulative guile' (Porter, 1997, p. 2). These women, often finding their way into organizations as personnel managers, have thrown their weight behind EO policies. Moreover, such women are evidently influenced by what Nikolas Rose (1989) has distinguished as a new form of subjectivity for workers. This involves a discourse of the self as shaped and developed by work, so that a career becomes the basis for self-fulfilment. Grey's study of accountants (1994) confirms the importance of such a 'project of the self' in promoting commitment to work. The confluence of these various ideologies, I suggest, lies behind the improved educational performance of young women and their pursuit of a range of qualifications, enabling them to challenge male power through the 'credentials lever'.

All this may suggest that a degree of gender homogenization[1] is indeed occurring. But against this I have demonstrated that long-established patterns of gender segregation and exclusion persisted in these workplaces; structures of segregation are dented but not displaced. As Rubery and Tarling state, 'the outcome of the big increase in female employment has not...been to homogenize the sectoral and industrial employment patterns of men and women' (1988, p. 109). They suggest that employers tend to use women to fill jobs that are more vulnerable to the effects of the business cycle and more prone to technological restructuring.

Rubery and Tarling view segregation in terms of employers' economic choices, but in this study I have also considered how men are able to resist gender homogenization. Gender boundaries are maintained by male utilization of positional and symbolic power. Symbolic aspects of gender differentiation are particularly tenacious; workplaces are important sites for the construction of masculinities and femininities. Individual women and men are led into replicating patterns of gendered difference at work through processes both of (imposed) gender stereotyping and of (active) feminine and masculine identification. The rules and norms of employment are still laid down by men, largely policed by men, and reflect the practices of dominant masculinities. Crompton and Le Feuvre (1997) argue that women who wish to progress in the hierarchy must behave as surrogate men.

The other important factor which supports segregation is women's responsibility for domestic work and childcare. My research suggests that changes in this respect are still rather minimal. Women continue to bear the brunt of responsibility for household work. The women I interviewed themselves believed this was the main obstacle to gender inequality. Changes are needed on two fronts to rectify this situation: the domestic division of labour must be reconstructed to allow as much sharing of tasks and responsibility as is feasible; while organizations need to alter their parameters to become 'family-friendly', facilitating the juggling of domestic and employment tasks among couples which is already under way, and making sure that parental duties do not serve to disqualify women – or men – from employment and advancement.

Unfortunately at present the opposite seems to be occurring. Organizations are becoming more 'greedy', demanding more of their employees' effort and time. It is not surprising that over the past ten years there has been a steady stream of stories about high-flying 'women who had it all' who subsequently gave up prestigious jobs to concentrate on motherhood. Coward (1992), among others, charts the guilt and pressures felt by mothers who strain to perform well both in their jobs and at home. Coward's suggestion that there may be a trend of retreat from employment into domesticity is not supported by my research; it may only be women married to affluent middle-class men who have a real option of making this move. But certainly I spoke to women, especially older ones, who expressed themselves as tired (literally and metaphorically) of bearing the strain of two jobs day in, day out: for such women early retirement or part-time employment was an enticing, though not necessarily attainable, prospect. In actuality men are more able to take advantage of early retirement schemes: at Albion it was the norm for men to retire in their mid-fifties. As Arber and Ginn (1991) have shown, women typically have lower pension entitlements, making it economically difficult for them to retire early, even if they wish to.

The desire of some women to escape the double burden, however, raises the issue of gender fragmentation and divisions among women. The reader will note that in this concluding chapter I have spoken of 'women' in general as though they shared common experiences. And indeed, in carrying out my research it was the commonalities in women's attitudes, behaviour and histories that struck me rather than the differences. This is undoubtedly in part an artefact of the research design. The use of a questionnaire in interviewing was likely to draw attention to common aspects of experience. The decision to interview full-time employees ruled out an important aspect of differentiated experience among women.[2] The lack of minority ethnic women in my sample meant I could not study what has come to be seen as the most potent source of difference. Nevertheless, the study offered the chance to consider differences of age and of class, although it is true that the sample, both in terms of class origin and current occupational status, tended to be drawn from the middle groupings and not the extremes of the class structure.

While occupational difference and family background had clearly influenced individuals' experiences and attitudes, I suggest that commonalities of experience, in terms of subjection to the dynamics of gender and class in the workplace, were more notable. Women faced the same problems and constraints: job insecurity; increased workloads and pressure; restricted opportunities; problems over childcare; sexism from powerful males. If we accept that gender (and class) are relational, and that these relations take differing forms as they are played out in specific sites, then within any given site the experience of femaleness and maleness is likely to take a regular form. All women were subject to the same structures of gender segregation, sex-typing and exclusion within these workplaces. Of course, they also bring to work experiences of gender relations as played out in other sites (the family, leisure relations) which may be rather different. But relations of gender and power in the workplace subject all of them – and similarly all men – to common constraints, both material and symbolic. As Gherardi states,

> Male and female . . . are indivisible positions of reciprocal relation. Both men and women are prisoners of gender, albeit in different ways, in asymmetrical situations of power. (1996, p. 187)

Of course there are different ways of being a woman and a man even within a single workplace (Collinson and Hearn, 1996b). This research has drawn attention to one aspect of this. Certain men and women seem happy to accept more traditional gender roles within the workplace, playing out forms of hegemonic masculinity and emphasized femininity (Connell, 1987). Such men are likely to have the major breadwinner role (sometimes with a non-employed wife), to resent female competition and to assert males' prior right to jobs, stereotyping women as unfit for certain activities. Traditional women are less ambitious for promotion, happy to adopt caring 'feminine' functions, accept subservience to dominant males in the workplace and would often prefer to work part-time. These attitudes seem to stem from family life, and contrast with the more feminist-influenced orientations displayed by many women or the attitudes of the 'new' or anti-sexist types of men in the sample. Yet it must be stressed that these forms of masculine and feminine identity are not fixed, as, for example,

Hakim's work seems to imply. Women's aspirations and attitudes change as they enter different life-course phases and encounter different situations.

Differentiation of experience also stems from the ways in which women and men of different class or ethnicity are differently inserted into the dynamic of gender. The significance of ethnicity is discussed later in this chapter. With regard to class, I have pointed to a growing polarization in the experiences of managerial and professional women and their less privileged sisters. The former are the more obvious beneficiaries of feminization and feminism as they can use their class resources (material and cultural capital) to buy out of some of the worst effects of gender (by employing nannies, cleaners and live-in child minders, for example). But such elite women were little represented in this particular study and among my interviewees higher-grade and lower-grade women alike reported gender discrimination.

Age is also an important source of division, as Walby (1997) argues. The young women interviewees were more likely to have longer-term plans and aspirations, while older women were more likely to feel trapped by circumstances and the effects of past choices. But the younger women in my study were not the well-qualified young professionals whose position is the base of Walby's argument. Younger women without higher education will continue to operate in the restricted labour market encountered by their mothers, although not facing quite the same pressures towards domesticity. Thus the division between the younger and older generations of women that Walby distinguishes is strongly influenced by class.

There can be no doubt that divisions among women will continue. Rubery and Tarling, suggesting that such labour market differences 'are taking on greater significance' (1988, p. 121), list divisions between full-time and part-time workers, those with union recognition and those without (a division outside the scope of this study), and between adults and young beginners. All these polarizing tendencies are at play. Nevertheless, I am arguing that within a given site particular groups of women and men engage in common with structures of gender and power; to that extent it *does* make sense to speak of common experiences of gender. But such common experiences do not necessarily give rise to common gender identifications; feminine and masculine identities are fluid and variable, being influenced both by global processes of gendered change (such as feminization and feminism), by the interpolation of other dynamics, such as those of class, age and ethnicity, and by the experience of different aspects of gender relations within other contexts.

Globalization, class and change

One such global influence is the process of national and regional economic restructuring, involving sectoral change in the economy, the rise of long-term unemployment and changes in the nature of employment relations. As Wheelock argues, 'a process of class and gender recomposition of the labour force has gone on alongside the process of economic restructuring' (1994, p. 81). National restructuring must itself be viewed in relation to the evolution of a more internationalized and competitive capitalist world economy, with a reconstruction of the division of labour on a global basis.

Globalization has a number of effects at workplace level which have been highlighted in my research. First, I have argued that the relations of wage labour have been affected by the increased competitiveness of 'lean, mean' globalizing consumer capitalism. This has brought an increasing sense of insecurity to hitherto more protected groups of employees, such as office staff and public-sector professionals, as organizations restructure their employment hierarchies and 'downsize' to get rid of slack. This has important effects on how people experience not just their jobs but their future living patterns. As Hutton emphasizes (1995), households are going to have to live with job insecurity:

> By the year 2000, full-time tenured employment, around which stable family life has been constructed along with the capacity to serve 25 year mortgages, will be a minority form of work.

The threat of job loss makes it more difficult for employees to resist changes at work: these include increased workloads (resulting in stress) and an emphasis on individual performance monitoring. Indeed, on the basis of my research and other work which supports it (Garrahan and Stewart, 1992; Beynon *et al.*, 1994: Darnell and Evans, 1995; Danford, 1996), I wish to argue that the

current phase of capitalist development, marked by heightened
international competition, global dominance of multinationals
and increased emphasis on services as a basis of profit, is generating a characteristic new regime of control. This is being developed
within many organizations, especially those which are seen as
market leaders.

This regime is marked by attempts to monitor and control
workers on an increasingly individual rather than collective basis
(through tactics such as performance appraisal, audits or computerized measurement of output); and thereby to create a sense of
fear and insecurity in employees to ensure compliance in efforts
to increase productivity. While fear and insecurity have long been
common in manufacturing industries, the tactics of individual
measurement and evaluation which are being employed in service organizations are changing the nature of white-collar work.
Also individuals now experience these strategies being targeted
more directly at themselves as individuals.

These developments have important gender implications. Systems of appraisal and assessment can be seen as gendered, reflecting male imperatives and thus disadvantaging women. Also the
requirement of organizations that employees 'prove' their worth
by dedicating increasing amounts of time to their jobs fits well
with certain forms of middle-class masculinity. In Collinson and
Hearn's description, 'such masculinities may be constructed
around a life vocation, an obsession with technology, the working
of long hours and the need to maximise earnings' (1996b, p. 67).
Married women, constrained by domestic responsibilities, find it
hard to emulate their male colleagues in this competition.

The changes discussed above connect globalization to a further
stage of proletarianization. Certainly, this was the expressed view
of some of the white-collar employees I interviewed. This may be
seen, however, as a limited form of proletarianization, which
involves the conditions of work rather than the economic rewards
received for it (although there was a sense among some occupational groups of a relative decline in pay levels, also linked to
feminization). But the key features of this white-collar decline,
as subjectively reported, were increased insecurity, diminished
autonomy and tightened control. While these features of wage
labour are not new, and have been the lot of manual workers since
industrialization, the change is the extension of these experiences

to the intermediate service-sector groups who dominated in my study. I have imputed this partly to the fact that in post-industrial forms of capitalism the extraction of more relative surplus (to increase profits) is concentrating on service-sector employment as the majority form of work; and partly to the manipulation by Conservative governments of the public sector, as a way to establish new norms of desirable employment practice, at the same time as cutting the public-sector wages bill.

While some have seen the latter objective as primary, I wish to emphasize the importance of the ideological project of the New Right. The attempt to reconstruct work relationships and social identities in line with the principles of meritocracy, competitiveness and market primacy, establishing much more firmly the hegemony of capitalism and stamping out the socialist 'enemy within', has been a crucial legacy of the Thatcher epoch. Part of such a project is the reconstruction of the subjectivity of the traditional classed worker as an entrepreneurial self (Du Gay, 1996). But, as we have seen, the crushing of collectivism has not been totally successful.

The logic of globalization, then, changes the nature of core class relations in the workplace; it has also altered the overall configuration of the class dynamic in terms of the sets of positions within it. Post-industrial capitalist societies are undergoing class transformation as sectors of production shift to other parts of the globe and intensified competition increases the level of unemployment. The key aspects of such class recomposition are the emergence of a large labour surplus class (the popularly named 'underclass'); the decline in size of the manual working-class; the increase of what used to be known as the 'middle classes', an extremely heterogeneous group employed in the service sector, ranging from managers and professionals to clerks and retail workers.

Certain aspects of this reconfiguration of class positions were mirrored in my research. First, though absent (by definition) from the study, the presence of the labour surplus class loomed over the lives of my interviewees, providing an inescapable warning of the costs of stepping out of line. Fear of unemployment inhibits employees' ability to resist the new regime of control. Living in the midst of unemployed communities (which ring the cities of the North East like the thorny hedge round the enchanted castle), hard-pressed employees locate themselves socially in distinction from the labour surplus class – and count themselves lucky. This is a potent example of the way class experience is shaped by dis-identification, as Skeggs so correctly discerns (1997a).

As manual jobs vanish (a long-term continuous process in the North East), most wage labourers are now in service employment, especially women. The lower or intermediate service groups who formed the bulk of my sample may perhaps be seen as an emer-gent service proletariat: their working conditions are still some-what superior to those of manual workers, but I have pointed to the ways in which these workers are being squeezed. While they tend to compare their situation favourably with that of their more obviously 'working-class' parents, their lifestyles and lifechances are still markedly different from those of the elite 'service class' as described by Goldthorpe and others (Goldthorpe, 1982; Lash and Urry, 1987; Crook *et al.*, 1992). These are the 'ordinary people' of the present and future, subject to the vicissitudes of wage labour relations. However, they are more heterogeneous than the old industrial proletariat and there is no necessity that they will share the political orientations, organizational traditions of unionism or class identifications of their predecessors.

There are continuities and changes here. I have suggested that the class transformations discussed above add complications to processes of class identification. Individuals perceive the class structure as changing, its boundaries as blurred, and find it increas-ingly difficult to place themselves within it. Many are placed in positions of class hybridity (having moved class position them-selves or having parents with different class backgrounds). They have also been subject to a discourse of classlessness which the majority reject but which nevertheless presents class as problem-atic, stigmatizing. Despite this, the sense of being rooted in class communities persists for many of my interviewees and has been fostered by processes of political socialization within families which have ensured that support for trade unions remains stronger in the North East. While my research, thus, does confirm the notion of fragmentation of class identities, I have argued that this neither means an end to class (for class *as a relation* is not to be reduced to class *as a source of identity*) nor an end of collectivism. The combined effects of confusion around class, class hybridity and the ethos of individualism fostered by Thatcherism *do* weaken old class loyalties at the more abstract level; but in given sites such as workplaces, the potential for identification of common interests, of being part of a 'we', remains strong.

In such circumstances the need for some kind of collective representation within the workplace, such as that provided by unions, is heightened rather than diminished. Without unions, as so many of my respondents made clear to me, employers could 'walk all over employees':

> 'If management were only ones wielding power they'd just steamroll every thing through regardless of staff.'

> 'It's going to be like Big Brother then. It would be like George Orwell, they'd just tell you to do that and if you don't, you're not there. At the end of the day you're always going to need somebody with clout or an organization big enough to back you up. People can't stand up for themselves.'

The bleak dystopian vision of this last statement rams home the message: there is a need for some countervailing form of power in the workplace which must take a collective form. Individual resistance alone will not suffice. But, at the same time, it will not be sufficient for unions, heartened by evidence of increased popular support and the return of a Labour government, to fall back into their old ways. Among the working people of the North East there is emerging a distrust of hierarchies of all kinds (and here unions have fatally tended to replicate the internal structures of the capitalist forms they oppose) and a growing commitment to democracy. Women, part-timers, temporary workers, occupational groups who are in a minority within an organization (along with other marginalized groups such as minority ethnic groups or disabled employees whose voice is not heard in this study), are no longer prepared to be 'tret as second-class citizens'.

They will no longer tolerate unions giving priority to an historically dominant group of white male skilled workers; and should unions continue to do so they will lose the allegiance of other groups. At the same time, as argued in Chapter 10, unions need to think carefully how to present policies which will reconcile male workers to the changed times, if they are to avoid male disillusionment with the union. Nobody gives up power without some resistance and temporary trade-offs may have to be made. In the longer term what is required is the recasting of class meanings and their associated political programmes. The working class has always had two sexes and its political vehicles have ignored this to their own ultimate peril. New political agendas do not necessarily mean the abandonment of class demands or rhetoric and the adoption of some idea of 'rainbow alliance' or the imagery of the 'new social movements'; but class demands and rhetoric must widen and change as the realities of the lived experience of class are constantly changing and reforming.

Ethnicity: a significant absence

The lived experience of class, moreover, intersects with the experience of other processes of social differentiation. In this book I have studied the interaction of two forms of differentiation, gender and class, in a given site. But the global tendencies I have been discussing in this final chapter are multifaceted. Global change also involves new forms of ethnic hierarchy and racialization *within* nations and changes in relations and hierarchization *among* nations. As Ward argues,

> Class and race mediate the processes of global restructuring as capital-ists seek women of color and working class women to meet their needs for a flexible labour supply. (1990, p. 3)

Ethnic hierarchization is reflected in my study through the absence of minority workers in organizations where jobs were sought after and still relatively secure. To locate the North East's minority workers would require investigation of more insecure, possibly illegal, forms of employment, of enclaves of work within the ethnic economy and of the lives of the region's labour sur-plus class. Minority members are more likely to be unemployed than the 'white' majority. In 1994, African-Caribbean men had an unemployment rate of 31 per cent, Bangladeshi men of 42 per cent, compared to 15 per cent of white, while the figures for women were 18 per cent, 40 per cent and 9 per cent respect-ively (Modood *et al.*, 1997). But class and gender are also strongly implicated in the experience of minority workers, as exemplified, for example, in the growing divide between the fate of young African-Caribbean British women, many of whom are making use of educational success to compete for professional jobs, and that of their brothers; or in the differential experiences of British South Asians of Pakistani, Bangladeshi or East African origin, whose subsequent employment and prosperity has been greatly affected by their class origins (Mirza, 1992; Modood, 1992).

There is a need to continue tracing out the precise patterns of differentiation and inequality that are being formed and reformed within workplaces as a response to processes of global change. The patterns are volatile, and we can expect major changes in the next decades. The election of a Labour government in May 1997 after two decades of New Right control adds a new element to the British situation, the outcomes of which are hard to predict. But it is important that we continue to try to study the way gender, class and ethnicity come together in whatever changes do occur. As Connell remarks:

> To understand gender, then, we must constantly go beyond gender. The same applies in reverse. We cannot understand class, race or global inequality without constantly moving towards gender. (1995, p. 76)

Power, inequality and change

In this book I have developed an account of power which enables us to study the processes by which actions transform structures, just as structures limit actions. Thus this approach illuminates both structure and action in the fashion called for by Roseneil (1995). This is the virtue of a resource-based model of power. The message has been one of cautious optimism: power is multifaceted, power relations can shift and the exercise of power can be resisted. In offering a multi-dimensional account of power, I have tried to steer a course between two unsatisfactory extremes.

First, we should beware of the facile account of power offered by some postmodernists, especially postmodern feminists. In an attempt to rectify early feminist theorizing which presented women as passive victims, feminists have overcompensated in representing women as free agents, continually reconstructing their own gendered identities. Such accounts dwell on the free-floating nature of identities and the ability of women to empower themselves by the deployment of their sexuality and their ability to choose from an array of gendered options. Such voluntaristic accounts ignore constraints on agency and the asymmetry of prevailing power relations. Bordo sharply criticizes this as 'a characteristically postmodern inclination to emphasise and celebrate resistance, the creative agency of individuals, and the instabilities of current power relations rather than their recuperative tendencies' (1993, p. 294).

But equally unsatisfactory is the tendency to fetishize existing power relations, especially the power of capital. Theorists of globalization, in particular, have fallen into this error, presenting a fatalistic and deterministic vision of contemporary class dynamics. This may be exemplified by the gripping and chilling visions offered by Zygmunt Bauman. Having previously suggested that capital had emancipated itself from labour, no longer requiring it in a production role but only for consumption (1992), his recent work presents a section of the population as totally redundant in capital's terms (1997). The world is divided between jet-setting global capitalists and their managerial and professional agents, enjoying unprecedented levels of conspicuous consumption and geographical mobility, and a socially excluded surplus class penned up and immobilized in the ghettoes and no-go areas of our cities.

This kind of pessimism frequently seizes those who contemplate the evolution of globalized capitalist economics. By contrast, Hirst and Thompson (1996) offer a needed critique of the globalization scenario. While they accept that there has indeed been 'a progessive internationalization of money and capital markets since the 1970s' (p. 196), they argue that the thesis that national governments have lost all power to restrain the activities of transnational companies is unsubstantiated by real evidence. A vision of the limitless power of transnational capitalism is thus unwarranted; and indeed we may argue that where governments have ceded power, it is partly because they lacked the will to do otherwise, as was certainly the case with the British New Right.

This is not to deny the reality of capitalist power, which I have emphasized in Chapter 10. I accept the critique offered by Eagleton (1996) of some current work on social divisions which, he argues, tends to render invisible the material and political realities of capitalist power. For him such power is 'the invisible colour of daily life itself, which determines our existence – sometimes literally so – in almost every quarter, which decides in large measure the destiny of nations and the internecine conflicts between them'. He charts the uneasiness with which many intellectuals confront that power:

> It is as though almost every form of oppressive system – state, media, patriarchy, racism, neo-colonialism – can be readily debated, but not the one which so often sets the long-term agenda for all of these matters, or is at the very least implicated with them to their roots. (pp. 22–3)

I have argued in this book that capitalist power is indeed deeply implicated with the persistence of all forms of social hierarchy and inequality, although it should not be seen as the *cause* of them. But such power must not be seen as absolute. To believe that, as Williamson argues in her discussion of a 'world out of control' (1997), is to collude with the ideology of the powerful that there is no alternative. Against such determinism it is important to assert that change is not only possible but evident. Perhaps, as Polly Toynbee argues, we need to look again with less postmodern scepticism at the notion of progress:

> We really do have a better, freer society with much more choice and opportunity for most people. Yearning for an imaginary golden bygone era is a national disease that infects our politics and deceives us. Why must we always be told things are morally worse?[3]

In this book I have tried to demonstrate how power relations are indeed, if slowly, altering in the direction of 'better, freer' relations of gender. A multi-dimensional model of power gives a more accurate account of the workings of the dynamics of gender and class than those offered by the one-sided accounts described above, enabling us to study the complexity, variability and fluidity of power relations.

While the balance of gendered power has seen a shift towards women, I have presented a more pessimistic view of capital/labour relations. The consolidation of capitalist power has undoubtedly been fostered by the political events of the past two decades. But even capitalist power can be resisted by the utilization of symbolic and collective resources. Trade unions still have a crucial future role in such resistance. The coming to power of a

Labour government, while I was writing the last sections of this book in the spring of 1997, has at least raised possibilities of change. It is significant that three weeks after the Labour victory the TUC was invited back to Downing Street to consult with the Prime Minister after years of exile. A few months later the sacked trade unionists of the GCHQ governmental intelligence centre returned to their former workplace in a ceremonial parade to mark the new government's pledge to lift the ban on unions imposed by the Conservatives in 1984. Such developments suggest that a space may be opening for counter-discourses and definitions which may challenge capitalist hegemony over symbolic resources.

Consolidated power of any type is extremely hard to overturn, but not impossible. Under the aegis of feminism women have risen and continue to rise against centuries of male dominance. Of course, as we know, women and men make history under constraints, under conditions not of their choosing: but they can, and do, make history.

Notes

1   See Chapter 3, p. 30.
2   In fact, the ten part-time women I interviewed at TradeFare, although displaying much more fragmented work histories, did not otherwise differ much from their full-time colleagues in their responses.
3   Polly Toynbee in *Radio Times*, 17–23 May 1997, p. 10.

Appendix

A The samples

At all organizations apart from TradeFare random samples were drawn from employee lists: at Albion these were lists of all full-time employees, at the other three organizations lists covering the chosen occupational categories. Part-timers were excluded. Where employees did not wish to be interviewed or were unattainable because of sickness, absence or resignation, comparable substitutes were drawn from a second random sample. Initial response rates varied from 78 per cent at the hospital to 50 per cent at Pillco. Those who are favourable to unions are probably slightly over-represented as they were the least likely to refuse to be interviewed. I could not use random samples at TradeFare because of the intricacies of scheduling labour in retail (see Du Gay, 1996); instead they selected interviewees for me on a rough quota basis (covering different ages, jobs in the store, as well as the required balance of gender and full-time or part-time status). Here the bias is likely to have been the other way, with the personnel managers selecting pro-company workers.

However in each occupational sample a range of political opinions was found, which indicates that bias was not too large. Moreover, the results of the study are broadly in line with other surveys of union members, for example, Fosh and Cohen, 1990; Rees, 1992; Whitston and Waddington, 1992; Penn and Scattergood, 1996. As women and men were selected in exactly the same way comparisons between them can be taken as valid.

I interviewed the majority of the respondents myself. Again for scheduling reasons, Mark Erickson interviewed ten of the TradeFare workers for me. The interviews were designed to last about half an hour, although sometimes they over-ran. Because of the difficulties surrounding access and the decision to interview during work time, I had to try to be as little disruptive as possible, in organizations where staffing was tight and time at a premium. The interview schedule was therefore designed to be administered as a questionnaire if need be, so that it could be completed in the respondents' own time. This only became necessary at Albion where nine respondents filled it in themselves. The answers to questions on these nine questionnaires were much briefer than the responses elicited by the interviewing method: but they were not significantly different in content, covering the same range of responses as the other Albion employees.

B   The interview schedule/questionnaire

The interview schedule evolved slightly as it was used. Below is the final version employed at TradeFare, the Bureau and Pillco. Slightly different versions were employed for men/women, members/non-members of unions.

Questionnaire on Work and Attitudes to Trade Unions

A   Demographic Details
A1   Sex
A2   Marital Status
A3   Age
A4   Do you have any children?
        If you do, how many?
        What are their ages?
A5   What kind of childcare arrangements do you have/did you have?
A6   Do you have any responsibility for caring for any other relatives?
        If so, who are they?
A7   Are you currently the sole earner in the household?
        Please list any other earners

B   Work History
B1   At what age did you complete full-time education?
B2   Please describe all the jobs you have had since leaving full-time
        education
        Dates   Type of Job   Employer   Location
B3   What is your current job?
B4   Have you had any breaks in your working career, because of
        training, or because of unemployment or for any other reason?
B5   How would you describe your feelings about your present job?
B6   Are your earnings: essential for the household/important but not
        essential/not especially important?
B7   In your job do you work: mainly with men/mainly with women/
        about equally with both?
B8   How would you compare the position of men and women in your
        workplace?
B9   What would you say are your main reasons for going to work?
B10   Do you have any ambitions to advance further in your job or
        career?
        If you do, what are they?
B11   Are there any worries or problems you have at present about
        your job or career?
B12   What would most improve the quality of your working life?
B13   a)   What was your father's main occupation?
        b)   What was your mother's main occupation?

C Trade Union History

C1   In your current job are you a member of a trade union?

C2   Which union?

C3   When did you join the union? before taking the job/when you took the job/later/much later

C4   What were your reasons for joining the union?

C5   Which of these most corresponds to your attitude towards unions? very committed/quite committed/neutral/quite hostile/ very hostile

C6   a) Is your husband/wife a union member?
b) Would you consider him/her active within the union?

C7   Is there any family background of union membership?

C8   If you feel committed to the idea of trade unions, do you have any idea how that commitment came about? Or if hostile, where did that come from?

C9   If you worked anywhere else before this were you a union member

D Trade Union Activities

D1   In your current union have you been involved in any of the following activities?
   a)   Reading a union magazine
   b)   Attending a union meeting
   c)   Attending any educational activity organized by the union
   d)   Attending any social event
   e)   Voting in a union election
   f)   Standing in a union election
   g)   Acting as a union representative
   h)   Taking part in any type of industrial action (if so give details)
   (If you have previously been in any other union please fill in D2, otherwise go to D3)

D2   In any of the other unions you have been a member of have you been involved in any of the following activities?
   a)   Attending a union meeting
   b)   Acting as a representative or officer (if so give details)
   c)   Taking part in any kind of industrial action (if so give details)

D3   If you needed help from your union would you know whom to contact?

D4   Would you consider yourself active in the union?

D5   If you answered NO can you mention any factors which prevent you from being active? (please specify)

D6   Can you think of anything that might encourage you to be more involved?

D7   Would any of the following encourage you to participate more fully in the activities of your current union? (please tick any which applies to you)

a) More information about trade union activities and procedures
b) More courses and training schemes
c) More social events
d) More of your friends being involved in the union
e) Meetings being held in work time
f) Meetings being held in a more convenient place
g) Fewer domestic responsibilities
h) Provision of childcare facilities by the union
i) Employers being less hostile to unions
j) Less worry that being active in the union might block promotion chances

E   Attitudes to Trade Unions

E1 Would you describe yourself as satisfied with your present union
branch? If not why not?

E2 Do you feel it represents your interests satisfactorily? If not why
not?

E3 Do you consider the policies of the national union to be correct?
If not why not?

E4 What are the main things you as an individual require from a
trade union?

E5 The following activities are carried out by trade unions (not
necessarily by your own union). In each case suggest whether the
activity is: very important/important/fairly important/not
important/or whether unions should not do this
a) Campaigning for better pay
b) Campaigning for better working conditions
c) Campaigning for health and safety at work
d) Working for better rights for part-time workers
e) Working to provide childcare provisions
f) Providing education and training facilities
g) Providing legal support
h) Providing financial benefits and perks
i) Organizing social events
j) Working for equal opportunities for women
k) Campaigning against racial discrimination
l) Campaigning against redundancy
m) Campaigning against public sector cuts
n) Trying to influence government policies
o) Rallying support for the Labour Party

E6 Are there are any policies or activities such as any of these you
would like to see your own union more involved with in the
future?

E7 Do you believe that the unions should ever use strikes as a method
to gain their objectives?

If you answered YES should they strike in any of the following circumstances?

a) to get more pay
b) to improve working conditions
c) when a member has been unfairly dismissed
d) when a company wishes to ban the union
e) when redundancies are threatened

E8 Do you believe unions should have a say in influencing decisions within your company or organization in the following areas?

a) pay and conditions
b) implementation of new technology
c) redundancies
d) investment policies and financial decisionmaking

Should they have seats on management boards?

E9 Do you agree with the statement that the unions have too much power?

E10 It has been suggested that in the future there will be no need for unions. Do you agree? If you answered no, what are your reasons?

E11 Do you consider your union represents the interests of men and women equally effectively?

E12 Do you think that women take as much interest in the union as men?

E13 Do you know of any EO policies your union has adopted to help get a better deal for women?

E14 Do you agree with the idea of having special reserved seats for women on union committees?

E15 Is there anything your union could do which would help improve women's position? (please specify)

F Yourself

F1 Do you agree with the idea that Britain is now a classless society?

F2 Do you identify yourself as belonging to a particular class? If so which?

F3 How would you describe your family social background?

F4 In your opinion do inequalities (for example in terms of pay, opportunities, work conditions) still exist between men and women workers?
If you answered YES, do you think these inequalities are greater: between men and women workers/between the different classes?

F5 Do you see yourself more as a woman or as a worker?

F6 Preferred retirement age

Bibliography

Abercrombie, N., and Urry, J. (1983). *Capital, Labour and the Middle Classes*. London: Allen & Unwin.

Allen, S. (1997). 'What is work for? The right to work and the right to be idle.' In R. Brown (ed.) *The Changing Shape of Work*. London: Macmillan.

Arber, S., and Ginn, J. (1991). *Gender and Later Life*. London: Sage.

Arber, S., and Ginn, J. (1995). 'The mirage of gender equality: occupational success in the labour market and within marriage.' *British Journal of Sociology*, 46 (1), 21–44.

Bailey, J. (1992). *Social Europe*. London: Longman.

Barrett, M. (1992). 'Words and things: materialism and method in contemporary feminist analysis.' In M. Barrett and A. Phillips (eds), *Destabilizing Theory*. Cambridge: Polity.

Bassett, P. (1987). *Strike Free*. London: Macmillan.

Batstone, E. (1984). *Working Order*. Oxford: Blackwell.

Bauman, Z. (1992). *Intimations of Postmodernity*. London: Routledge.

Bauman, Z. (1997). 'Glocalization or globalization for some, localization for others.' Paper presented at BSA Annual Conference, York University.

Beaumont, P. (1987). *The Decline of Trade Union Organization*. London: Croom Helm.

Beaumont, P. (1992). *Public Sector Industrial Relations*. London: Routledge.

Beck, U. (1992). *Risk Society*. London: Sage.

Bell, D. (1973). *The Coming of Post-Industrial Society*. New York: Basic Books.

Benn, M. (1987). 'In and against the European left: socialist feminists get organized.' *Feminist Review*, 26, 83–90.

Beynon, H. (1975). *Working For Ford*. Wakefield: EP Publishing.

Beynon, H., and Blackburn, R. (1984). 'Unions: the men's affair.' In J. Siltanen and M. Stanworth, *Women and the Public Sphere*, London: Hutchinson.

Beynon, H., Hudson, R., and Sadler, D. (1994). *A Place Called Teesside*. Edinburgh: Edinburgh University Press.

Bird, D., and Corcoran, L. (1994). 'Trade union membership and density 1992–3.' *Employment Gazette* (June), 189–92.

Blackburn, R., Jarman, J., and Siltanen, J. (1993). 'The analysis of occupational gender segregation over time and place: considerations of measurement and some new evidence.' *Work, Employment and Society*, 7 (3), 335–62.

Bordo, S. (1993). *Unbearable Weight: feminism, western culture and the body*. Berkeley: University of California Press.

Boston, S. (1980). *Women Workers and the Trade Union Movement*. London: Davis-Poyntcr.

Bottomore, T., and Brym, R. (cds) (1989). *The Capitalist Class*. Hemel Hempstead: Harvester Wheatsheaf.

Bradley, H. (1987). 'Degradation and resegmentation: social and technological change in the East Midlands hosiery industry.' PhD, University of Durham.

Bradley, H. (1989). *Men's Work, Women's Work*. Cambridge: Polity.

Bradley, H. (1994). 'Divided we fall: unions and their members.' *Employee Relations*, 16 (2), 41–52.

Bradley, H. (1996). *Fractured Identities*. Cambridge: Polity.

Bradley, H. (1997). 'Gender and change in employment: feminization and its effects.' In R. Brown (ed.), *The Changing Shape of Work*. London: Macmillan.

Bradley, H., and Fenton, S. (1999). 'Reconciling culture and economy: ways forward in the analysis of ethnicity and gender.' In L. Ray and A. Sayer (eds), *Culture and Economy*. London: Sage.

Braverman, H. (1974). *Labor and Monopoly Capital*. New York: Basic Books.

Briskin, L., and McDermott, P. (eds) (1993). *Women Challenging Unions*. Toronto: University of Toronto Press.

Brown, P. (1995). 'Cultural capital and social exclusion.' *Work, Employment and Society*, (9) 1, 29–51.

Brown, R. (1995). 'The changing nature of work and employment.' In L. Evans, P. Johnson, and B. Thomas (eds), *The Northern Region Economy*. London: Manscll.

Burchell, B. (1994). 'The unequal distribution of job security.' Unpublished paper, University of Cambridge.

Burris, B. (1996). 'Technocracy, patriarchy and management.' In D. Collinson and J. Hearn (eds), *Men as Managers, Managers as Men*. London: Sage.

Campbell, B. (1993). *Goliath*. London: Methuen.

Carson, G. (1997). 'The power of talk.' Paper presented at British Sociological Association Annual Conference, York University.

Carter, J. (1997) 'Ethnicity, equality and the nursing profession.' PhD, Bristol University.

Cavendish, R. (1982). *Women on the Line*. London: Routledge.

Chaney, D. (1990). 'Subtopia in Gateshead: the metrocentre as a cultural form.' *Theory, Culture and Society*, 7, 49–68.

Clark, A. (1982, first edition 1910). *Working Life of Women in the Seventeenth Century*. London: Routledge.

Clarke, J., and Critcher, C. (1985). *The Devil Makes Work*. London: Macmillan.

Clegg, S. (1990). *Modern Organizations*. London: Sage.

Clement, W., and Myles, J. (1994). *Relations of Ruling: class and gender in post-industrial societies*. Montreal: McGill-Queens University Press.

Coates, G. (1996). 'The art of persuasion: organizational togetherness in the 1990s.' Discussion Papers in Sociology, No. S96/12, University of Leicester.

Cockburn, C. (1981). 'The material of male power.' *Feminist Review*, 9, 41–58.

Cockburn, C. (1983). *Brothers*. London: Pluto.

Cockburn, C. (1985). *Machinery of Dominance*. London: Pluto.

Cockburn, C. (1989). 'Equal opportunities: the short and long agenda.' *Industrial Relations Journal*, 20, 213–25.

Cockburn, C. (1991). *In the Way of Women*. London: Macmillan.

Collinson, D., and Hearn, J. (eds) (1996a). *Men as Managers, Managers as Men*. London: Sage.

Collinson, D., and Hearn, J. (1996b). '"Men" at "work": multiple masculinities/multiple workplaces.' In M. Mac an Ghaill (ed.), *Understanding Masculinities*. Milton Keynes: Open University Press.

Connell, R. (1987). *Gender and Power*. Cambridge: Polity.

Connell, R. (1995). *Masculinities*. Cambridge: Polity.

Coole, D. (1996). 'Is class a difference that makes a difference?' *Radical Philosophy*, 77, 17–25.

Coward, R. (1992). *Our Treacherous Hearts*. London: Faber & Faber.

Crompton, R. (1993). *Class and Stratification*. Cambridge: Polity.

Crompton, R., and Gubbay, J. (1977). *Economy and Class Structure*. London: Macmillan.

Crompton, R., and Jones, G. (1984). *White-Collar Proletariat*. London: Macmillan.

Crompton, R., and Le Feuvre, N. (1992). 'Gender and bureaucracy: women in finance in Britain and France.' In M. Savage and A. Witz (eds), *Gender and Bureaucracy*. Oxford: Blackwell.

Crompton, R., and Le Feuvre, N. (1997). 'Paid employment and the changing system of gender relations: a cross-national comparison.' *Sociology*, 30 (3), 427–45.

Crompton, R., and Sanderson., K. (1990). *Gendered Jobs and Social Change*. London: Unwin Hyman.

Crook, S., Pakulski, J., and Waters, M. (1992). *Postmodernization*. London: Sage.

CSO (1995). *Regional Trends*, 30. London: HMSO.

Cunnison, S., and Stageman, J. (1993). *Feminizing the Unions*. Aldershot: Avebury.

Danford, A. (1996) 'Japanese management techniques and British workers.' PhD, Bristol University.

Darnell, A., and Evans, L. (1995). 'The economic record since 1975.' In L. Evans, P. Johnson, and B. Thomas (eds), *The Northern Region Economy*. London: Mansell.

Davies, C. (1996). 'The sociology of professions and the profession of gender.' *Sociology*, 30 (4), 661–78.

Davis, K. (1991). 'Critical sociology and gender relations.' In K. Davis, M. Leijenaar and J. Oldersma (eds), *The Gender of Power*. London: Sage.

Davis, K., Leijenaar, M., and Oldersma, J. (1991) (eds). *The Gender of Power*. London: Sage.

Dennis, N., and Erdos, G. (1992) *Families Without Fatherhood*. London: Institute of Economic Affairs.

Devine, F. (1992). *Affluent Workers Revisited*. Edinburgh: Edinburgh University Press.

Devine, F. (1997). 'Privilege, power and the reproduction of advantage.' Paper presented at BSA Annual Conference, York University.

Du Gay, P. (1996). *Consumption and Identity at Work*. London: Sage.

Eagleton, T. (1996). *The Illusions of Post-modernism*. Oxford: Blackwell.

Edley, N., and Wetherell, M. (1996). 'Masculinity, power and identity.' In M. Mac an Ghaill (ed.), *Understanding Masculinities*. Milton Keynes: Open University Press.

Edwards, R. (1979). *The Contested Terrain*. London: Heinemann.

Elger, T. (1991). 'Task flexibility and the intensification of labour in UK manufacturing.' In A. Pollert (ed.), *Farewell to Flexibility?* Oxford: Blackwell.

Ellis, V. (1988). 'Current trade union attempts to remove occupational segrgation in the employment of women.' In S. Walby (ed.), *Gender Segregation at Work*. Milton Keynes: Open University Press.

Esping-Andersen, G. (ed.) (1993). *Changing Classes*. London: Sage.

Fairbrother, P. (1991). 'In a state of change: flexibility in the Civil Service.' In A. Pollert (ed.), *Farewell to Flexibility?* Oxford: Blackwell.

Fairbrother, P. (1994a). 'Privatization and local trade unionism.' *Work, Employment and Society*, 8 (3), 339–56.

Fairbrother, P. (1994b). 'Workplace trade unionism in the state sector.' Paper presented at 12th International Labour Process Conference, Aston University.

Fenton, S. (forthcoming). *Ethnicity: Social Structure, Culture, Identity*. London: Macmillan.

Filby, M., and Shelton, P. (1996). 'In search of the generic health support worker: the restructuring of non professional support roles in the state hospital sector.' Unpublished paper, UCE Birmingham.

Fosh, P., and Cohen, S. (1990). 'Local trade unionists in action.' In P. Fosh and E. Heery (eds), *Trade Unions and Their Members*. London: Macmillan.

Foster, J. (1974). *Class Struggle and the Industrial Revolution*. London: Methuen.

Fox, A. (1974). *Beyond Contract*. London: Faber.

Fraser, N. (1989). *Unruly Practices*. Minneapolis, MN: University of Minnesota Press.

Fraser, N. (1995). 'From redistribution to recognition? Dilemmas of justice in a post-socialist age.' *New Left Review*. 212, 68–93.

Freely, M. (1996). 'Five alive.' *Guardian*, 2 December.

Friedman, A. (1977). 'Responsible autonomy and direct control over the labour process.' *Capital and Class*, 1, 43–57.

Fulcher, J. (1995). 'British capitalism in the 1980s: old times or new times.' *British Journal of Sociology*, 46 (2), 325–38.

Gall, G. (1997). 'Developments in trade unionism in the financial sector in Britain.' *Work, Employment and Society*, 11 (2), 219–35.

Gallie, D. (1996). 'Trade union allegiance and decline in British urban labour markets.' In D. Gallie, R. Penn, and M. Rose (eds), *Trade Unionism in Recession*. Oxford: Oxford University Press.

Gallie, D., Penn, R., and Rose, M. (eds) (1996). *Trade Unionism in Recession*. Oxford: Oxford University Press.

Gallie, D., and White, M. (1993). 'Employee commitment and the skills revolution: first findings from the Employment in Britain survey.' London: PSI.

Garrahan, P., and Stewart, P. (1992). *The Nissan Enigma*. London: Mansell.

Garrahan, P., and Stewart, P. (eds) (1994). *Urban Change and Renewal: the paradox of place*. London: Avebury.

Geertz, C. (1995). *After the Fact*. Cambridge, MA: Harvard University Press.

Gherardi, S. (1996). 'Gendered organizational cultures: narratives of women travellers in a male world.' *Gender, Work and Organization*, 3 (4), 187–201.

Giddens, A. (1973). *The Class Structure of the Advanced Societies*. London: Hutchinson.

Giddens, A. (1984). *The Constitution of Society*. Cambridge: Polity.

Giddens, A. (1994). *Beyond Left and Right*. Cambridge: Polity.

Glucksmann, M. (1995). 'Why "work"? Gender and the "total social organization of labour."' *Gender, Work and Organization*, 2 (2), 63–75.

Goffman, E. (1959). *The Presentation of Self in Everyday Life*. New York: Doubleday Anchor Books.

Goffman, E. (1964). *Stigma*. Englewood Cliffs, NJ: Prentice-Hall.

Goldthorpe, J. (1982). 'On the service class, its formation and its future.' In A. Giddens and G. Mackenzie (eds), *Social Class and the Division of Labour*. Cambridge: Cambridge University Press.

Goldthorpe, J., and Heath, A. (1992). 'Revised class schema.' Working Paper No. 13, Joint Unit for the Study of Social Trends.

Goldthorpe, J., and Marshall, G. (1992). 'The promising future of class analysis.' *Sociology*, (26) 3, 381–400.

Gorz, A. (1982). *Farewell to the Working Class*. London: Pluto.

Grey, R. (1994). 'Career as a project of the self and labour process discipline.' *Sociology*, 28 (2), 479–98.

Hakim, C. (1979). 'Occupational Segregation by Sex.' Research Paper No. 9, Department of Employment.

Hakim, C. (1991). 'Grateful slaves and self-made women: fact and fantasy in women's work orientations.' *European Sociological Review*, 7 (2), 101–21.

Hakim, C. (1992). 'Explaining trends in occupational segregation: the measurement, causes and consequences of the sexual division of labour.' *European Sociological Review*, 8 (2), 127–49.

Hamilton, R. (1978). *The Liberation of Women*. London: Allen & Unwin.

Hammond, J., and Hammond, B. (1979). *The Skilled Labourer*. London: Longman.

Handy, C. (1984). *The Future of Work*. Oxford: Blackwell.

Haraszti, M. (1977). *A Worker in a Worker's State*. Harmondsworth: Penguin.

Harrop, J., and Moss, P. (1995). 'Trends in parental employment.' *Work, Employment and Society*, 7 (1), 97–120.

Hartmann, H. (1976). 'Patriarchy, capitalism and job segregation by sex.' *Signs*, I (3), 137–68.

Hearn, F. (1971). *Domination, Legitimation and Resistance*. Westport, CT: Greenwood Press.

Heery, E., and Kelly, J. (1988). *Union Women: a study of women trade union officers*. London: London School of Economics and Imperial College of Science and Technology.

Henwood, M., Rimmer, L., and Wicks, M. (1987). *Inside the Family*. London: Family Policy Studies Centre.

Herzog, M. (1980). *From Hand to Mouth*. Harmondsworth: Penguin.

Hirst, P., and Thompson, G. (1996). *Globalization in Question*. Cambridge: Polity.

Hochschild, A. (1983). *The Managed Heart*. Berkeley, CA: University of California Press.

Hochschild, A. (1997) *The Time Bind*. New York: Metropolitan Books.

Hollands, R. (1990). *The Long Transition: class, culture and youth training*. London: Macmillan.

Hollands, R. (1994). 'Back to the future? Preparing young adults for the post-industrial Wearside economy.' In P. Garrahan and P. Stewart (eds), *Urban Change and Renewal: the paradox of place*. London: Avebury.

Holloway, G. (1997). 'Finding a voice: on becoming a working-class feminist academic.' In P. Mahony and C. Zmroczek (eds), *Class Matters: 'working-class' women's perspectives on social class*. London: Taylor & Francis.

Hollway, W. (1996). 'Masters and men in the transition from factory hands to sentimental workers.' In D. Collinson and J. Hearn (eds), *Men as Managers, Managers as Men*. London: Sage.

Homans, A. (1987). 'Man-made myths; the reality of being a woman scientist in the NHS.' In A. Spencer and D. Podmore (eds), *In a Man's World*. London: Tavistock.

Hossfield, J. (1990). '"Their logic against them": contradictions in sex, race and class in Silicon Valley.' In K. Ward (ed.), *Women Workers and Global Restructuring*. Ithaca, NY: ILR, Cornell University.

Humphries, J. (1983). 'The emancipation of women in the 1970s and 1980s.' *Capital and Class*, 20, 6–27.

Hunt, J. (1982). 'A woman's place is in her union.' In J. West (ed.), *Work, Women and the Labour Market*. London: Routledge.

Hutton, W. (1995). 'High risk strategy.' *Guardian*, 3 October.

Hyman, R. (1991). 'European unions: towards 2000.' *Work, Employment and Society*, 5 (4), 21–39.

Hyman, R., and Price, R. (eds) (1983). *The New Working Class? White-collar workers and their organization*. London: Macmillan.

Jenkins, C., and Sherman, B. (1979). *The Collapse of Work*. London: Eyre Methuen.

Jenson, J., Hagen, E., and Reddy, C. (eds) (1988). *Feminization of the Labour Force*. Cambridge: Polity.

Jewson, N., and Mason, D. (1986). 'The theory and practice of equal opportunities policies: liberal and radical approaches.' *Sociological Review*, 34 (2), 307–34.

Johnson, T. (1972). *Professions and Power*. London: Macmillan.

Jones, B. (1989). 'When certainty fails: inside the factory of the future.' In S. Wood (ed.), *The Transformation of Work?* London: Unwin Hyman.

Jowell, R., Brook, L., Prior, G., and Taylor, B. (eds) (1992). *British Social Attitudes: the ninth report*. Aldershot: Social and Community Planning.

Kanter, R. M. (1977). *Men and Women of the Corporation*. New York, NY: Basic Books.

Kitzinger, C., and Wilkinson, S. (1993). 'The precariousness of heterosexual feminist identities.' In M. Kennedy, C. Lubelska, and V. Walsh (eds), *Making Connections*. London: Taylor & Francis.

Kumar, K. (1978). *Prophecy and Progress*. Harmondsworth: Penguin.

Kumar, K. (1995). *From Post-Industrial to Post-Modern Society*. Oxford: Blackwell.

Land, H. (1994). 'The demise of the male breadwinner.' In S. Baldwin and J. Falkingham (eds), *Social Security and Social Change*. London: Harvester Wheatsheaf.

Large, P. (1989). 'They have seen the future – and it reminds them of ancient Greece.' *Guardian*, 3 February.

Lash, S. (1984). *The Militant Worker: Class and Radicalism in France and America*. London: Heinemann.

Lash, S., and Urry, J. (1987). *The End of Organized Capitalism*. Cambridge: Polity.

Lash, J., and Urry, J. (1994). *Economies of Signs and Space*. London: Sage.

Lawrence, E. (1994). *Gender and Trade Unions*. London: Taylor & Francis.

Ledwith, S., Colgan, F., Joyce, P., and Hayes, M. (1990). 'The Making of Women Trade Union Leaders.' *Industrial Relations Journal*, 21 (2), 112–25.

Lewenhak, S. (1977). *Women and Trade Unions*. London: Ernest Benn.

Liff, S., and Wacjman, J. (1993). 'What problems are EO initiatives an answer to?' Paper presented at Labour Process Conference, Blackpool.

Linhart, R. (1981). *The Assembly Line*. London: John Calder.

Lockwood, D. (1958). *The Black-Coated Worker*. London: Allen & Unwin.

Lockwood, D. (1975). 'Sources of variation in working-class images of society.' In M. Bulmer (ed.), *Working-class Images of Society*. London: Routledge & Kegan Paul.

Lyon, D. (1988). *The Information Society*. Cambridge: Polity.

Mahony, P., and Zmroczek, C. (eds) (1997). *Class Matters: 'working-class' women's perspectives on class*. London: Taylor & Francis.

Mallier, A., and Rosser, M. (1987). *Women and the Economy*. London: Macmillan.

Mann, M. (1986). 'A crisis in stratification theory?' In R. Crompton and M. Mann (eds), *Gender and Stratification*. Cambridge: Polity.

Marchington, M., and Parker, P. (1990). *Changing Patterns of Employee Relations*. London: Harvester Wheatsheaf.

Marshall, B. (1994). *Engendering Modernity*. Cambridge: Polity.

Marshall, J. (1984). *Women Managers: travellers in a male world*. Chichester: Wiley.

Marshall, J. (1995). *Women Managers Moving On*. London: Routledge.

Martin, R. (1995). 'Plus ca change...? The Social Change and Economic Life Initiative.' *Work, Employment and Society*, 9 (1), 165–81.

Mason, D. (1992). 'Some problems with the concepts of race and racism.' Discussion Papers in Sociology No. S92/5, University of Leicester.

McCarthy, M. (1971). 'Women in trade unions today.' In L. Middleton (ed.), *Women in the Labour Movement*. London: Croom Helm.

McCarthy, W. (1994). 'Of Hats and Cattle: or the limits of macro-survey research in industrial relations.' *Industrial Relations Journal*, 25 (4), 315–22.

McDowell, L. (1997) *Capital Culture*. Oxford: Blackwell.

McNay, L. (1992). *Foucault and Feminism*. Cambridge: Polity.

Mirza, H. (1992). *Young, Female and Black*. London: Routledge.

Mitter, S. (1986). *Common Fate, Common Bond: Women in the global economy*. London: Pluto.

Modood, T. (1992). *Not Easy Being British*. Stoke-on-Trent: Trentham Books.

Modood, T., Berthoud, R., Lakey, J., Nazroo, J., Smith, P., Virdee, S., and Beishon, S. (eds) (1997). *Ethnic Minorities in Britain: diversity and disadvantage*. London: PSI.

Morgan, D. (1992). *Discovering Men*. London: Routledge.

Morley, L. (1997). 'A class of one's own: women, social class and the academy.' In P. Mahony and C. Zmroczek (eds), *Class Matters: 'working-class' women's perspectives on class*. London: Taylor & Francis.

Murray, C. (1990). *The Emerging British Underclass*. London: Institute of Economic Affairs.

Musson, A. (1972). *British Trade Unions 1800–1875*. London: Macmillan.

Nichols, T., and Beynon, H. (1977). *Living with Capitalism*. London: Routledge.

O'Connell Davidson, J. (1993). *Privatization and Employment Relations*. London: Mansell.

ONS (1996). *Regional Trends* 31. London: HMSO.

OPCS (1991). *Census County Report: Tyne and Wear*. London: HMSO.

Osborne, D., and Gaebler, T. (1992). *Reinventing Government: how the entrepreneurial spirit is transforming the public sector*. Reading, MA: Addison Wesley.

Pahl, R. (1984). *Divisions of Labour*. Oxford: Blackwell.

Pahl, R. (1995). *After Success*. Cambridge: Polity.

Pahl, R., and Gershuny, J. (1979). 'Work Outside Employment: some preliminary speculations.' *New Universities Quarterly*, 34, 120–35.

Pahl, R., and Wallace, C. (1988). 'Neither angels in marble nor rebels in red: privatization and working-class consciousness.' In D. Rose (ed.), *Social Stratification and Economic Change*. London: Hutchinson.

Pakulski, J., and Waters, M. (1996). *The Death of Class*. London: Sage.

Parkin, F. (1979). *Marxism and Class Theory*. London: Tavistock.

Payne, J. (1989). 'Trade union membership and activism among young people in Britain.' *British Journal of Industrial Relations*, 27 (1), 111–32.

Penn, R., and Scattergood, H. (1996). 'The experience of trade unions in Rochdale during the 1980s'. In D. Gallie, R. Penn, and M. Rose (eds), *Trade Unionism in Recession*. Oxford: Oxford University Press.

Perkin, H. (1985). *The Origins of Modern English Society*. London: Ark.

Peters, T. (1987). *Thriving on Chaos*. London: Macmillan.

Peters, T. (1992). *Liberation Management: necessary disorganization for the nano-second nineties*. London: Macmillan.

Phillips, A. (1987). *Divided Loyalties*. London: Virago.

Plummer, K. (1992). *Modern Homosexualities*. London: Routledge.

Pollert, A. (1981). *Girls, Wives, Factory Lives*. London: Macmillan.

Pollert, A. (1991). 'The orthodoxy of flexibility.' In A. Pollert (ed.), *Farewell to Flexibility*? Oxford: Blackwell.

Porter, H. (1997). 'Smashing the glass ceiling.' *Guardian*, 26 May, 2–4.

Porter, M. (1983). *Home and Work Consciousness*. Manchester: Manchester University Press.

Ramsay, K., and Parker, M. (1992). 'Gender, bureaucracy and organizational culture.' In M. Savage and A. Witz (eds), *Gender and Bureaucracy*. Oxford: Blackwell.

Reay, D. (1997). 'The double-bind of the "working-class" feminist academic: the success of failure or the failure of success.' In P. Mahony and C. Zmroczek (eds), *Class Matters: 'working-class' women's perspectives on class*. London: Taylor & Francis.

Rees, T. (1992). *Women and the Labour Market*. London: Routledge.

Roberts, I. (1997). 'The culture of ownership and the ownership of culture.' In R. Brown (ed.), *The Changing Shape of Work*. London: Macmillan.

Robinson, F. (1994). 'Something old, something new? The great North in the 1990s.' In P. Garrahan and P. Stewart (eds), *Urban Change and Renewal: the paradox of place*. London: Avebury.

Robinson, O. (1988). 'The changing labour market: growth of part-time employment and labour market segregation in Britain.' In S. Walby (ed.), *Gender Segregation at Work*. Milton Keynes: Open University Press.

Rorty, R. (1994). 'Towards a liberal Utopia: an interview with Richard Rorty.' *Times Literary Supplement*, 24 June, 24.

Rose, M. (1996). 'Still life in Swindon: case-studies in union survival and employer policy in a "sunrise" labour market.' In D. Gallie, R. Penn, and M. Rose (eds), *Trade Unionism in Recession*. Oxford: Oxford University Press.

Rose, N. (1989). *Governing the Soul*. London: Routledge.

Roseneil, S. (1995). 'The coming of age of feminist sociology: some issues of practice and theory for the next twenty years.' *British Journal of Sociology*, 46 (2), 199–205.

Rosser, J., and Davies, C. (1987). '"What would we do without her?" Invisible women in the NHS administration.' In A. Spencer and D. Podmore (eds), *In a Man's World*. London: Tavistock.

Rubery, J., and Tarling, R. (1988). 'Women's employment in declining Britain.' In J. Rubery (ed.), *Women in Recession*. London: Routledge.

Rubery, J., and Wilkinson, F. (1994). *Employer Strategy and the Labour Market*. Oxford: Oxford University Press.

Savage, M. (1992). 'Women's expertise, men's authority: gendered organization and the contemporary middle classes.' In M. Savage and A. Witz (eds), *Gender and Bureaucracy*. Oxford: Blackwell.

Savage, M., Barlow, J., Dickens, A., and Fielding, T. (1992). *Property, Bureaucracy and Culture: middle class formation in contemporary Britain*. London: Routledge.

Savage, M., and Witz, A. (eds) (1992). *Gender and Bureaucracy*. Oxford: Blackwell.

Sawicki, J. (1991). *Disciplining Foucault*. London: Routledge.

Sayer, K., and Fisher, G. (1997). 'Something vaguely heretical: communicating across difference in the country.' In P. Mahony and C. Zmroczek (eds), *Class Matters: 'working-class' women's perspectives on class*. London: Taylor & Francis.

Scott, A. (1994). *Willing Slaves?* Cambridge: Cambridge University Press.

Scott, A. M. (ed.) (1994). *Gender Segregation and Social Change*. Oxford: Oxford University Press.

Scott, J. (1994). 'Class analysis: back to the future.' *Sociology* 28 (4), 933–42.

Scott, J. W. (1988). *Gender and the Politics of History*. New York, NY: Columbia University Press.

Seifert, R. (1992). *Industrial Relations in the NHS*. London: Routledge.

Segal, L. (1990). *Slow Motion – Changing Masculinities, Changing Men*. London: Virago.

Sianne, G., and Wilkinson, H. (1995). *Gender, Feminism and the Future*. London: Demos.

Siltanen, J. (1994). *Locating Gender*. London: UCL.

Skeggs, B. (1997a). *Formations of Class and Gender*. London: Sage.

Skeggs, B. (1997b). 'Classifying practices: representations, capitals and recognitions.' In P. Mahony and C. Zmroczek (eds), *Class Matters: 'working-class' women's perspectives on class*. London: Taylor & Francis.

Smith, P., and Morton, G. (1993). 'Union exclusion and the decollectivization of industrial relations in contemporary Britain.' *British Journal of Industrial Relations*, 31 (1), 97–114.

Spencer, A., and Podmore, D. (eds) (1987). *In a Man's World*. London: Tavistock.

Spencer, I.., and Taylor, S. (1994). *Participation and progress in the labour market: key issues for women*. Research Series No. 35, Department of Employment.

Stephenson, C. (1994). 'Worker consent to lean, flexible production in a depressed regional economy.' PhD, Sunderland University.

Still, J. (1997). '*Homo economicus* in the twentieth century: *ecriture masculine* and women's work.' *History of the Human Sciences*, 10 (3), 109–25.

Stuart, A. (1990). 'Feminism: dead or alive?' In J. Rutherford (ed.), *Identity*. London: Lawrence & Wishart.

Thompson, E. P. (1967). 'Time, work-discipline and industrial capitalism.' *Past and Present*, 38, 56–97.

Thompson, E. P. (1968). *The Making of the English Working Class*. Harmondsworth: Penguin.

Tilly, C. (1996). *Half a Job: bad and good part-time jobs in a changing labour market*. Philadelphia, PA: Temple University Press.

Walby, S. (ed.) (1988). *Gender Segregation at Work*. Milton Keynes: Open University Press.

Walby, S. (1992). 'Post-post-modernism? Theorizing social complexity.' In M. Barrett and A. Phillips (eds), *Destabilizing Theory*. Cambridge: Polity.

Walby, S. (1997). *Gender Transformations*. London: Routledge.

Walkerdine, V. (1990). *Schoolgirl Fictions*. London: Verso.

Walsh, V. (1997). 'Interpreting class: auto/biographical imaginations and social change.' In P. Mahony and C. Zmroczek (eds), *Class Matters: 'working-class' women's perspectives on class*. London: Taylor & Francis.

Ward, K. (ed.) (1990). *Women Workers and Global Restructuring*. Ithaca, NY: ILR, Cornell University.

Warde, A., and Hetherington, K. (1993). 'A changing domestic division of labour? Issues of measurement and interpretation.' *Work, Employment and Society*, 7 (1), 23–45.

Watson, D. (1988). *Managers of Discontent: trade union officers and industrial relations managers*. London: Routledge.

Webb, J. (1996). 'Gender, work and transitions in the local state.' Paper presented at the Cambridge Social Stratification Seminar, Clare College.

Webb, J. (forthcoming). 'The politics of equal opportunity'. *Gender, Work and Organization*.

Webb, J., and Liff, S. (1988). 'Play the white man: the social construction of fairness and competition in equal opportunities policy.' *Sociological Review*, 36, 532–51.

Wedderburn, D., and Craig, C. (1974). 'Relative deprivation at work.' In D. Wedderburn (ed.), *Poverty, Inequality and Class Structure*. Cambridge: Cambridge University Press.

Wertheimer, B., and Nelson, A. (1975). *Trade Union Women*. New York, NY: Praeger.

West, J. (1996). 'Figuring out working women.' In R. Levitas and W. Guy, *Interpreting Official Statistics*. London: Routledge.

Westwood, S. (1984). *All Day, Every Day*. London: Pluto.

Westwood, S. (1996). '"Feckless fathers": masculinities and the British state.' In M. Mac an Ghaill (ed.), *Understanding Masculinities*. Milton Keynes: Open University Press.

Wheelock, J. (1994). 'Is Andy Capp dead? The enterprise culture and household responses to economic change.' In P. Garrahan and

P. Stewart (eds), *Urban Change and Renewal: the paradox of place*. London: Avebury.

Whitston, C., and Waddington, J. (1992). 'Why sign up? New trade union members' reasons for joining.' Research Report No. 6, Warwick University: IRRU.

Williams, R. (1968). 'The meanings of work.' In R. Fraser (ed.), *Work: twenty personal accounts*. Harmondsworth: Penguin.

Williams, S. (1996). 'Meeting the needs of the individual: the nature and diffusion of recent trade union modernization policies in the UK.' PhD, Sunderland University.

Williamson, B. (1982). *Class, Culture and Community*. London: Routledge & Kegan Paul.

Williamson, J. (1997). 'Out of control.' *Guardian Weekend*, 15 February, 6.

Willis, P. (1977). *Learning to Labour*. Farnborough: Saxon House.

Willis, P., Jones, S., Canaan, J., and G. Hurd (1990). *Common Culture*. Milton Keynes: Open University Press.

Willott, S., and Griffin, C. (1996). 'Men, masculinity and the challenge of long-term unemployment.' In M. Mac an Ghaill (ed.), *Understanding Masculinities*. Milton Keynes: Open University.

Witz, A. (1992). *Professions and Patriarchy*. London: Routledge.

Wood, S. (1989). 'New wave management.' *Work, Employment and Society*, 3 (3), 379–402.

Index